CW00552928

DREAM ROAD

DREAM ROAD

A journey of discovery

Percy Trezise

ALLEN & UNWIN

First published in 1993
Allen & Unwin Pty Ltd
9 Atchison Street, St Leonards, NSW 2065 Australia

National Library of Australia
Cataloguing-in-Publication entry:

Trezise, Percy.
    Dream road.

    Bibliography.
    Includes index.
    ISBN 1 86373 403 1.

    [1]. Aborigines, Australian.   [2]. Aborigines, Australian – Religion.
    [3]. Aborigines, Australian – Art.   [4]. Aborigines, Australian –
    History.   I. Title.

306.0899915

Maps drawn by Valda Brook

Set in 10.5/12pt Garamond IBX
by Graphicraft Typesetters Ltd., Hong Kong
Printed by Dah Hua Printing, Hong Kong

10 9 8 7 6 5 4 3 2 1

Contents

Acknowledgments

During the thirty years of exploration and field work that have led
to this book, I have been ably assisted by many more people than I
can possibly name. To all of them I offer my sincere appreciation,
especially my wife Beverley who typed and retyped, and kept the billy
on the boil.

My greatest debt is to the Aboriginal people, who contributed
virtually all the knowledge contained within this book. Their wisdom,
mythology, and art have vastly enriched my life, and I dedicate this
book to them, and hope it will be a vehicle to enrich the lives of all
mankind.

Percy Trezise
Cairns, 1993

Introduction

Dream Road is the story of a personal investigation of the first Australians, which has extended over more than thirty years and continues still. It was never intended to be a formal scientific investigation—it has been a journey among men and women, trying to see life through their eyes.

When my journey commenced it was generally believed that the Aborigines had been here less than 10 000 years, and that they were a backward race; unchanging people in an unchanging land. So it was fortunate that early in my journey I fell in step with a very remarkable man. He was about my age and had been born under a clump of pandanus palms as Goobalathaldin, a member of the Lardil tribe on Mornington Island in the Gulf of Carpentaria. He became known to all Australians as Dick Roughsey.

It was Dick and his clansmen who guided my steps along the roads of Dreamtime, who took me into the inner sanctums of their complex and rich culture, and gave me a new perspective on life. For a quarter of a century we explored for and found the beautiful temples of Dreamtime in the lost world of Quinkin country in Cape York peninsula.

The art in the stone temples and the mythology are the visual and oral history of an astonishing people who were highly intelligent, energetic, resourceful and responsible. When information from the art and the mythology is added to the scientific knowledge derived from anthropology, archaeology, geology and climatology, patterns emerge which reveal that the first Australians have been here for more than 100 000 years, may have been here upwards of half a million years, and by 40 000 years ago, led the world in art, religion and technology.

It is a story without parallel in the rest of the world because nowhere else were there the abundant species of marsupials, especially the marsupial megafauna of the Ice Ages, the gentle giants of Dream-time, that made it all possible.

At the beginning of European colonisation in 1788, the British decision to declare Australia *terra nullius*, an unoccupied continent, was a political decision which effectively deprived the native Australians of their humanity. It inferred they were subhuman, that they had no organised social systems, no religion and no system of land tenure.

The basic white doctrine of *terra nullius* gave those Christian people licence to murder the Aboriginal people by any means and dispossess them of their clan lands, and to avoid the moral and political consequences of their actions.

It was probably more than 200 000 years ago that early man arrived and began populating Australia. Over the millennia they flourished sufficiently to produce a race of philosophers and mythologists who developed a civilisation of high degree, based on spiritual, not material, values.

When the first Europeans came to Australia the Aborigines had evolved a society and way of life which will eventually be recognised as one of the most extraordinary, in many ways the most idyllic, ever evolved by man. All their needs, both spiritual and material, were catered for and assured, and they lived in total harmony with their environment.

Because of their seemingly impoverished material possessions, Europeans regarded the Aboriginal people as savages of low intelligence, as children of nature having barely attained the status of humanity. The gossamer-fine fabric of their spiritual civilisation was not recognised, and its fragile structure was destroyed before it was known to exist.

The Aboriginal concept of their clan lands was that the land belonged to the ancestral spirits, and the people belonged to the land.

My first exposure to Aboriginal rock art was in 1960, when I went with Xavier Herbert and my two sons, Matthew and Stephen, to inspect several painted galleries found by road builders the previous year. They were in Cape York peninsula, near Laura, a small town inland from Cooktown.

In that area the Laura River flowed north-west through a wide sandstone gorge. There were huge slabs of pink sandstone on a terrace above the river and we climbed up to search among them. The sandstone blocks, some as big as houses, were scattered in an open forest of bloodwood, stringy-bark and quinine scrub, at the base of a scree slope topped by a red scarp which towered above us on the south side. To the north the terrace fell away, abruptly at first, then more gradually down to the river, seen as a meandering line of greener trees about a kilometre away.

We found the first paintings in a large, open shelter under a twenty-metre-high block of sandstone, which was split diagonally from top to bottom. The back wall of the shelter was covered with a mosaic of figures in rich earth colours of reds, yellows and white, portraying people, kangaroos, emus, fish, snakes, echidnas, and strange anthropomorphs, which I learned later were Quinkins. They were superimposed in layers in what seemed the utmost confusion, but it was an exciting and beautiful sight; the rich ochre colours blended with those of the uneven rock surfaces matched the colours of the landscape about us. The art fitted naturally and harmoniously into its surroundings, and the figures hinted at a great mystery about their creation and meaning.

We found three more sites in what appeared to be a complex of living shelters, and one ceremonial site which contained four tall, attenuated human figures. There were three men and a woman, all were wearing headdresses and were nearly three metres tall. They were executed in dark red ochre as linear figures, with elaborate inner decoration of barred lines, and probably portrayed ancestral beings. They appeared to be much older than the figures in the other three sites.

We were convinced that such a refined form of art could not be just an isolated occurrence, the sites would be part of a large body of such art and be traditional to the entire sandstone region. My occupation as an airline pilot took me almost daily over the area, so I decided to watch out for similar likely sites to mark on air navigation charts for later ground investigation.

PAPUA
NEW GUINEA

TIMOR
Arafura Sea

Torres Strait
Cape York

INDIAN

OCEAN

Darwin

*Gulf
of
Carpentaria*

CAPE

YORK

*Mornington
Island*

PENINSULA

CORAL

SEA

GREAT BARRIER REEF

NORTHERN
TERRITORY

QUEENSLAND

Tropic of Capricorn

WESTERN
AUSTRALIA

SOUTH
AUSTRALIA

Brisbane

NEW SOUTH
WALES

Perth

Adelaide

Sydney

VICTORIA

Melbourne

Scale:

0   1000

kilometres

TASMANIA

Hobart

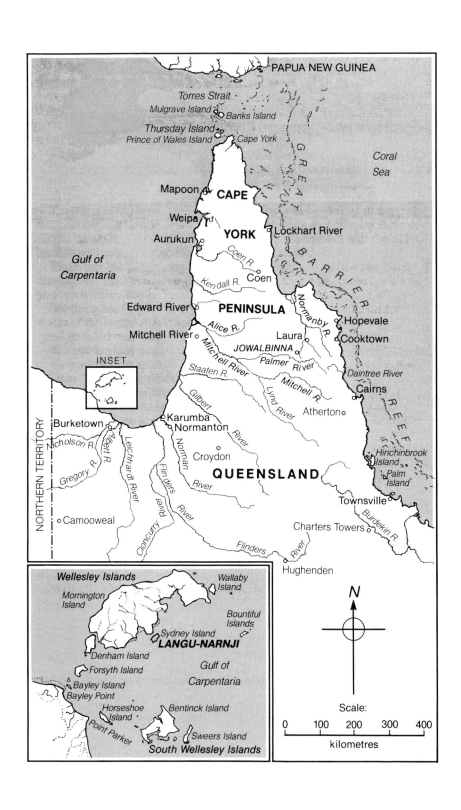

PAPUA NEW GUINEA

Torres Strait
Mulgrave Island
Banks Island
Thursday Island
Prince of Wales Island
Cape York

Coral
Sea

Mapoon
CAPE

Weipa

YORK

Aurukun

Lockhart River

Coen R.

Gulf of
Carpentaria

Kendall R.
Coen

Edward River

PENINSULA

Alice R.

Normanby R.

Hopevale

Mitchell River

Laura

Cooktown

Mitchell River

JOWALBINNA

Palmer River

Mitchell R.

Daintree River

Staaten R.

Lynd River

Cairns

INSET

Gilbert

Atherton

REEF

Burketown

Karumba
Normanton

River

Nicholson R.

Albert R.

Norman

Croydon

Hinchinbrook
Island

Leichhardt River

Gregory R.

River

QUEENSLAND

Palm
Island

NORTHERN TERRITORY

Flinders

Townsville

o Camooweal

Cloncurry

River

River

Burdekin R.

Charters Towers

Flinders

River

Hughenden

Wellesley Islands

Wallaby
Island

Mornington
Island

Bountiful
Islands

Sydney Island

LANGU-NARNJI

Denham Island

Gulf of

Forsyth Island

Carpentaria

Bayley Island
Bayley Point

Horseshoe
Island

Bentinck Island

Point Parker

Sweers Island

South Wellesley Islands

N

Scale:

0   100   200   300   400
kilometres

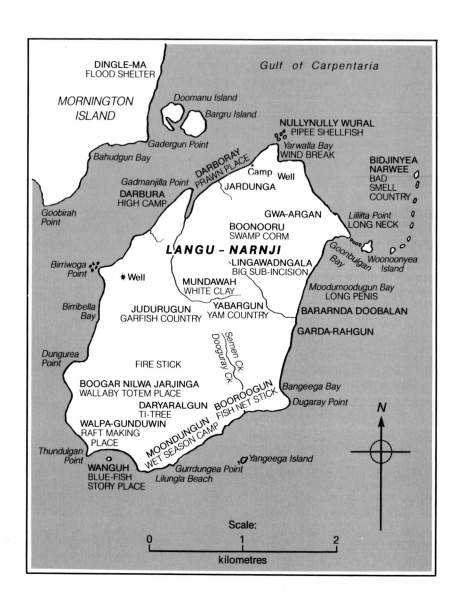

DINGLE-MA
FLOOD SHELTER

Gulf of Carpentaria

MORNINGTON
ISLAND

Doomanu Island

Bargru Island

NULLYNULLY WURAL
PIPEE SHELLFISH

Gadergun Point

Yarwalla Bay
WIND BREAK

Bahudgun Bay

DARBORAY
PRAWN PLACE

Camp   Well

BIDJINYEA
NARWEE
BAD
SMELL
COUNTRY

Gadmanjilla Point

JARDUNGA

DARBURA
HIGH CAMP

Goobirah
Point

GWA-ARGAN

Lillilta Point
LONG NECK

BOONOORU
SWAMP CORM

L'ANGU – NARNJI

Goonbulgan
Bay

Woonoonyea
Island

Birriwoga
Point

LINGAWADNGALA
BIG SUB-INCISION

Well

Moodumoodugun Bay
LONG PENIS

MUNDAWAH
WHITE CLAY

Birribella
Bay

JUDURUGUN
GARFISH COUNTRY

YABARGUN
YAM COUNTRY

BARARNDA DOOBALAN

GARDA-RAHGUN

Dungurea
Point

FIRE STICK

Semen Ck.
Dooguray Ck.

BOOGAR NILWA JARJINGA
WALLABY TOTEM PLACE

Bangeega Bay

DARYARALGUN
TI-TREE

BOOROOGUN
FISH NET STICK

Dugaray Point

WALPA-GUNDUWIN
RAFT MAKING
PLACE

MOONDUNGUN
WET SEASON CAMP

N

Thundulgan
Point

WANGUH
BLUE-FISH
STORY PLACE

Gurrdungea Point
Lilungla Beach

Yangeega Island

Scale:

0   1   2

kilometres

Palmer River limestone mortuary figures.

Hand stencils—mankind's signature.

1

The peopling of Australia

Until late Cretaceous times the Australian continent had been part of the southern super-continent called Gondwanaland. It was then the age of the dinosaurs and other reptiles, but early forms of the order of marsupial mammals were already developing in the South American, Antarctic and Australian regions of Gondwanaland. When Australia broke away from Antarctica about 45 million years ago it was home to diverse populations of reptiles, monotremes, marsupials, birds, insects and other forms of animal and plant life.

During the Miocene epoch, about fifteen million years ago, Australia's northern shelf, Sahul, collided with the Sunda shelf of Asia. At that time it was a lush, moist land, covered with great forests, lakes and rivers. It was an Eden awaiting human inheritance, but it was to be a long wait, as the small creatures who were to evolve into humans were only commencing their development in far-off Africa. The continent commenced a slow drying out.

Fortunately for the small-brained, primitive marsupials, deep channels between islands of the Indonesian archipelago always provided a barrier against superior placental mammals, which would have overwhelmed the marsupials, as happened to most of the marsupials in South America, when it made contact with North America. Placental mammals occupied all the Indonesian islands, but only rats and bats were able to cross the final barrier of sea, before mankind made the crossing to Australia.

More than a million years ago, a race of man, *Homo erectus*, came to occupy the Indonesian archipelago, and slowly evolved into early *Homo sapiens*, whose descendants would eventually inherit the fifth continent, Australia. When, and by what means they crossed the final sea barrier, will always be speculation, but a map of those Pleistocene times showing the lower sea level, and the Leeuwin Current which

1

flowed through it, demonstrates that the crossing of the final channel was not only possible, but inevitable.

The Leeuwin Current is a band of warm, low-salinity water of tropical origin, about fifty kilometres wide and about two hundred metres deep, that flows southward. The current is thought to originate in tropical waters of the West Pacific and to sweep down through the Indonesian archipelago onto Australia's north-west shelf. From there it travels down the coastline from Exmouth to Cape Leeuwin where it turns east and, at times mingling with other currents, reaches Tasmania. It is strongest during autumn and winter, and speeds of one to three knots per hour have been measured. In the narrower channels of the Pleistocene Age, beyond ten thousand years ago, it was probably a swifter current. It was always the fast track into Australia.

Whenever it was that the early people of Java and other islands commenced to exploit their marine environments, using bamboo rafts or other watercraft, they would have become candidates for immigration to Australia, whether they wanted to or not. The first Australians probably came unwillingly, by accident, upwards of half a million years ago.

The early fishermen would have soon become aware of the dangerous seasonal current, just as the people on the nearest islands to Australia would have become aware of a land mass lying just beyond the horizon, where every monsoon season they saw towering thunderstorms mass above it, and at night the distant flashes of sheet lightning.

It would have been logical for later people, under stress from overpopulation, and armed with the knowledge of the Leeuwin Current sweeping toward a land just beyond the horizon, to plan migration to it. They would have built rafts large and sturdy enough to carry family groups, equipped with food, and water in skin bags. Eventually, some even brought their dogs, the pale-footed descendants of the Asian wolf, which they had domesticated long before.

The Australia which greeted early man was vastly different from that of today. Ancient Australia was much larger, joined by the Sahul shelf to New Guinea at the top, and to Tasmania at the bottom. It was about one-seventh larger than now.

To enter that southern Eden, early man has only to leave his watercraft somewhere on the north-west Sahul shelf, follow a west-flowing stream to its head, cross a low divide, and follow another stream east to one of the many freshwater lakes scattered over the forested interior of Australia.

The optimum conditions of climate and food supplies, would have enabled early man to wander at will, and within a few thousand years spread over and occupy the entire continent.

What the first Australians looked like can be seen in the ancient skull of Willandra Lakes Hominid, number 50. He had a massive, thick-boned skull with beetling brow ridge and sloping forehead, which encased a 1300cc brain. From the remnants of the elbow and leg, we can deduce that he had a massive body. With all the normal phosphates replaced with silicates, the ancient skull of WLH 50 has probably been gazing blankly at his surroundings for more than a hundred thousand years.

I had first heard of Robust skulls when on fishing trips to the Murray and nearby Wakool rivers in the early 1950s. We fished on a property owned by Bruce Martin, who was much interested in Aboriginal prehistory. While fishing he talked about ploughing up various skulls on the old sandridges in the wheat fields, and maintained that two distinctly different races of people had once lived together in the region; one with a rounded, thin-boned skull, the other with a very heavy and thick-boned skull, with sloping forehead. Bruce had tried to interest a local medical doctor in one of the Robust skulls, but it had mouldered and disintegrated at the back of the doctor's garage.

The Robusts slumbered on for many more years until Alan Thorne found one of them gathering dust in a Melbourne museum, and traced it back to Kow Swamp, near the Murray River, where he excavated many more Robust skeletons.

Much later arrivals were the Lake Mungo people, and they were fully modern *Homo sapiens sapiens*, with thin-boned, fully rounded skulls, and their gracile skeletons of slight build were a total contrast to the robust might of early man. They had probably evolved somewhere in Asia, and reached Australia, riding on the Leeuwin Current, in a specu-lative time range of 70000 to 40000 years ago. The cremated and smashed bones of their burials indicate that they had religion and a concern about life after death, more than 26000 years ago.

That these two distinctly different races, the Robust and the Gracile, eventually hybridised to produce the modern Australian Aborigine, is evidenced by the modified Robust skeletons from Kow Swamp, which were dated from 13000 to 10000 years old. As Thorne com-mented, the ancient Willandra Lakes hominid made them seem almost Gracile.

Prehistorians indicate that everywhere in the world the Robust people appeared first, having evolved in Africa, followed much later by the Graciles, probably from Asia. The amalgamation of these two basic races commenced all over the world many millennia ago.

Aboriginal oral history records much conflict between the two races, over territory, women, and cannibalism. A myth from Mount Olga in Central Australia relates how the last of the cannibal Robusts was killed by a womera-flung spear, the long-range weapon undoubtedly in-vented by the Graciles to overcome the powerful Robusts, just as the

Cro-Magnons invented it in Europe about 35 000 years ago, to defeat the Neanderthals.

Changing weather patterns in Australia would have played a major role in the long period of time during which the Robust and Gracile peoples amalgamated. A study of weather patterns of the late Pleistocene Age by J.M. Bowler, indicate the dramatic changes:

- 120 000 to 60 000 years ago, conditions were about the same or marginally better than those of today.
- 60 000 to 40 000 years ago, a very humid, temperate climate prevailed offering optimum conditions for flora, fauna, and man.
- 40 000 to 17 000 years ago, a drying out occurred. Bowler suggests that by 20 000 years ago most of the interior of Australia would have been shifting sand-dunes.
- 17 000 to 15 000 years ago, there was a period of severe aridity with searing droughts.
- 15 000 years ago to present, a slow recovery from aridity with a gradual increase in humidity to the present climate took place. Climatologists also indicate a more intense humid phase from about 8000 to 5000 years ago, permitting a more rapid recolonisation of formerly abandoned arid country.

By assembling the evidence available from the sciences of palaeontology, geomorphology, archaeology, and anthropology, and then adding to it other evidence gathered from Aboriginal mythology and rock art, one can discern a chronological pattern of events emerging which indicates the course of life for countless generations of first Australians.

Sometime before 120 000 years ago, Robust *Homo sapiens*, descendants of Java Man arrived in northern Australia, perhaps first by accident, then by deliberately riding on the Leeuwin Current, on rafts or canoes. They discovered a continent cooler and wetter than that of today. With rainforests, sclerophyll forest, savannah woodlands, lakes and river systems, it was habitable all over. With the Leeuwin Current sometimes extending as far as Tasmania, it would have been possible to populate the entire western and southern coastlines in only a few decades, and may be the explanation for some of the differences between the Tasmanian and mainland populations.

With no barriers of water or desert to deter them, they would have spread out and occupied most parts of the continent within a few thousand years. Evidence of that early population will be found, as Bowler suggests, under the sand-dunes covering the ancient inland river systems and lakes.

The food supply available to the Robust people was enormous and probably had no equal anywhere else in the world. All the different species of marsupial megafauna, especially the huge diprotodons,

4

were small-brained and relatively slow-moving, with no obvious means of defence against man the hunter. The construction of the marsupial brain prevents the animals from ever learning by experience; the same wallaby or wombat can be caught day after day in the same trap.

Diprotodons and other large species would have been chosen and killed selectively, with the hunters cutting up and carrying away the meat they needed, or the family horde camping by it until it was finished. Meat can be preserved for up to two weeks by keeping it in a heated ground oven.

Extremely large, hafted stone hatchets have been found on ancient horizons in many places over Australia and New Guinea, and as has been suggested long ago, they would have been used to kill the megafauna. We found a sharp, edge-ground, hafted stone-axe, down three metres in our Sandy Creek excavation, which was eventually dated by Mike Morwood to about 32 000 years B.P. We have found similar slender, edge-ground axes on the surface, so the same implement had been manufactured and used continuously for over 30 000 years.

The types of food included in the diet of early man may have depended largely on whether they initially had the use of fire. Many yams and other vegetable foods need to be cooked to rid them of poisons. Evidence from Europe suggests that *Homo erectus* had the occasional use of fire between 300 000 to 400 000 years ago, but hearths were not common until the Neanderthals appeared about 100 000 years ago. Fire could be obtained from natural sources of lightning strikes or volcanic activity. The ability to make fire at will was an acquisition of enormous significance to early man, and the sudden increase of charcoal in Lake George sediments about 120 000 years ago, may be mute evidence of the occasion in Australia.

The skeletal evidence for the antiquity of Lake Mungo Graciles is presently less than 40 000 years, but proof of a more ancient presence is sure to be found. The knowledge of how to make fire may have been among the invisible baggage of the Graciles when they arrived, and it's possible that they were responsible for the Lake George charcoal.

Whenever the Graciles arrived they found a fairly lush environment with abundant food supplies. The Robust people they encountered were probably in fairly large bands of family hordes, living a very contented nomadic existence, shifting camp mainly for a change of diet, and under few stresses.

The relationship between the two races would have been one of avoidance, especially by the Graciles, who were much smaller in stature and numbers. With a large continent habitable all over, a temperate climate, abundant food and water, there was no reason for conflict; but raids after women would have been certain.

If the Graciles had arrived by 60 000 years ago, there were many thousands of years of superabundance for both races to live in harmony. Those Garden of Eden millennia became the Dreamtime of Aboriginal race memory. But those conditions were not to last.

The climate began to dry out and this is evidenced by the fact that the megafauna began to eat saltbush and other vegetation very similar to that found here today. The desiccation probably commenced about 40 000 years ago, and was so gradual that flora and fauna adapted to it over a period of several thousand years, with surface water retreating gradually to permanent waterholes far apart; but there was no prolonged drought.

When the drought came it was totally devastating, because by then the remaining surface waters were too far apart, and once the vegetation within walking distance of water had been eaten out, the megafauna were all doomed.

At present there is insufficient data to make any estimation, other than speculative, of the human population of the continent at the onset of the great droughts. If they had enjoyed 20 000 years of optimum living conditions Australia-wide, there would have been a lot of people, probably two or three million. The stresses and conflict would have been enormous, and would have increased every decade as the flora and fauna retreated to refuge areas on reliable rivers, lakes, the coast and coastal ranges.

Many clans, especially in the central regions of the continent, must have found themselves trapped on dwindling water supplies, and either perished there, or set off with the last of the water in skin bags in a desperate and probably fatal attempt to find another waterhole. That some adapted and grimly survived is evidenced by a 23 000-year-old occupation date for central Australia, and that some of the Dieri clan survived around Lake Eyre until the twentieth century.

The Robust and the Gracile peoples may have been easily able to avoid each other during the lush millennia, with a limited gene exchange between them. When huge areas were devastated by drought however, they would have been forced together to share the dwindling waters, and large-scale miscegenation, and cannibalism, would have commenced.

Most of the large freshwater lakes which offered refuge areas at some time during the arid millennia, either dried out, became saline, or were inundated by sea water at the end of the Ice Age. Those drowned by the sea included lakes on the Tasmanian land bridge, Spencer Gulf in South Australia, and several lakes on the northern Sahul shelf, the largest of which was located largely within the boundaries of what is now the Gulf of Carpentaria.

This Sahul lake was mapped by Tom Torgersen in 1985, and its size estimated at 165 000 square kilometres, ranking it as one of the world's largest freshwater lakes, but its maximum depth would have been less than sixteen metres, and average depth less than five metres. Before 36 000 years ago the area would have been dry, but after that it would have reached its maximum size about 26 000 years ago. Its catchment area would have extended up to Papua New Guinea and to Mt Isa and from Tennant Creek to the Great Dividing Range on Cape York peninsula—an area of 1.1 million square kilometres.

Freshwater frogs and turtles, which exist today only in Papua New Guinea, West Irian and Arnhem Land, were dispersed through the lake. The lake probably also affected the migration and distribution of people as the whole environment would have been more habitable than previously thought.

The large Sahul lake would have been the main refuge for the people of Cape York peninsula and eastern Arnhem Land. As the great droughts tightened their grip, the clans left belongings like the edge-ground axe at Sandy Creek (see Chapter 11), and followed rivers running into the great lake, to take up new clan countries around its 2000 kilometre coastline, where they would remain for many millennia, leaving their former clan lands to the shifting sands.

About 8000 years ago, rising sea levels breached the Arafura sill of Sahul Land and sea water rushed in to drown the lake and refill the Gulf, probably the greatest catastrophe ever to engulf the survivors of the Pleistocene droughts.

The central deserts have only slightly recovered and stabilised from the great arid phase, with re-established clan territories being very large and thinly populated.

Outside the desert regions the rest of the continent recovered and clan territories were reoccupied and became more densely populated than the deserts. The rock art of the Cape York peninsula is spectacular evidence of the reflourishing of the Aboriginal people of Australia.

'The most dramatic figures were two almost life-size dark red men
spreadeagled across many other figures.'

2

Wind in the bloodwoods

Aerial surveys revealed the main tracts of sandstone which stretched north from near Cooktown on the east coast, and west to the Palmer River, and which covered about 10 000 square kilometres. Geology maps indicated two layers of sandstone, both being formed as beds of ancient inland seas. The lower layer, of the Jurassic Age, was a heavy conglomerate of sand and water-worn pebbles. The top layer, of the Lower Cretaceous Age, was composed mainly of smooth sandstone in varied colours of cream, grey, pink and red. Outcrops of ferruginous concretions embedded in the lower layer contained many colours of ochre, which had been used to paint the smooth walls of shelters in the top layer of sandstone.

Over ensuing millions of years streams eroded the softer areas, carving out deep gorges and valleys, leaving the harder parts as plateaux, with vertical scarps of pink, red and grey, capping a sloping and often scree-covered base of low hills. The entire country was covered with a fairly heavy open forest of eucalypts and acacias, making it a beautiful wilderness. With unbounded enthusiasm we set out to explore it all, blissfully unaware that three decades later we would still be at it.

The first trip to the Cooktown area yielded a new discovery, although only a minor one when compared to the Split Rock galleries. The main value of the first expeditions was in learning how to navigate and traverse the rugged terrain and how best to deal with the normal inconveniences of heat, fatigue, green ants, scrub bulls, snakes, and huge, feral boars, dangerous descendants of those released by Captain Cook.

The first find, in Isabella Creek gorge, we named Platform Gallery, as it contained a few rough sleeping platforms, made from bush timber and paperbark, these made necessary by a damp floor. The few paintings were of men and women, and more of the strange spirit figures. It was a land where legend still dominated, and when we found that the spirit figures were called Quinkins, which still inhabit the wild hills, we began calling it Quinkin country.

Our entire family was eventually caught up in the excitement of discovery, and school holidays became family expeditions to explore more of the aerial prospects. Stephen, the younger of the two boys, discovered the spectacular Crocodile galleries when he was ten, and his older brother Matthew could not rest until he capped it by finding the most complex and beautiful gallery of all, Pig Gallery—so named because an excellent painting of a pig was an outstanding figure. Their mother, Beverley, and two sisters, Vicki and Anna, were not to be out-done and each discovered galleries and named them.

The excitement of discovery never diminishes; each gallery is different in some way from all the rest. We found ancient engravings covered with brown silica, and the different styles in layers of super-imposed paintings suggested the art body had been created over an extremely long period of time, from remote times right up to the present century. We felt certain that the paintings would have an associated mythology, representing the religion and other beliefs of the vanished tribes. I began searching for Aboriginal people who might know something about the paintings and the mythology.

There were about sixty Aboriginal people camped along the river near Laura. Among them were a few old men who exhibited marks of initiation: pierced nasal septums and ear lobes, a front top tooth missing, and cicatrice scars on arms and torso. They were friendly but shy, and were evasive when questioned about the paintings, obviously unwilling to place any trust in a white man. I did not have to look far back into history to discover reasons for this mistrust.

The first Europeans to pass through Quinkin country were members of the ill-fated Edmund Kennedy expedition of 1848, and the William Hann expedition in 1872. Both reported clashes with groups of armed warriors. Hann seemed to be constantly 'dispersing' them, but the most significant event of the Hann expedition was the reporting of traces of gold in the Palmer River, the southern boundary of Quinkin country. Within a few months prospector James Venture Mulligan had precipitated the Palmer gold rush, and 1873 saw Quinkin country invaded by thousands of armed, gold-hungry European and Chinese miners. A war of attrition between black and white commenced immediately, and a few short years saw a traditional way of life that had developed and flourished over countless millennia, dwindle and vanish forever.

I had one close Aboriginal friend at the time, Dick Roughsey, whom I was helping commence a career as an artist. Dick's people were the Lardil of Mornington Island, in the Gulf of Carpentaria, and his tribal name was Goobalathaldin, meaning literally 'rough sea'. I first met him at Karumba Lodge, where he was working as a yardman. It was situated at the mouth of the Norman River and overlooked the grey Gulf waters. The Lodge was our overnight stop on the two-day Ansett weekly stations' run out of Cairns. We flew a DC3 into about seventeen Gulf settlements like Normanton, and into large cattle stations and Aboriginal missions.

At the time Dick was making and selling boomerangs to visiting tourists, his decorations exhibiting quality draftsmanship, and I decided to help him. Traditional art among the Lardil was confined to bodypainting with ochre and bird down, with similar decoration of weapons and ceremonial objects. There were no rock shelters on Mornington and no tradition of bark painting. However, as bark paintings were readily saleable I suggested to Dick he should begin by painting on bark the myths and legends of his own tradition.

I obtained messmate bark and ochre colours for him, and left him to his own devices, offering advice and encouragement when necessary. His natural talent was soon apparent and within six months Goobalathaldin had his first exhibition in Cairns. It was highly successful, and a few months later I went to Mornington Island with Dick to assist other Lardil artists.

We spent much of the time in the bush collecting and preparing bark, hunting, fishing and discussing tribal traditions and mythology. I spent more time as a student than a teacher. Aborigines have a very complex kinship system and are uneasy with anyone whose relationship to them, whether real or implied, is not clearly defined. Anyone with whom they are closely associated for any length of time must be given a place in the kinship system, and the entire tribe then know how to behave towards them.

Naturally I was classed as Dick's brother in the Leelumbanda clan (southwind Lardil), in the Booralungi subsection, with Dreamings of brolga and stingray. I was given the name of Warrenby, a legendary Lardil warrior and leader. This was communicated to me during a spectacular ceremonial corroboree during which they performed the Warrenby dances and sang the associated song cycles. It had taken them about two weeks to make all the colourful ceremonial gear, especially the tall tapered headdresses made of bark and human-hair string, which were decorated with red ochre, white clay and small balls of white bird down, and topped with a bunch of swaying emu plumes. Several hapless emus, black cockatoos, and scores of white corellas contributed to the ceremony that was to set my feet firmly on my own Dream Road. However, it would be several more years before I had learned enough to be shown the treasured sacred site, the Dreaming of Margara, the wallaby woman, although my wife Beverley was called Margara from that time on.

I thought Dick should be able to break the ice with the Laura

Aboriginal people for me, and an opportunity arose when Frank Woolston, a friend from Brisbane, wanted to record an Aboriginal shelter in Cape York. After some discussion we chose Platform Gallery, discovered earlier with Xavier Herbert. I arranged for Dick to fly over and join us.

Before going Laura way we spent a day and night in Cooktown to seek information from Gugu-Imudji men, and to replenish our supplies. Dick struck up an acquaintance with a Gugu-Almura man, Mitchell McGreen, whose tribal name was Papi-tharagen. His clan country was around Barrow Point, about a hundred kilometres northwest of Cooktown. Dick thought that Mitchell had a sound knowledge of tribal tradition and mythology, and as he also knew the Laura people, suggested we take him with us. Mitchell was keen for the adventure, so I agreed.

We planned to explore an area north of our major find of the previous year, where Steve and I had found two major galleries. They were located on Crocodile cattle station and we had named them Crocodile One and Two. An aerial survey had revealed many large blocks of sandstone lying on a terrace on the other side of the plateau.

We camped by the Laura River and prepared our gear to backpack into the hills next morning. We climbed into the high country up a steep razorback ridge, which in places offered spectacular views up and down the broad Laura valley, and south to the smoky ranges of the Great Divide. Hours later we were glad to shed our heavy gear in the painted shelters of the Crocodile galleries where we intended to camp, before going on to explore the new area.

My three companions were astonished by the powerful figures in the Crocodile galleries. There was a large red kangaroo with white outline and interior line decoration, painted over other faded figures, some of which appeared to represent waterlilies. The eastern end of one of the shelters was cylindrical and the back wall and ceiling were covered with a mass of figures superimposed in layers. We could identify a dark red and white echidna, a large orange yam, a yellow scrub turkey partly over a dark red emu, and several segmented crescent shapes which Mitchell thought were the big white grubs found in trunks of grasstrees and called 'jumboon'. There were several figures which offered no clue to what they represented, and I realised it would be necessary to acquire an intensive and intimate knowledge of all the local flora and fauna, and local Aboriginal traditional culture, before we could hope to interpret the art body.

Easily recognisable were the many human figures in every layer, men and women, varying in size from a few centimetres tall to larger than life. There were also many hand stencils, mainly in white and often placed on top of a figure as though in association with it. The most dramatic figures were two almost life-size dark red men

12

spreadeagled across many other figures. They were outlined and decorated with thick white lines and had glaring white eyes. They appeared to be the last addition to that section, and were intrusive and threatening. Dick and Mitchell felt certain they were associated with sorcery.

There was a second, outer shelter at the eastern end and it also contained paintings. A line of dark red horseshoe tracks meandered up the wall and across the ceiling, mute evidence of European contact. The main figures were a five-metre-long snake, and two big men, both lying horizontally and each a having a long narrow object between lower arm and body; they were pale yellow with dark red outlines. Both were barefooted but appeared to be wearing shirts and had grey-blue eyes, and dark red ovals on top of their heads. We speculated they might represent white or Chinese men of the gold rush days.

We packed lunch and set out to explore the new area. It proved to be extremely steep and rugged open-forest country, choked with long grass, undergrowth, fallen timber and green ants. The first prospect, a house-sized slab of sandstone just below the western end of the scarp, contained a small shelter with two well-drawn, life-size tortoises in red ochre and white, and a few small engraved stick-men. We worked eastwards along the scarp, Frank and Mitchell exploring the upper levels, and Dick and I the large outlier slabs scattered along the lower slopes.

By late afternoon the numerous shelters had yielded only a few more stencils and small painted figures. Rounding a large slab I came on Dick performing a vigorous 'green antic' dance. After slaughtering his tormentors he flopped sweating and moaning to the ground. 'I give up, Warrenby. I'm a flat-country man and my knee been touching my chin all day. I'm done in.'

He looked really distressed, so I hailed the others and suggested we call it a day. We had covered a big semicircle and our camp at Crocodile was only about two kilometres south across the plateau.

Dick went up to join the others while I went on to look at a last mass of slabs a hundred metres distant. In the first small shelter a large horizontal cream and red man glared out at me, and a little further on I could see a shelter with a large gallery of paintings. My shouts brought the others rushing back, their weariness forgotten in the excitement of a new discovery.

It had been a much-used camping shelter and contained about sixty figures. Large, well-drawn kangaroos in dark red with white decoration were painted over faded figures of human ancestral beings with rayed headdresses. Other human figures in white and pink were curiously shaped, and their interiors elaborately decorated with red lines and dots. A large barramundi fish was painted in a similar style. A two-metre-long cream kangaroo with red outline and interior line decoration was particularly well drawn; it had a short spear protruding from its back. Some of the more recent figures were obviously painted for sorcery purposes, such as for singing somebody to death. Under a ledge we found a bark food basket and small stone tools.

The sun was down among the bloodwoods, so we headed for camp, well satisfied with the day's work. We decided we should call it Woolston Gallery. By the time we reached night camp both Dick and Mitchell, unused to steep country, had again run out of steam, so we left them collapsed on their swags and went for water.

Hot sweet tea helped their recovery, and we noticed then that although our Aboriginal companions were cheerful and at ease in the galleries during the day, they became uneasy as the gloom of a moonless night gathered and flickering firelight animated the painted figures on the walls. Just before dark a black butcherbird had landed on a dead tree in front of the shelter and sat peering at us, first with one eye, then the other. Dick and Mitchell exchanged apprehensive glances and said the bird might have been a spy sent to look us over.

After dinner of bully beef stew we sat round the fire and Dick told us how his old people placated the spirits when they visited strange country: they called out loudly who they were, why they were there, and advertised their peaceful intentions. Mitchell was a mine of information on mythology and told us his Genesis story involving the freshwater tortoise Dreaming at Cape Flattery, north of Cooktown. Behind beach sand-dunes the oval top of a large granite boulder obtrudes from the sand. It was the carapace of Dugol, the tortoise:

In the beginning, when all animals were people, they gathered together at Cape Flattery to hold the first big dance. They came from all over the land, and spoke different languages. They had been called together by a message-stick carried around by Jaju the kangaroo rat.

Among those who came were Dugol the tortoise, Guraway the emu, Bonjul the frilled lizard, Wandar the white cockatoo, Ngalculli the red kangaroo, Barwoor the rock wallaby, Kargna the goanna, Balinga the echidna, Kalpala the long-eared kangaroo, Wallanga the death adder, Girrapati the dugong, and Goorlu the sea urchin.

The people practised for their big corroboree. Dugol the tortoise was the drummer and Jaju the kangaroo rat the main songman with clap-sticks. The people were very thirsty after preparing the dance ground and practising, but when they went to the waterhole it was dry. Someone had drunk all the water.

They were running about looking for water when Wallanga the death adder came along and told them he had seen the woman Dugol drink all the water. The people had a meeting and decided to spy on Dugol to discover where she had hidden the water. They told Kargna the goanna to climb a tree and see if he could sight Dugol, but Kargna could not see far enough. Guraway the emu set off to spy; he hid behind bushes and called out, 'Can you see me?'

The others said, 'It's no good. You are too big and we can still see you.'

Kalpa the kangaroo then went and hid himself, but again the people said, 'No, we can still see you.'

They tried everyone out as a spy, but none could hide themselves well enough. Finally Wallanga the death adder set out. He crawled into the bushes and hid under dead leaves and grass before calling out, 'Can you see me?' The people could not see Wallanga, so he crawled away to spy on Dugol the tortoise.

Wallanga watched Dugol. He returned and told the people that Dugol had the water hidden in bags along her thighs. They held a meeting to decide how to get the water back. Ngalculli the red kangaroo said: 'I am the first dancer. When I get near I will kick her and tear the bag.'

But Guraway the emu said, 'No, you will be too slow, it will be better if I kick Dugol and rip her bag open with my big toe.'

The dancing started and soon everyone was thirsty, their throats dry from dust. Near the end of the dance Guraway moved closer to Dugol where she sat drumming and kicked at her thigh. Water poured out like a river and all the people stopped dancing and rushed for the water.

After the big corroboree was finished the people exchanged gifts. Dugol gave her large shell to the saltwater turtle, and turtle gave her small shell to Dugol. Balinga the echidna gave his fat to Dugong and his spines to Sea Urchin. Sea Snake gave his skin to Carpet Snake; they all exchanged gifts. Then they all went off to change into animals, birds, fish, reptiles, insects, plants and all other living things. Some went to live on land and some in water, and they stayed there forever.

The first big dance ground is now a freshwater lagoon called Ngabar. It's the home of many tortoises. In the dry season when the water begins to dry up the tortoises drink all the water they can, storing it in bags under their thighs. Then they dig down into the mud and bury themselves until the rains come again.

Dick told his tribal legends of Thuwathu the Rainbow Serpent and Gidegal, the greedy moon man. Mitchell called the evil supernatural spirits Quinkins, but to Dick they were Mulgans or Narbiahs. Whatever their names, the reminiscing ensured that they were lurking about outside, and Dick and Mitchell took no chances with the Quinkins in those hills. They arranged their swags so as to have Frank and myself on one side and the fire on the other. Frank suggested they should sleep with their boots on so that if a Quinkin dragged one of them away in the night we could track their heel drags in the morning. They took it in turns to keep the fire going all night. Weary limbs, a lullaby of mopokes and wind in the bloodwoods soon had us fast asleep.

Next morning we were out early to continue exploring nearby areas, but found nothing of note. I planned to return to the Crocodile sites to do an intensive recording later in the year, when water would be a problem, so we filled plastic containers at the dwindling soak to store in the shelter.

We visited Split Rock on the way to Laura and arrived at the sleepy little hamlet near sundown. Kites were wheeling over the old shed which used to be the railway goods shed before the line was dismantled. Blue heeler dogs sprawled in the dust in front of the old corrugated-iron Laura pub. Big mango trees shaded the pub veranda where a few cattlemen in high-heeled boots and broad-brimmed hats were sitting on wooden benches, or hunkered on their heels drinking stubbies of beer. A store-cum-post office and a police station-cum-residence comprised the rest of Laura. We got some cold beer and went down to camp on the Laura River, about a kilometre away.

Next day we set about establishing a friendly relationship with people of the Laura encampment, located a kilometre upstream. The camp was on a river terrace above high flood level, and consisted of a single row of squalid galvanised iron shanties, the Queensland Government's concept of adequate housing for the dispossessed first Australians, but flowerbeds and vegetable plots evidenced their continuing independence. A pack of savage and emaciated dogs of all shapes, sizes and colours erupted from the luxurious weed growth to surround our car and snarl defiance at our intrusion. Their tattered ears supported a fine crop of ticks, and scarred shoulders and flanks were graphic evidence of fierce battles with boar pigs that the people hunted.

An ancient tribal woman, one of the old bush people, sat naked in the dust, her thin arms around a terrified infant. Small curly-haired heads peeped cautiously round corners, and an elderly man in stockman's rig emerged from the gloom of a house to curse and belabour the dogs with a womera. The atmosphere of cautious suspicion was dispelled when Mitchell got out of the car and greeted the man as uncle.

The dogs retired grumbling and unconvinced to their dustholes and we were soon surrounded by a small group of shy but curious men, women and children. We were introduced to them by Mitchell and then retired to the shade of a giant milky pine to talk and explain our mission. The women and children sat in the shade of the houses, unobtrusively observing every detail of our appearance and actions.

Dick was soon on familiar terms with the men. His gregarious good nature and intelligent wit won the friendship of all. He related events of our long friendship and carefully explained my mission to discover and record their ancient cave art, before it was lost forever. While doing this, Dick, a wise judge of character, was carefully noting the undercurrents of feeling existing between the men, and estimating their likely value as tribal authorities. He was watching the 'eye talk'.

Before returning to our camp we invited several of the old men to come down in the evening for a meal and a yarn. I had brought some fruit for the children and while this was being distributed we drove off accompanied by an escort of barking dogs who pursued us for a reasonable distance before trotting back, proud of their final expulsion of the intruders.

The last glare was in the western sky when four old men came walking through the paperbarks in the river bed. They were very dignified in their acceptance of our hospitality, and became more relaxed after food and mugs of hot sweet tea. Dick established their identities as George Pegus, aged about seventy, of the Gugu-Yalanji tribe, with the clan name of Joogumu, meaning grey box tree; Willy Long, also over seventy and of the Olcula tribe, with the name of Toomacalin, white gum tree; Jerry Shepherd and Joe Musgrave, both of Taipan snake tribe, from further up the peninsula.

George Pegus and Willy Long were good mates who were to prove themselves very knowledgeable and reliable. George's early years had been spent in tribal life in clan country around the Palmer and Laura rivers. Later he joined his father cattle droving, and became a stockman on the developing cattle stations. Willy Long had lived a traditional life on his clan country between the Alice and Coleman rivers, until he was about fifty, when he 'came inside' during World War II to work on cattle stations. Willy was fully initiated and spoke English poorly, but several tribal languages fluently. Both the old men bore themselves with great dignity and self-assurance, and displayed considerable patience in later years when teaching me their traditions and culture.

Jerry Shepherd was about sixty and was employed as a tracker at the Laura police station, and Joe Musgrave was soon to return to work on a cattle station. Both George and Willy were keen to join us in an expedition in the near future, and I arranged to call for them in a month's time.

We remained in the Laura area for several days and found a small gallery of paintings at the base of the eastern scarp of Mingaroo Hill. While Frank and I explored, Mitchell helped Dick cut and prepare more bark for paintings, until he had enough for exhibitions in Cairns and Brisbane later in the year.

Mitchell decided he would rather visit relatives in Mossman than return to Cooktown, so we dropped him off there on our way to Cairns. He reappeared regularly to go on numerous field trips.

'One painting was very curious . . . the misshapen body had a large ugly head, thin arms and legs, and a large three-pronged penis.'

3
Legends of the land

Willy Long was away when I returned to Laura a few weeks later, but George Pegus was ready to roll his swag and accompany me and son Matthew to an area north-west of Cooktown. I had previously found an important group of galleries on Bull Creek, a tributary of the Normanby River, and intended making a detailed recording of them. It was outside George's clan country, in Gugu-Imudji territory, but I wanted George's opinion of the paintings, and also to record some of his legends and bush lore.

It was a five-kilometre walk from the vehicle to the galleries. We set off in late afternoon, carrying swags and enough food for a couple of days. Grasstrees grew in thousands in the open eucalypt forest and we were threading our way through a group of them when George called my attention to several which appeared to be dying, their normally dark green crowns turning yellow. George pushed one of them over, and borrowing my tomahawk, proceeded to chop into the soft trunk. The inner heartwood was riddled with holes made by a large white grub, which George called 'jumboon'. They were really good tucker, said George, so we cut up more of the dying trees and collected a good number of grubs in the billy for future cooking.

Even in the daylight most of the shelters were dark and gloomy, and George was uneasy. After examining the various paintings he expressed the opinion that 'only bad men came here', meaning men bent on sorcery or other forms of magic. He pointed out that there was little charcoal or other signs of occupational debris in the shelters. One painting was very curious; it portrayed a man about 1.5 metres tall, painted in bright yellow with a dark red outline and interior decoration. The misshapen body had a large ugly head, thin arms and legs, and a large three-pronged penis. The arms were deliberately drawn without hands. George thought it represented either an evil Quinkin

19

or a warning of the deformities which could be inflicted on trans-gressors of the tribal laws, particularly those governing sexual behaviour.

We camped under a rock overhang and kept a good fire going, not for warmth but to enable George, whose rolling eyes expressed a wish to be elsewhere, to keep the Quinkins at bay. George cooked the jumboon grubs by lightly roasting them for five minutes on black coals at the side of the fire. When they were cooked he held them by the head and putting the grub in his mouth, bit off the head and threw it away. I followed suit and found they had a very pleasant flavour, like crushed almonds. I thought they were probably the larvae of longicorn beetles, and later on found adult beetles with the same grubs.

George had been thinking of the ugly Quinkin figure nearby and later that evening related a Gugu-Imudji story which may have had some relationship to the distorted male figure. It concerned the frilled-neck lizard, which often had a villainous role in stories:

> Bonjul the frilled lizard was travelling down from the north, accompanied by his two young sisters. They had travelled a long way and were very thirsty by the time they came to a sandy creek bed. The two girls sat in shade while Bonjul went along the creek looking for water. He found a damp place and dug down in the sand till he found water. Bonjul had a long drink and then made the hole a lot deeper.
>
> The two girls came along and asked Bonjul for water and said, 'We can't reach the water, the well is too deep.'
>
> 'Get your heads right down in the well and you will be able to reach it,' said Bonjul.
>
> The girls put their heads and shoulders right down in the well, their tails sticking up in the air. While his sisters were drinking Bonjul came up and had intercourse with both of them. The girls cried out, 'You are doing a very bad thing. You must stop.'
>
> But by then it was too late. When the rest of the people heard what Bonjul had done they put a curse on him, saying, 'From now on, any man who does this to his sister, or any other relative, will grow a forked penis, big ears and a big ugly head.'

There were many other interesting figures in the small galleries. The first I worked in contained a finely executed freshwater crocodile over two metres long. It was a dark red linear figure, intricately decorated with red lines which also portrayed some internal organs. A kangaroo, emu, and a fish, all in white with red outline and decoration, also had internal organs depicted. It was obviously an incipient X-ray technique, not as refined as the X-ray art of Arnhem Land.

Another shelter contained yellow and red bichrome figures of three men and an echidna. The echidna had entrails depicted, and two of the men had their hair tied in a bundle at the back; the third man was smaller and had a wild 'Afro' hairstyle or headdress. They were more reminiscent of Arnhem Land than Cape York figures, and with the incipient X-ray style may have represented an Arnhem Land influence which had somehow reached Cape York peninsula in the past.

After spending two days there while I made drawings and took photographs, George was very glad to leave the place. When talking later with Gugu-Imudji men in Cooktown, I heard him describe the place as having 'too much bloody Quinkins'.

George decided to stay in Cooktown to see something of Harry Mole, another old mate of his living there. Harry had been police tracker at Laura for more than sixty years. He thought he had been about twelve when taken to Laura by members of a punitive expedition who had slaughtered virtually all his people, the Gugu-Warra tribe. That occurred near Jack Lakes, about one hundred and seventy kilometres north-west of Cooktown.

I was planning a three-week trip to the Laura area in November, and made arrangements to collect both George and Harry from Cooktown before going there. Harry appeared very old and frail, but George assured me that he had a great store of tribal knowledge and would be able to stay and look after our camp while we were away in the hills.

It turned out that I was to see a lot of George before we actually set out on that trip. My plans to get a team of the colourful Lardil dancers to Cairns for a corroboree had been approved by Reg Ansett and would take place in August. During the elaborate preparations to stage the corroboree it occurred to me that it would cement my friendship with George if I got him down to see the corroboree and meet my Lardil mates. I sent out the necessary message-sticks and George duly arrived by air, to be billeted with the Lardil men and enjoy the six stage performances they put on for the enthralled audiences of Cairns.

The excitement proved too much for George as he wound up in hospital with pneumonia. We visited him in hospital and my family looked after him afterwards, and by the time we set out on our November trip we were firm friends.

Driving north with George was to enter a land of legend—a living land whose rocks and trees possessed spirits to murmur secrets to those who wished to hear. George had been away from his country for a couple of months, and it was not George Pegus who sat beside me, but Joogumu, grey box tree, returning to his country.

George was a big man, who had grown rather portly during his long spell in hospital and convalescence. Thick, curly iron-grey hair and kindly face showed little trace of his more than seventy years, and his deep-set liquid brown eyes were as keen as when he speared his first kangaroo. He was looking forward to bush tucker—he called it hard tucker—food that would make him strong again after becoming soft and flabby on white man's food. We talked of those things as we went along, of wild duck in the early dawn, of plains turkeys, pigeons, barramundi and other fish in the waterholes, and we planned raids on flying fox colonies.

Once past Mt Molloy we were in George's country. The rough dirt road wound around the base of granite mountains, through poor country supporting an open forest of stunted eucalypts and termite mounds. It was early November and the drought-stricken land bleached under a relentless sun. Creek crossings which normally had a little water were dry and dusty, their banks fringed with drooping pandanus listlessly awaiting the wet season.

About fifteen kilometres south of Mt Molloy George asked me to stop. He pointed to a tall pillar of pale granite standing like a sentinel on top of a boulder-strewn hill some four kilometres west of the road. 'That rock,' he said, 'is Milkee the frog-mouthed owl. His father, Ngalculli the red kangaroo, is curled up at his feet.' George related the travel story of Ngalculli and Milkee as we drove along.

Ngalculli and the rest of the red kangaroo mob were travelling down from the north, coming from up past Princess Charlotte Bay. At the same time all the bird men were out hunting kangaroos. The young men and boys were sent off to drive the kangaroos toward the older men, who would spear them. Goodbulboon the butcherbird told Milkee to go with the young men.

'No, Grandfather,' Milkee said, 'I want to stay here and spear a kangaroo myself.' The older men finally agreed to let Milkee stay, but told him to keep well behind.

The kangaroos came in a big mob and the bird men began to spear them. Milkee waited until the biggest kangaroo came along at the back of the mob. Milkee speared the big kangaroo; it was old Ngalculli. Ngalculli pulled the spear out and smelt it, looking about and sniffing the air to see who had speared him. Ngalculli saw Milkee. He grabbed him, put him in a bag on his back and hopped away.

When the bird men missed Milkee they looked about for tracks but could not find any. Goodbulboon sent two swallow men, the Warrenjugu brothers, to look for his tracks. The swallow brothers flew off, each making a big semicircle. They met again without finding any trace of Milkee. The swallows flew another big circle and met again. 'No he is not there. He must be going another way.'

Ngalculli kept travelling south with Milkee; he had made him his son. Each night he made a flat place to camp, then continued on next day. One of his camping grounds was near the St George River.

The Warrenjugu-jugu had flown a long way south and sat down and waited. They heard Milkee cry out, 'Milkee, Milkee,' and saw him being carried along in the bag on Ngalculli's back. The swallows flew up then swooped down and each caught hold of one of Milkee's arms and flew off with him. They put Milkee behind a tree on the hill and left him there. Ngalculli came and rested there and they both turned to stone.

The story covered part of the Dream road of Ngalculli, which had been shown to George by his father, who had been a big man in the

Gugu Yalanji tribe. He was called Narmuwalbidgee, with the sacred name of Yanbun. They had wandered through the country when George was a boy and he was shown the Dreaming places, where to find water high in the hills, and where the old people had camped in rock shelters among the huge granite boulders. I resolved to find out more about the northern parts of Ngalculli's Dream road when the opportunity occurred.

We continued the dusty drive north until George again called a halt about three kilometres south of Desailly Creek. He had told me a legend concerning Gidja the moon-man, and wished to show me the story place. He pointed to Mount Elephant about five kilometres to the north. Near the top of the mountain there was a huge outcrop of grey granite with a diagonal split, which viewed from the east looks like a head-on view of an elephant—but to George it was the awful place where Gidja had cooked and eaten his two grandsons:

One time Gidja was travelling with his daughter Boolbuh the coucal, and her husband Yalngool the wedge-tailed eagle. Boolbuh had two sons, the Bil-bil or rainbow lorikeets.

Gidja went out hunting. High on the mountain he saw a rock wallaby and threw his spear at it; the spear cut the tip off the wallaby's tail. Gidja took the piece of tail back to camp and told his daughter she could have the wallaby if she sent the two Bil-bil boys to carry it.

Gidja took the boys up the hill to show them where the wallaby was supposed to be lying. He took them to the huge rock on the hillside; the rock had a great crevice in it and he told the boys to go inside and look for the wallaby. As soon as the Bil-bil went inside Gidja took out his fire-sticks; he gathered dry grass and wood and began spinning the fire-sticks to make fire and cook the boys. The Bil-bil boys heard the fire-sticks squeaking together and came out to see what caused the noise. They asked Gidja what it was.

'It is only parrots sqeaking. Go right inside and find the wallaby.' He pushed the boys back inside the crevice, lit a big fire at the entrance, and cooked them.

When the Bil-bil boys were cooked Gidja pulled them out of the crevice and ate all of them except the feet. By the time he reached the feet he had no more room left in his stomach, so he wrapped them in paperbark and put the parcel in a tree before returning to camp.

Boolbuh asked Gidja where were her sons. 'They must be playing about somewhere,' he replied. 'They will come soon.'

When the boys did not return Boolbuh went looking for them; she tracked Gidja back up the hill and looked about. Boolbuh found the bark parcel of feet. She sat down and cut her head with sharp stones and cried for her lost boys.

Boolbuh went back to camp and told her husband Yalngool, that Gidja had eaten their sons. Yalngool took up his spears and chased after the fleeing Gidja; he caught him and speared him until he was dead.

The sun was almost directly overhead as we climbed the winding road up the Desailly Range. Shimmering heat waves made lakes on the road ahead, but the mirages would not become reality for some weeks yet. The only breeze was caused by the passing of small whirlwinds which skirled across the road to vanish among hot rocks on the hillside. No living creature stirred from whatever shade it had found.

We were crossing one of the several tributaries of the St George River, all of them dry, when George pointed out another story place. It was time for lunch and some of the cool contents of the waterbag, so I pulled up in the scant shade of an ironbark and we got out to stretch our legs. About two kilometres across the valley to the east of the road, Noolgu the red owl sat on top of Birra hill and watched while we ate lunch. Then George told the story of Noolgu:

The two Noolgu brothers, the red owl men, were hunting fish. They were stunning fish in a waterhole of the Palmer River, using the poisonous bark and roots of freshwater mangroves growing on the banks. Digging-sticks and stone axes were used to cut and pound the bark and roots and the bundle of them was dragged back and forth through the waterhole with a rope and then left to steep in the deepest part.

The owl men sat in shade and waited for the poison to bring fish to the surface gasping for air. They saw a boy coming; it was their grandson Jimlinch, the cuckoo. He asked whether they had caught any fish yet, and they said, 'Not yet, but they will surface soon.'

Jimlinch walked around the waterhole. He saw the first fish come to the surface gasping for air, and tried to spear them. The owl men told him to stop as the fish would soon be easy to catch, but Jimlinch kept on trying to spear them.

Again and again they told him to stop, and when he would not stop the younger brother said, 'What will we do to stop him frightening the fish?'

The older brother said, 'We will have to kill him.'

They went down and grabbed Jimlinch and held him underwater until he drowned. Then they wrapped his body in poison bark and pushed it under roots in the water.

The owl brothers wrapped their fish in paperbark parcels. They were now sorry they had killed Jimlinch and were afraid of what the rest of the people would do about it. They decided to run away to new country further up river.

When the people found Jimlinch dead they looked about for tracks. They found the owl men's tracks and sent a party of warriors to follow and punish them. The warriors tracked the owl men for days and days until they caught up with them on Boongar Creek.

The owl men saw the warriors coming with ready spears and turned to run away. The vengeance party threw their spears and killed the older owl man, whose body fell into the creek and and turned into a large boulder. The younger owl man ran up Birra hill but the bird warriors caught him at the top and killed him. They lifted the owl man up and put him on top of a big rock and said, 'Now you stay there forever. Stay and look always west, back to the place where you killed Jimlinch.'

I was curious as to the identity of Jimlinch, and George explained that he was the rufus-breasted cuckoo who always arrived just before the wet season. He gave an imitation of his call—six or seven shrill whistles with a monotonous descending scale. Noolgu, the red owl, still sits on Birra hill and the westering sun reddens his breast like blood from spear wounds as he gazes west to the place of his crime back in Dreamtime, when all living things were still people.

All that long day we drove through the parched country and George re-created the Dreamtime, bringing the ancestral beings and totemic heroes back to life. I saw the Dreaming places and heard the stories of Marngu, the old tortoise woman, the rainbow serpent Nuramulli, and the creek he made as he crawled away dragging the spear thrust into him by Munnobungle the eel. Doolka the bandicoot danced again, and we came to the place where huge black heaps of dead flying fox warriors, now turned to stone, slumbered uneasily in the summer sun. They were about twenty kilometres south of Cooktown and called the Black Mountains, but actually they were huge piles of giant, rounded granite boulders, covered with black lichen; but to George they were the Kalkajagga, and he told the Gugu-Bullanji story of their creation:

> In the time when all animals and birds were people, the Joonging, or flying fox people, stole three more married women from the bird people. They were always stealing bird women, so the old men of the bird people, old Emu, Turkey, Brolga, Cockatoo and other men held a meeting.
>
> Gooranji the emu said, 'The Joonging warriors have taken three more of our young women. What are we going to do about it?'
>
> 'We must fight the Joonging and get our women back,' said all the other men.
>
> Gooranji said, 'There are a lot of flying fox people. We must send out scouts to find their main camp and see how many warriors they have.' They sent parties of young men in all directions to spy on the Joonging people.
>
> From the top of a hill a party of bird men saw the main camp of the Joonging—it stretched to the horizon in all directions. When they reported back to the old men, Gooranji said, 'The Joonging have too many warriors, we can't fight them. We will have to use the magic fire-sticks to light a big fire around them, a magic fire which burns without smoke or noise, just flame, to take them by surprise.'
>
> When the wind was right the bird warriors lit a big bush fire right round the flying fox camps. The Joonging people ran about everywhere trying to escape. Some grew wings and flew over the fire, but most fell down in big heaps and were burned to death.

As we drove through the Kalkajagga pass the heat waves shimmered over the black hills and the bodies of the Joonging seemed not to have cooled down at all.

'During the following weeks they pointed out in the galleries many of the sorcery figures.' Left to right: *Caesar Le Chu, the author and Willy Long at Mushroom Rock.*

4
The old men

Cooktown was still asleep when I drove out to the settlement in the warm November dawn to pick up George and Harry Mole to take them to Laura. They had just finished breakfast and I helped them roll swags and pack their gear in the station wagon, keeping a wary eye on the bristling dogs as I did so. The mistrust of whites by Aborigines was strikingly manifested in the behaviour of their mean and mangy, but loyal, dogs.

Harry had been away from Laura for nearly two years and was pleased to be going back, and he and George were reminiscing as we passed familiar places. It was only a two-hour drive in the relative coolness of early morning. Near King's Plains a large mob of wild pigs crossed the road in front of us and I leapt out with the rifle to shoot a small one for the Laura camp, but they vanished quickly into long grass.

The Laura settlement was deserted when we drove in, a couple of huge gaunt tomcats being the only sign of life. The waterhole below the huts had dried up and the few families were living in tents a couple of hundred metres upstream. We picked up Willy Long and drove a kilometre up stream to camp on a deep waterhole, spending the afternoon making a comfortable camp as we intended to stay a week before shifting to a new area.

The temperature had soared during the day and we were glad to get into the waterhole for a swim when the sun vanished, blood red in the low dado of smoke haze. We sat in the shallow water and discussed legends until the first of the flying fox hordes came flapping by in search of sweet blossom. I was anxious to start taping legends while the old men were still fresh, and after dinner we sat around the recorder in the bright light of a full moon and listened to Harry Mole telling his 'bora' story. Harry's main Dreaming was the dingo, and his story related the Cape York peninsula section of the dingo Dream road, including the death and rebirth of the legendary dog, the re-enactment of which formed an important part in the initiation ceremonies of dingo boys.

Dick had told me that the Lardil legend said the dingo had come from the west to Mornington Island and there were two dingo Dreamings, one on Denham Island and the other near Charlie Busch Bay on Mornington Island. Harry's dingo story also travelled from the west:

Old Eelgin the grasshopper woman and Gaiya the giant devil-dog came from the west. Gaiya was huge, much bigger than a horse. Old Eelgin was boss of that dingo, and she used him to hunt and kill men for food. When Gaiya was hunting and got on the track of someone, his awful howling could be heard from far off, and his galloping shook the ground and sounded like distant thunder.

One day when Gaiya was away hunting, two young men came along to Eelgin's camp. They were the Chooku-chooku, or butcherbird brothers. Old Eelgin saw the young men coming and called out, 'Hello, here are two of my grandsons. Where are you going?'

'We are out hunting for meat,' the older brother said.

'Good, you can camp here, boys.'

But the Chooku-chooku were afraid of Gaiya and said, 'Where is your big dog, Granny?'

'It'll be all right,' Eelgin said. 'He is away hunting and won't be back until tomorrow at sunrise. You can camp here.'

But the brothers did not trust Eelgin and said, 'No, we have a long way to go and will travel on now.'

As soon as they were out of sight down the creek the butcherbird brothers began to run away swiftly.

Gaiya came back some time after the boys had gone, and Eelgin scolded him. 'Where have you been? You're too late now. There were two nice fat young men here, but they've gone. Come and I will put you on their tracks.' And Eelgin set her devil-dog on the tracks of the butcherbird brothers.

The brothers knew that Gaiya would soon be after them and they travelled on and on, not stopping to rest, running as fast as they could. When they heard the dreadful howling of Gaiya coming faintly on the wind they ran faster, heading towards the east.

Gaiya chased the butcherbird boys right across Cape York peninsula. Always they heard his howling coming down the wind; he was getting closer and closer and they knew they could not get away.

The two brothers ran on until they were near Barrow Point. Here they came to a big rocky pass through the hills. The pass was called Bulinmore. The younger brother said, 'I can run no further. What will we do now?'

'We'll try and spear him. You climb up that side and I'll climb up this side. We'll hide and when he comes through we'll spear him.'

They then climbed up the sides of the pass and hid among rocks. The howling dog came on, following their tracks. Old Eelgin was following on behind, hobbling along on a stick and sooling her dog onward, sooling him on.

The Chooku-chooku brothers listened to the dog coming, still far away. He came closer and closer and the howling became louder and louder. The younger brother said, 'There he is! I'll spear him.'

But the older brother said, 'No, that's only his tongue. Wait!'

Again the younger brother said, 'There he is! Now I'll spear him.'

But again the older brother said, 'No. That's only his head. Wait and spear the dog behind.'

When the dog's shoulders appeared in the pass the older brother began spearing Gaiya. He speared and speared him, and when he had finished the younger brother started spearing from the other side. He kept on spearing until Gaiya was dead.

The butcherbird brothers then climbed down and called to all the people to come and cut up and share the meat of the giant dog. The brothers cut off the tip of Gaiya's tail. The spirit of Gaiya was in that tail, and the older brother said to it, 'Now go back and meet your boss.'

Eelgin was hobbling along behind, sooling her dog on. She saw Gaiya coming and, glad to see her dog said, 'Ah, so my dog has come back. Did you catch those nice fat boys?'

But the spirit Gaiya was angry with Eelgin for having set him on the tracks of the butcherbird men, and bit her on the nose.

Eelgin cried out, 'Why did you bite me?'

The butcherbird brothers then came along and killed Eelgin.

They said to her spirit, 'Now you go down to the salt-arm near Barrow Point and stay there; that will be your Dreaming place.'

The spirit of Eelgin lives in a big rock in the salt-arm and the marks where Gaiya bit Eelgin can be seen on the noses of all grasshoppers.

In the meantime the people were cutting up Gaiya, and they asked the clever man, Woodbarl the white cloud, what parts he wanted.

'I want the kidneys and the head,' Woodbarl said. 'You people have all the flesh, but give me the bones also.' Later he gathered up all the bones and took them away to the top of a mountain. He also took the skin.

From the bones Woodbarl made two small dingoes, one male and one female. He blew down the mouths of the dogs and they came alive. Woodbarl said to the male dingo, 'Come on, you howl now.' The dingo howled. 'All right, lift up your back leg now. All right, you are a good one. From now on you are a dingo and you won't eat people. You will be a friend of people.'

Today the dingo is a friend of people; Eelgin has her home in the rock near Barrow Point; butcherbirds have beaks like spears, and Woodbarl has his spirit home on Woolcooldin Island.

The telling of the story was, as always, interrupted by questions or amendments from the other old men, particularly if their own stories differed greatly from that being related. Willy's dingo story obviously differed considerably from Harry's version, so I recorded it a week later. The very next day we found an excellent large painting of a dingo in a group of galleries.

I had not previously recorded a full version of the rainbow serpent saga on the peninsula, but George knew the southern section and Harry the northern, and after much discussion I recorded the following:

The land was all flat in the beginning; there were no mountains at all, other than a huge one called Borabunnaru. Goorialla, the great rainbow serpent, travelled up from the south until he stopped in this country at a place called Narabullgan, now called Mt Mulligan. Goorialla made Narabullgan from his droppings and fashioned the big waterlily lagoon on top. The coal seam that white men have been digging was the remains of his campfire. He camped in big caves on top of the mountain.

Goorialla sat on top of Narabullgan and listened on the wind. He listened to the four winds and heard the voices of many people floating on the wind. He listened a long time and finally said, 'This is not my country. All these people speak a different language to me; I will go further north and look for my own people.'

Mt Mulgrave was the next stopping place. Here he made, again from his droppings, a long granite mountain in the shape of a snake. Goorialla camped there to rest awhile, then he continued on north. When Goorialla reached the Palmer River he again listened to the wind. He could hear people away up north and they were speaking his language. He travelled on to Fairlight and made a big limestone hill, high and sharp like a windmill, and with five windows, each looking in a different direction. Goorialla climbed up and looked in each direction before going on northwards.

The next stop was at Fairview, on top of a broad ridge. He decided to make another big waterlily lagoon there. He turned round and round trying to make the hole deeper, but the ground was too hard so he left it and went northward. When he came to Scrubby Creek he decided to build a big gunyah and camp there until some of his own people came along. One day he heard singing coming down the wind; he listened carefully and heard 'Ahrrrr, AHrrrr, AHrrrr'.

'Those are my people singing,' he said. 'They are holding a big bora.'

Goorialla travelled north and the singing came louder on the wind. When he reached the place where the Kennedy and Normanby rivers meet, he saw his own people. Goorialla went up quietly and hid in long grass. He could see men dancing—emu, cockatoo, brolga, jabiru, ibis, kangaroo and all the other big men. They were dancing and singing the bora.

Pink-pink the double-barred finch saw grass moving and called out that someone was coming. Kookaburra heard him and sent one of his children over to see who was there. When the child came near, Goorialla spoke quietly to him. 'Now you go back and tell them there is no one here. I want to watch the men dance.' So the boy went back and said he could not see anybody.

The big men began dancing again. The singers had didjeridoos, which were not used as drone pipes but which were sung and yelled through.

Goorialla watched the dancing for a long time, and then came out of his hiding place and was greeted by the people.

Goorialla said to the men, 'You're not dancing properly, and you're not dressed properly. Now you watch me.'

He put a lump of bee's wax on the back of his head and then stuck cockatoo feathers in it to make a rayed headdress. He put on pandanus armbands, a pearl-shell pendant, beads made from yellow grass-stems, and put a white bone through his nose. Then he painted designs on his body with white clay and began to dance.

All the men watched Goorialla and then copied him. They danced and danced until they were finished. Goorialla went off and made a gunyah and went to sleep. All the people went to their bark gunyahs to sleep.

During the night a big storm came up. Heavy rain began to fall, lightning flashed, and the wind blew strong. Two young rainbow lorikeet men came running along; they were the Bil-bil brothers and were looking for shelter. They went to the gunyah of their grandmother, the old star woman, and asked for shelter.

'You can't get in here boys, I have too many dogs.'

They asked Goorangi the emu, who said, 'No, I have no room, I have too many children.' Wherever the boys asked they could get no shelter.

They tried Goorialla, who said, 'No, I have no room.'

'But it's raining very hard now, Grandfather. We must have shelter.'

'All right, you wait. I'll make my gunyah bigger, and then you can come in.'

He opened his mouth, opened it very wide, right up to the roof, and said, 'All right, you come in now.'

The two boys ran inside, right into Goorialla's mouth, and he swallowed them.

After he had swallowed the Bil-bil boys, Goorialla began to worry about what the rest of the people would do when they found them missing. He decided to move on and began to travel north again. He kept going till he came to Barrow Point on the coast. Here was Borabunaru, the only mountain in the world; it was huge and had sheer cliffs all around its base. Goorialla climbed on top of the mountain and went to sleep with the two young Bil-bil inside him.

When the people saw that Goorialla had gone they looked about and found tracks.

Goorangi the emu said, 'Goorialla has swallowed the Bil-bil. We must follow him and get them back.' All the people tracked Goorialla to the foot of the great mountain.

The people tried to climb the mountain—old Emu, Brolga, Turkey, Tortoise, Possum, Barramundi, they all tried, but kept falling back down again. Then two tree goannas, the Wongu men, came along. Goorangi spoke to them. 'We can't climb the mountain. Would you try and rescue them?'

'All right, we can climb up and rescue them, but there will be big trouble and Goorialla will be very angry, so all you people go away, go and change into birds and animals and other living things.'

All the people ran away. The Wangu men then found some white quartz from which they each made a knife. They began to climb the mountain, climbing on and on, getting higher and higher. They came to the top and saw Goorialla lying fast asleep; he was snoring.

The Wangu men crept up to Goorialla. 'You cut him open on that side,' said the older brother, 'and I'll cut him open on this side.'

They cut him open from his neck right down to his tail, and saw the Bil-bil boys inside Goorialla. They had changed into rainbow lorikeets, one male and one female. The Wangu said, 'All right. You can come out. You are rainbow lorikeets now; you have wings and can fly sway.'

So the Bil-bil flew away and the Wangu climbed down off the mountain. They ran away to join the rest of the people and changed themselves into tree goannas.

Goorialla snored and slept on. A cold wind began to blow; it blew through the empty stomach and woke him up. He looked about and said, 'There is something wrong with me, someone has cut me open and taken my dinner away.' He became very angry and roared and threshed about. He tore the great mountain to pieces and hurled it all over the country. The pieces of the great mountain formed the hills and mountain ranges as they are today, and only a small hill remains where that first great mountain stood.

Afterwards Goorialla went down to the sea by Barrow Point. He went into the sea and stayed there. If people try to pass the place in a boat old Goorialla acts like a magnet and drags them under the water. The shooting star is the eye of Goorialla as he watches over everything.

The moon was now high in the sky and we watched the flying foxes come swooping down over the waterhole to skim the surface and scoop up water on the wing. George said that was when Narwool the freshwater crocodile got his share of juicy flying fox, lying with only his eye knobs above the water waiting to snap up an unlucky flying fox. He suggested we take the shotgun with us next day as we would be passing the flying fox camp.

The plaintive wailing of curlews came drifting on the light wind as we lay on our swags. George said the birds were rounding up straying, unborn baby spirits. Willy said the curlew's name was Nuyumul, and tomorrow night he would tell us how Nuyumul and Algarumba, the bandicoot, first brought fire-sticks to this country.

No alarm clocks are needed when camping on the Laura River. First light brings a cacophony of birdcalls which will wake the heaviest sleeper. The blue-wing kookaburra begins the chorus with loud raucous chortlings, followed by his more melodious cousin, the laughing kookaburra. They wake the banana-birds and then all the lesser fry, and within minutes the vivid dawn air throbs with bird song. Raucous sulphur-crested cockatoos shout from the treetops and mobs of rainbow lorikeets flash flame across the sky. Their shrilling eagerness makes lying in bed seem slothful.

Harry stayed to mind camp and doze in the shade while I set off with George and Willy to explore another aerial prospect about twelve kilometres east of camp and located on a low sandstone plateau covered with eucalypt forest.

One of the old tracks from the gold rush days went close to the plateau and we were able to bump slowly along it, winding in and out among the trees. About six kilometres from camp we came on the flying fox colony. A permanent spring supported a residual patch of vine forest and the tall trees were festooned with several thousand fruit-bats of the smaller red-collared variety. The place was noisome both in smell and sound, and the bats kept up a continuous screeching and flapping of wings to fan themselves as they hung upside down. George assured me the red variety were the best eating and did not smell badly like the larger black bats. He was looking forward to a feast in the evening.

As we drove along George talked about Joonging the flying fox: "im bin human being one time, 'e teach murri (man) how to camp, married people in middle, single man there, single girl over other side. Old Joonging still camp that way.' Willy said that Joonging also showed man how to protect himself in wet weather. During periods of heavy rain flying foxes hang under the fronds of pandanus palm heads, and conveyed to man the idea of building shelters from similar materials. George described how the mother flying fox carries her baby on her underside attached to a teat while it is small, and on her back as it grows larger. When she alights among blossom or fruit, the baby swings about among the branches helping itself; the mother whistles it back when she wants to move on.

We had to walk the last three kilometres. It was already hot, so I left George and Willy to track me along at their own pace. When I reached the top of the plateau and saw many house-high slabs of sandstone containing shelters I knew we had struck it rich again. Although the galleries were not large or extensively painted they contained some particularly fine figures, including a very large dingo and two life-size echidnas. I had assembled my grid and was doing scaled drawings when George and Willy arrived.

Poor old portly George was feeling the heat, but long, lean and dignified Willy appeared not affected. Sheets of old paperbark matting had been used by former occupants to soften the rock floor and the old men sat on them to study the paintings while I drew them. George called the echidna Bulinmore, and said it was very sacred, only father's father could eat the succulent animal. I asked George whether the echidna had a story, and after remembering for a while, he related it:

When the people were camped at Wahwingee, a waterhole on the north branch of the Palmer River, they all went out in the bush to hunt for honey. Bulinmore, the echidna, found a honeybee hive in a hollow tree. He had no stone axe to cut the tree open and get honey, but Gulna the black cockatoo came along and Bulinmore asked for a loan of his axe. Gulna would not lend his stone axe, however, because the law of that time ruled that the stone axe of the father belonged to his children, and could not be lent to anyone.

Bulinmore asked all the people as they came along, he asked kookaburra, brolga, emu, plains turkey, he asked everyone, but no one would lend him a stone axe. Bulinmore became very angry and went back to his camp at Wahwingee. He went to the waterhole and drank all the water he could hold; there was a little bit left so he sat in it and covered it up.

When the people came back from hunting they were very thirsty from eating honey, and went straight to the waterhole where they found Bulinmore covering the water. The people asked him for water saying, 'Come on Bulinmore, give us some water for our thirsty children.' Bulinmore just grunted and would not move.

The people talked together about what they should do. They decided to spear Bulinmore. Gathering their spears they stood all around Bulinmore and speared and speared him until the spears stood out thickly all over. Then they dragged him out, turned him over and cut him open. Water poured out of Bulinmore in a great flood and filled the waterhole again. Now the people called out, 'Shoo—oo. From now on no one can block the water. Water belongs to everybody. Shoo—oo. From now on we will lend our stone axes to anyone who needs them. We will all share everything.'

The painting of Bulinmore on the wall in front of me had a solid red ochre body, outlined with white. Short white stripes all over the body indicated his spines. His head was turned slightly as though listening to ensure that his ancient story was told aright. In a small shelter opposite, Gaiya the devil dog, with ears pricked forward and bushy tail streaming behind, seemed to be in relentless pursuit of the valiant butcherbird boys.

I continued with scaled drawings while the old men fossicked about or dozed in the shade. On a sheet of paperbark in a shallow crevice Willy found a small edge-ground stone axe, a couple of trimmed stone knife blades, and a grass dillybag which crumbled to dust when touched. We named them the Scattered Group galleries.

The afternoon sun had lost some of its fierceness when we arrived back at the flying fox camp. Their incessant chatter rose in volume as we walked in under the laden trees, and erupted into screeching bedlam when George fired both barrels into the mass of russet and black bodies. Dead flying foxes rained down and further shots were drowned in a wave of noise and flapping confusion.

We gathered up about fifty of the small animals, enough to feed the settlement and ourselves. We were putting them in sugarbags when Willy yelled suddenly and dropped a bundle of flying foxes to caper about with surprising agility for a man of his age. A supposedly dead flying fox had fastened its dog-like teeth into his thigh. Only George and I appreciated the humour of the situation.

I noted that the male flying fox has a penis very like a circumcised man, and when I mentioned it, George said, 'Well old Joonging bin human being one time.'

At the settlement we handed out the flying fox to eager hands and returned to camp with our share. I gathered wood while George and Willy prepared a ground oven to roast our catch. They dug a shallow pit in the sand of the riverbed and lined it with large pebbles; wood was piled on the stones and then more stones placed on and among the wood. When the fire was burning fiercely they threw the flying foxes into the blaze. The wings and fur were burnt off in a couple of minutes and the blackened bodies raked out to cool.

When the fire had burnt down they raked the coals from the pit and covered the hot stones with a bed of gum leaves. The flying foxes were placed on a flat rock and pounded with a large stone to smash all their bones, then placed on the leaves and covered with sheets of paperbark, which was then covered with sand and left for about an hour. In the meantime I had mixed and pounded a damper for bread and used coals raked from the oven to line a hole and cook it in the camp oven. With dinner cooking we stripped off and dived into the waterhole.

The smashing of the flying fox bones before cooking had intrigued me as I could not see how it would improve them as food with bits of shattered bone among the meat. I asked George about it, but he deferred to Willy, who explained that back in Dreamtime Joonging had been a very wise, important and powerful man, and it was essential to break the bones of all Joonging to give their spirit bodies soft bones, so they could not travel back from the spirit world to cause trouble for the people.

The flying foxes turned out to be delicious, although the dark meat did have a flavour of its own, perhaps due to their diet of blossom and fruit. Years ago I had adopted an attitude toward bush tucker; I like oysters, so anything in the grub or insect line becomes an oyster, any aquatic life, including tortoise, eel or crocodile, becomes fish, and anything that flies becomes wild duck. So wild duck and damper made a pleasant dinner that evening. Afterwards I reminded Willy to tell us of the legend of Algarumba the bandicoot and Nuyumul the curlew:

Algarumba the bandicoot and Nuyumul the curlew met each other on the Mitchell River, near the present Koolatah cattle station, and decided to travel together. Nuyumul had fire-sticks in his dillybag.

They travelled northward until they came to the junction of the Coleman and Crosbie rivers. Here they could smell something stinking. They looked about and found kangaroo meat hanging up in a circle of trees; the meat was raw and beginning to smell. Nuyumul said, 'This meat is going bad, when the people who own it come back they will be hungry; we had better cook it for them.' He got out his fire-sticks, rubbed up some dry grass into tinder and twirled his fire-sticks until he had fire. He said to Bandicoot, 'You go round that way and cook the meat, and I will go this way and cook it.'

The camp belonged to the flying fox people. It was spread around in a circle, married people in the middle section, single men on one side and single girls on the other. The flying fox still camp this way, and it was the flying fox people who showed everybody else the proper way to camp. The flying fox people were away up on the hill; they were letting the young men have intercourse with the young women so they could learn and get married.

When the flying fox people returned to camp they found Bandicoot and Curlew hard at work cooking all the meat. It was nearly finished and smelled good. The flying fox people said, 'Look at those young men working so hard for us; we must give them a present of a young girl each.'

'What will we do?' Bandicoot said to Curlew. 'Will we teach these young girls now?'

But Curlew was shy and said, 'There are too many people about; it's still daylight and they can see us.'

Bandicoot said, 'It will be all right, you'll see.'

They lay down with the two girls; as soon as the girls opened their legs, darkness poured out from between them. It became very dark as though a big storm was coming; the wind blew strong and rain fell. The flying fox people were afraid and got into their camps, calling out, 'What is happening? It should not be dark.'

Bandicoot said, 'Don't worry. It will get light again; you'll see the morning star soon.'

Bandicoot and Curlew finished with the two girls and the darkness passed away; it was just like an eclipse of the sun. The people came out of their camps and Curlew went among them handing out fire-sticks to everybody, saying, 'For you, married man; for you, single man; for you, boy. Now you have fire and need never be afraid of the dark again.'

The flying fox people did not know how to use the fire-sticks, so Curlew said, 'Now you watch me; watch my hands.' He first dug a small hollow in one of the sticks, then cut a groove down the side from the hollow so the powdered and smouldering wood could run down it. He ground dry grass, put it on a small piece of bark on the ground and placed the stick with the hole in it on the bark. He stood the other stick upright in the hollow and holding the bottom stick firm with his foot, twirled the upright stick back and forth in his hands while pressing it down on the bottom stick. The wood began to powder and run down the groove, getting hotter and hotter until it began to smoulder on the dry grass. Curlew then picked up the bark and grass and fanned it about in his hand until it burst into flame.

Since that time man has always had fire to cook his food and provide him with light and warmth at night.

We certainly needed no fire for warmth that night and we had a bright yellow moon for light, but a fire is the focal point of any camp and provides company for the lonely. A night social life for early man probably began when he acquired fire.

Man probably had the use of fire for a very long time, acquired from natural sources of lightning strikes and volcanoes, before he acquired the knowledge of how to make fire at will, and consequently the loss of fire in sudden rain storms was no longer a disaster.

The old men said that fire-sticks could be made from many different woods, including the flower stem of the grasstree, which was used as the bottom, or female stick. The most popular wood for fire-sticks came from the 'matchwood' tree, or 'fire-stick' tree, and may be the reason why the matchwood tree was so important in mortuary rites across northern Australia. A tree from which fire can be easily kindled could also kindle new life for the spirits of the dead.

It was still too hot to sleep so I asked Willy to tell us the Olcula version of the dingo legend, as he had been through the dingo bora ceremony, covering that part of the dingo Dream road.

The white-faced owl and the red mopoke were brothers. They were travelling north and crossed the Mitchell River at the ford near Koolatah cattle station. For three days they travelled north, killing and eating people for food. Near the Palmer River the owl brothers found a fresh camp where the ashes were still warm in the fireplaces. They looked about for tracks and followed them until they caught up with a young man, Alpudda the coucal; he was nice and fat so the owl men killed him with spears.

The owl men had two young mopoke girls to do all the cooking. The girls cut bark and made bark vessels to cook Alpudda. They cut him up and put pieces of meat in the bark vessels and added water and hot stones. Then they put more hot stones all round them, covered them over with large sheets of paperbark and heaped sand over the bark.

When the meat was cooked the girls scraped off the sand, removed the bark sheets and took out the vessels. There was a lot of soup in with the meat, so they made wads of soft fine grass and the owl people sat around mopping up the soup and eating it. They hung the meat in a tree for next day.

There was an old woman camped farther along the river and the owl men went and camped with her. The old woman was boss of a big dog; it was as big as a bullock and had a small pup.

All the owl people went hunting for more men to eat. They found a camp with fires and bark shades. Old woman mopoke sooled her dog along the tracks of men from the camp and it caught and killed one of them. The rest of the men ran away, crying out, 'Yackai, yackai, yackai.'

The dingo pup ran up to two men in another camp; they were Jimbal the tree goanna and Andidjeri the sugar glider. Jimbal kicked the pup, knocking it over, and the pup ran away howling.

Jimbal and Andidjeri knew the pup would soon come back with the big dog. They decided to make a swamp to bog the big dog so they could spear him. They used a magic quartz crystal to sing up the rain, running round in a circle. When the rain came they ran all over the circle, thrusting their spears into the ground to make it soft and boggy. When the bog was ready Jimbal and Andidjeri practised fighting and planned how to attack and kill the big dog. Andidjeri said, 'You and I will both spear him and then I'll jump on his back and hit him on the head with my big axe. Don't you spear me when I jump up on him.'

The men heard the dog coming when it was a long way off; he was howling as he galloped along. Jimbal and Andidjeri stood on the other side of the bog and waited. The huge dog came over a hill, saw the men and rushed at them, only to hit the swamp and get bogged. The two men hurled spears into him and then Andidjeri jumped on his back and killed him with a stone axe.

They pulled the big dog out of the swamp and cut him up, throwing the pieces all over the country. The pieces turned into small dingoes which would not attack people, and everybody had dingoes to help them in hunting.

37

Jimbal and Andidjeri killed all the owl people except the two girls. They took one young mopoke girl each and travelled north to their own country on the Coleman River.

After a nightcap of rum and river water I went to sleep pondering on the giant devil dingo legends. How long had the dingo been in Australia, and what manner of men had made the water craft to bring them here? Were the first dingoes larger than the present day species? Did one race of people who were cannibals use dingoes to hunt another race of people? Were the old women who owned the giant dog evidence of a matriarchal society, or did they indicate that dingoes were more useful to women hunters than to men? How long have some dingoes been feral animals, since they could only have arrived as the domestic animals of man?

Next morning the sky was overcast. George had told me earlier of a spectacular gallery he had seen when a young man. It was far better than anything we had yet seen; he described it as being very long and high—a horse could be ridden along inside it for the full length. The back wall was painted from the floor to the ceiling. It was located, he thought, on a branch of Ginger Creek, only about fifteen kilometres distant.

We went to the waterhole where it was shaded by big paperbarks and sat in water up to our chins to discuss the lost gallery. Harry Mole had never seen it but had heard of it. Many years before, Harry's uncle, a man called Dingo, had been camping along Ginger Creek with his first wife, Maggie. When Maggie ran off with another man, Dingo decided to kill her by sorcery. In a small shelter near the main gallery he used white clay to paint the figure of a woman, with a snake biting her on the heel, 'singing' Maggie to death as he painted.

After Maggie had died from the sorcery, Maggie's relatives in turn killed Dingo by sorcery. The event occurred about the time of the last bora, about fifty years previous. During the discussion which followed Harry's revelation, the old men lamented the fact that the only living part of their culture remaining was the practice of sorcery, and that men still die from it. During the following weeks they pointed out in the galleries many of the sorcery figures, which were in human form, and sometimes associated with snakes and catfish.

Most of the sorcery figures, male and female, were simple monochrome silhouettes, a few were more intricate, and some elaborately decorated. I asked George why some of the sorcery figures were inverted. He explained:

Well, this man is your enemy—but you can't catch him with a spear, he's too good a fighter; so you catch him this way. Upside down means he is going to be buried that way, which is the worst thing that can happen to anybody. It means that his spirit can't get out of the ground to travel to

Woolunda, the land of life after death. That's why most people are buried
trussed in a sitting position, so the spirit can come out their nose just
below the surface and get away.

Many of the sorcery figures had hand stencils on them, and other
additions like barbed spears through them, with extra barbs being
added later in different shades of paint, to reactivate the magic. One
dark red man had been struck all over his torso by a sharp implement,
probably a spear. There were apparently two types of sorcery figures.
The main ones, often life-size and in public view in living sites, were
used to 'sing' people from another clan; others placed in secrecy in
remote and hidden places were for pay-back killings within the
clan.

We were talking about some of the figures in Split Rock galleries
when Harry mentioned that they were not the main camping place in
recent times. The old Myalls had told him their main camp was on top
of the plateau, about two kilometres west of Split Rock, where it could
not be approached by the mounted Black Police.

As the current heatwave was proving too much for the old men, I
decided to explore the area alone next day. The sun had gone and we
were about to leave the water when Willy said, 'Look out, there's my
wife!' I couldn't see any women and knew his wife had been dead for
many years. Understanding dawned when Willy pointed with his chin
at two small red-legged sandpipers just arrived at the waterhole. The
sandpiper was one of his former wife's totems and her spirit bird had
arrived to check on him. When the birds flew over our heads Willy
ducked underwater and later came up to say, 'I'll have to watch out
tonight, she'll have my guts out quick-time.'

The spirits of the dead people are potentially harmful to the living,
and I noticed that Willy was always careful to observe the taboos
placed on him by his wife's death, such as not being able to eat kangaroo or barramundi.

Next day I left the three old men resting and set off to search for the
refugee camp on top of the plateau. The sun again created an inferno
as I climbed up among pink sandstone slabs. It was easy walking along
the top through an open forest of bloodwood and grasstrees, and a
light breeze made the heat more bearable. Far below to the north
a meandering line of darker green among the sea of grey-green
eucalypts marked the course of the Laura River, now just ponded
waterholes. Small flocks of black cockatoos were feeding on bloodwood nuts, their harsh eerie calls warning the rock wallabies that man
was coming.

I had expected to see large blocks of sandstone on the plateau, but
there was none until I came suddenly on an area where the top layer
of sandstone had fissured and tessellated into huge slabs resting on a
terrace about ten metres below the top level. A steeply sloping fissure

gave access and I slid down it to enter into a lunar landscape of tumbled slabs, heavily sculpted by wind and water.

I looked into a small igloo-shaped cave and saw many red hand stencils on the walls and ceiling, some very faded, and there were no traces of occupational debris. Around the corner a high wall of sandstone leaned outward to provide shelter for a mass of red stencils of hands, feet, weapons, stone axes and other implements. They were all on the bottom two metres of the wall, apart from a group of stencilled hands about ten metres above ground level. Although no trace of it remained it was obvious that a tree had once grown close against the cliff face.

Some of the stencilled feet belonged to small children, and their parents must have held them up to place a foot against the rock and spray a mouthful of red ochre round it. The stencil of a tommy-roundhead lizard was also there, and I imagined his disgust at having red ochre spat all over him. Some hand stencils had one or two fingers missing or doubled under, the latter more likely as there were no stencils with just the top joint missing. The old men had told me that hand stencilling was the same as 'putting your name on the wall', so perhaps the missing finger stencils ensured recognition at a later time.

I found seven more galleries, each containing twenty to thirty figures, the main motif being humans. The paintings seemed to be very old or very recent, suggesting that an old infrequently used site had suddenly been heavily populated in recent times. Harry's statement that this was one of the main Gugu-Yalanji camps during the early stages of the European invasion seemed to be correct. There was a small spring of water, and the limited number of steep access tracks were clearly visible from above, ensuring no surprise raids by mounted Black Police.

The older paintings were mainly in dark red ochres. Remnants of a large bichrome snake and a couple of faded human figures appeared to have a ceremonial origin. The more recent figures were in cream or pale yellow clay and appeared to be of a secular nature for sorcery, love-magic or hunting purposes.

The most westerly gallery was somewhat isolated from the main group, and appeared to be a ceremonial site only recently created, perhaps during the last period of occupation. There were only four figures, all in the same dark red ochre with white outlines and interior bars. A man, probably an ancestral being, had a headband and stretched ear lobes; he was about a metre high. The other three figures were birds, two were scrub turkeys, and the third either an incomplete scrub turkey still awaiting a tail, or an emu. I walked out of the shelter and was startled by a large black bird which dashed from under bushes and flapped noisily over my head; it was a scrub turkey.

Next day was cooler and I returned with George and Willy, bringing our swags, food and water, and recording gear to camp for a couple of days to record the galleries. They identified some of the figures for me, some were for sorcery, some for love-magic, and another was a painting of a bark mortuary basket used to contain bones for a secondary burial. One stencil was identified as that of a horseshoe axe. Willy explained that a cast horseshoe was a treasured find by the old people. They cut it in half by abrading it on sandstone to make two steel tomahawks. Next day he found half a rusted horseshoe in a shelter; its wooden haft had been eaten away by termites.

Night slipped quietly over the galleries and again brought the Quinkins pressing in on George and Willy. They came sliding thin attenuated bodies out of rock holes and crevices to sit with quiet menace around the outer edges of the firelight, watched covertly by the old men. However, they drew strength and courage from each other and from my presence, and we talked quietly in the hot night.

There were several pairs of kangaroo tracks painted in one gallery and they reminded me of similar tracks engraved in rock in the bed of the Laura River. Old Jerry Shepard, the police blacktracker, said that the tracks had been made 'to teach young men how to swear (curse) the kangaroo foot'. Jerry said he did not know how to 'swear the kangaroo', but that Willy could; Willy had previously declined to do this, probably because young uninitiated men were present, but now he readily agreed to do so.

Willy explained that only the red and grey kangaroos were hunted in this way, because they lived in mobs. The animal called the red kangaroo in Cape York peninsula is actually the antilopine wallaroo, due to the fact that the males of the species are of a reddish colour. The big hill kangaroos, or wallaroos, lived singly or in pairs, and were hunted with dingoes to bring them to bay. The agile wallaby was driven by fire, as part of the fire-stick animal husbandry, burning the grass in mosaic patterns to keep green grass available to their kangaroos and other animals. Apparently the kangaroos were reserved as the wet season meat supply, as Willy said they were harvested only during the wet season, the men going out during breaks in the rain:

> The men spread out, some go this way, some go that way, until they find a mob of kangaroos. All right, here they are. One man picks up a stick and follows along the tracks of the biggest male kangaroo. He swings the stick from side to side over the tracks and sings out loud, 'Wonk, wonk, wonk, millard. Wonk, wonk, amirrid. Wonk, wonk, larrard. Wonk, wonk, atubard, wonk, wonk, togard. Wonk, wonk, anitumid. Wonk, wonk, gebard. Wonk, wonk, oridard!'
>
> The hunter keeps swinging his stick and singing, 'I curse your eye, wonk, wonk, your neck, wonk, wonk, your ear, wonk, wonk, your shoulder, wonk, wonk, your heart, wonk, wonk, your tail, wonk, wonk, your foot.'

The kangaroo will take a huge leap sideways and head in a different direction. Other men wheel out in semicircles on each side till they cut the tracks again. 'Here it is! Wonk, wonk, millard. Wonk, wonk, amirrid.' The kangaroo can't go far, maybe half a mile, then he starts to stagger about as though he were drunk. No need to spear him, don't spear him, just walk up and hit him with that stick and carry him back to camp.'

Only the red and grey kangaroos are 'sung' in this way, not the emu or any other game. They are all speared.

The old men could give no satisfactory reason as to why this 'singing' weakens the kangaroo, but they were adamant about its sure success. Perhaps the relentless pursuit, combined with the monotonous 'wonk, wonk' which cannot be eluded by dodging about, causes the quarry kangaroo to realise he at last has been chosen, and he becomes paralysed with fear. They have probably been harvested the same way for so many thousands of years that even the kangaroos know the rules.

Dingoes use the same technique of relentless pursuit of a selected animal, and even when a wallaby leaps frantically through a group of its own kind sitting up watching the chase, the dingo keeps relentlessly after it, and it seldom escapes. Other wallabies watching seem absolutely assured that they are in no danger once the dingo has selected its prey.

We talked on late until Gidja the moon came winking up through the bloodwoods, silvering the silent bush and dispersing the lurking Quinkins, so we were able to go to bed and sleep unmolested. But George and Willy stoked the fire up for good measure.

After completing work in the Gugu-Yalanji main camp I spent the next few days recording Mushroom Rock and Mingaroo Hill galleries, walking into them early morning and out in late afternoon to avoid the worst heat. We again raided the flying fox colony and Willy got a wallaby and a plains turkey, so George was getting his hard bush tucker.

At dawn one morning I went down to our waterhole and found a dead cow in it. Weak from hunger and thirst the beast had become bogged and had expired there. There were also three plump black ducks paddling about, incautious in the early dawn. I told Willy and he took the shotgun and faded into long dry grass on the bank, and two minutes later had bagged the three of them.

The dead cow dictated a move to another waterhole, so we packed up and moved about fifteen kilometres upstream, closer to where I intended to work. Our new waterhole was smaller and deeper than the last, but to our great joy it was obviously full of fish and other aquatic life. We had wild duck to roast in the camp oven for dinner, and decided we would have a rest day tomorrow and spend a cool day fishing.

42

Next morning Willy repaired his traditional fish net. It was a circular scoop net about one and a half metres in diameter, made from lawyer cane and bush string. The waterhole was shaded by large flowering melaleucas, and a few small tree trunks lay in the water, providing habitats for fish.

The water was not much more than a metre deep and a bit muddy. George said the rifle-fish and bream kept the mud stirred up so they could hide from the voracious barramundi. We spent a couple of hilarious hours chasing the fish about. We herded them into a corner against a log, only to find that they promptly hurdled the log back into the water on the other side. So Willy stationed himself on the other side with the net while we herded them up again, and this time some of them landed in the net.

There were three or four large barramundi in the hole and Willy eventually speared one of them. We got an eel, some eel-tailed catfish, bream and rifle-fish, and I was able to examine some of the species that were portrayed in the galleries. We cooked them in a ground oven, and the fish, steamed in their own juice and slightly flavoured by melaleuca leaves and bark, were delicious.

All day hordes of screeching rainbow lorikeets had squabbled among the flowering paperbarks, and as I wished to do some tape-recording, I waited for sunset to drive them to bed and silence. However I had forgotten Joonging the flying fox; no sooner had the last of the Bil-bil gone shrieking off when the first Joonging arrived, followed by hundreds more, to continue flapping and haggling over the rich blossom and providing a noisy background on my tapes.

Willy had been schooling me for some time about life after death and the ceremonies associated with it, and having absorbed a good working knowledge of it, I set about recording it.

Willy had pointed out a low shrubby tree that grew to about ten metres high. In appearance it was similar to the local kurrajong, and like it, was deciduous. He called it the matchwood tree because it was the best wood for making fire-sticks. Its resinous wood burnt fiercely and gave off black sooty smoke.

The matchwood tree (*Erythroxylum ellipticum*) is the tree of life, and the tree of death, to many of the tribes of Cape York peninsula, and after death it is believed the spirit gains a new impetus from the tree to travel on to the land of life after death, via 'the Good Gate'.

When a child is born the mother buries the afterbirth under a matchwood tree; as soon as the child is able it is encouraged to climb a matchwood. When a person dies the body is taken to the clan burial ground, usually on a sandy ridge in the forest. The body is trussed in a sitting position, with the knees and elbows dislocated, and placed in a shallow grave so the head is close to the surface. A small matchwood tree, about fifteen to twenty centimetres in diameter, is uprooted and the top cut off to leave a metre high stump, which is stuck upside down in the top of the grave. The matchwood has a shallow, flat, root system with a main taproot anchoring it against the prevailing wind. The roots make a platform and the taproot is orientated to the west, pointing the way to Woolunda, the Aboriginal heaven.

On the third day after death the spirit emerges from the nostrils and ascends through the matchwood grave post to sit on the platform and look about. It is very confused, but revitalised by the passage through the magic wood, sees the taproot pointing west and flies 'swift and straight like a wild duck', to 'the Good Gate', the entrance to Woolunda.

The Good Gate is guarded by the presiding deity who has a secret sacred name, which must never be spoken aloud, and who is generally referred to as Big Uncle, 'big boss belong everybody—white man too'. Big Uncle stands in the relationship of mother's brother to everybody. Only those men who have been through the bora (the initiation ceremony of tooth avulsion) can gain admission through the Good Gate, as they have learned the secret names.

An inverted Y-shaped tree trunk is suspended over the entrance to Woolunda and this can be slammed down to deny entry to the uninitiated. The inverted Y-shape symbolises the thighs of the mother and passing through the gate symbolises being reborn into Woolunda. A constant stream of spirits approach the Good Gate, and to each one Big Uncle says something so incredibly funny that the spirit must open his mouth to laugh and Big Uncle can 'see the hole in his head', from the missing front tooth. He also checks the body cicatrices, concentric circles on chest and abdomen, which symbolise the entrance to Woolunda.

A spirit who has somehow missed or evaded the bora ceremonies will try to run past laughing with his mouth shut, but Big Uncle drops the tree trunk and blocks the way. The spirit without bora marks is turned away to wander about forever lost, and forced to drink 'maggotty water'.

After passing through the Good Gate the new spirit is given a bark container of sweet water to drink, then a bark basket containing as much honey as he can eat. Big Uncle then adorns the new spirit, putting on yellow pandanus armbands, a cockatoo feather headdress, strings of beads made from short pieces of yellow grass, a new string belt, a pearl-shell pendant, white paint, and a kangaroo rib-bone through the pierced nasal septum.

The earthly mother of the new spirit knows that someone belonging to her has come, for her breasts feel as though she is nursing a baby. If the earthly mother is still alive, a woman in correct kinship status, a grandmother or mother's sister, will stand in. After dressing the spirit Big Uncle hides him under a large sheet of paperbark, telling him to stay hidden and make no noise. He then brings the mother along and tells her to look under the bark. When the mother raises the bark she does not see anything, because the spirit clings flat like a bat to the underside of the bark. When the mother says she can see nothing there, Big Uncle turns the bark right over and the new spirit arises, reborn into the spirit world of Woolunda.

A corroboree is held to welcome the new spirit, and then a big feast. While they are eating, young girls come from all directions, 'from this way and that way', and the new spirit can marry as many as he wants. But Big Uncle breaks every bone in the spirit's body so that he cannot run away; he must remain there forever.

About a year after the initial burial in the sand ridge, much loved and respected people were exhumed. The long bones and skull were cleaned and red-ochred, and purified by smoking over a fire of smouldering matchwood logs. They were then bound up in a cylindrical bark coffin and carried about by relatives from camp to camp, and finally placed in a mortuary rock shelter or hollow tree.

Willy told of his bora ceremony when his front upper tooth was removed. One of the old men kept a thumbnail long and sharp, and used it to push the gum right back from the tooth. He then took a short stick of ironwood, pointed at one end, and placing the sharp end on the tooth, hammered the other end with a stone until the tooth was knocked out. He had to keep his mouth shut and was barred from speaking until the gum was healed.

Later on the same thumbnail was used to pierce the nasal septum, and a thick grass-stem was pushed through and twisted occasionally until the hole was healed, and the stem free. About that time the body cicatrices were cut with a stone flake and rubbed with ashes to raise a weal. The cutting of the cicatrices was sometimes made easier and less painful by the application to the skin of a certain species of hairy caterpillar, which causes intensive swelling and deadens pain. The caterpillar is found in grass at the end of the wet season.

Willy said the burial grounds were easily identified by the inverted matchwood grave posts, which lasted for generations as, like ironwood, matchwood will not catch alight in a grass fire. We eventually came across a burial ground, with fourteen matchwood posts still standing. They were scattered over about a hundred square metres, apparently in family plots with three to five posts in each cluster. None was recent and most appeared older than matchwood posts still standing from Palmer gold rush days.

It was interesting to note that the Aboriginal concept of life after death had so many similarities to Christianity and other religions. In previous conversations with Dick and others we had especially considered the universal belief of the spirit of the dead exiting the body on the third day after death.

We thought it may be associated with the lunar cycle, as in Aboriginal mythology the moon was responsible for humanity losing its once held immortality. Gidja the moon man had been killed and hurled into the sky, where he lived and died each month, so we had watched a full lunar cycle to see for how long Gidja remained dead before coming to life again.

The moon became full, then rose later each night, getting thinner and thinner, until finally on a Thursday morning we saw him just above the sunrise, thin and stooped like an old man. There was no sign of Gidja on Friday or Saturday, but Sunday evening he was back, just above the sunset, a thin disc on its back, symbolically like a baby cradle. On the third day Gidja had risen again.

'Willy told of his bora ceremony . . . Later on the same thumbnail was used to pierce the nasal septum.' Toomacalin (Willy Long).

'In the Pig Gallery . . . A long-necked bird sat on his arm and pecked into his armpit. It had been stroked with such passionate hatred that the paint had run from its neck.'

5

Sorcery versus Snider rifles

Later that year I returned with my son Matthew to do a detailed recording of Woolston Gallery, and to continue exploration of that region. Aerial surveys had revealed a likely-looking scatter of huge slabs on a steep hillside about two kilometres east of Woolston and I felt sure they would contain some galleries.

Matt was keen to find a better gallery than that found by his brother, Stephen. It took us four hours to carry our gear and sufficient water into the gallery to camp for three days. We boiled the billy and had lunch, then set off to explore the new prospects.

It was hard going on the steep slope, among a tangled mass of fallen timber and undergrowth around the huge blocks of sandstone. We found shelters but they contained only light evidence of occupation and a few hand stencils. We were beginning to lose hope when Matt saw red ochre paint on the curved corner of a large shelter. We scrambled up to it and were delighted to see a large array of big figures painted all over the back wall.

The most striking figure was that of an emu over two metres tall, painted in white with a red outline. Below the emu were several larger than life-size figures of men; they were all horizontal, painted in dark red with white outlines and interior bars. Each had a long object under one arm and all appeared to be booted. They appeared even more threatening than the dark red figures in Crocodile Gallery, and I was again struck by the thought they might represent men with rifles, particularly as they were among the last additions to the gallery.

I was examining some large dark red kangaroos in the southern end of the gallery, when I heard Matt calling excitedly from about forty metres across a shallow gully. He had found a magnificent gallery with scores of large and colourful figures painted one over another in a pro-fusion of rich ochre colours in every shade of red, yellow and white.

The shelter had an easterly aspect and the cylindrical-shaped interior provided maximum protection against rain, wind and sun. It was about twenty metres long and the back wall was two to three metres high, then the ceiling curved over and out for five metres before curving down again. The paintings covered the entire back wall and were the brightest array of technicolour figures seen in any gallery yet found in Cape York peninsula.

There were about a hundred and twenty identifiable figures in the gallery, almost half of which were human beings, including several more of the large, menacing, booted figures with rifles. There were several kangaroos, including one with a joey in the pouch, together with emus and other birds, fish, crocodiles, dingoes, pigs, various weapons, and even a large red and white beetle.

The two pigs were in the top layer of paintings; one of them, in monochrome dark purple-red, was a rather impoverished figure and was probably painted when the strange new animal first appeared. The later pig was remarkably well drawn and decorated, the body a pretty light red ochre, outlined and decorated with white. The artist who painted it was clearly very familiar with pigs.

Early European explorers like Edmund Kennedy, William Hann and James Mulligan, did not mention wild pigs, so their numbers may have been severely controlled by Aboriginal hunters and their dingoes. This control was relaxed when the worldwide epidemic of influenza devastated the people of Cape York peninsula in 1920, and a couple of years later remnants of the tribes were rounded up and sent to missions around the coast, leaving only the dingoes as predators of the pigs.

A missionary at Aurukun, Geraldine MacKenzie, recorded the pigs appearing there in the late 1920s, and thought they had originated from some pigs released at the tip of the peninsula some fifty years earlier. At Lockhart Mission, on the east coast, the pigs were first seen moving north in the early 1930s. In *Aurukun Diary*, Geraldine MacKenzie described the arrival of the wild pig:

> An excited, elderly Aborigine returned one day from hunting about eleven miles northeast of the mission. He described to Bill a wild animal he had met in the bush, which made a track like the cloven hoof of a young calf. It made a noise 'like this one'; and he imitated most unmistakably the grunting of a pig. Bill laughed and told him the pig was good meat and he should kill it. In time the people did. They learned they must not hunt it alone. The wild pig could be very dangerous, quite unlike the timid, defenceless wallabies the people hunted along the coast.
>
> That first, simple step away from the purely hunting life was to catch, tame and rear young wild pigs, to be a good feast when full grown. Men from Kendall River, toward the southern end of the Reserve, would be met making their way up to the mission with a tame pig or two trotting behind them as well as their dogs.

Aerial view of Split Rock.

Caesar Le Chu and Dick Roughsey at Split Rock.

Two sorcery figures of Black Police troopers at Crocodile Gallery.

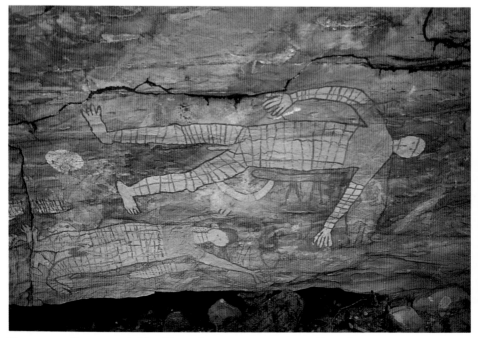

Two sorcery figures, probably white police troopers, at Crocodile Gallery.

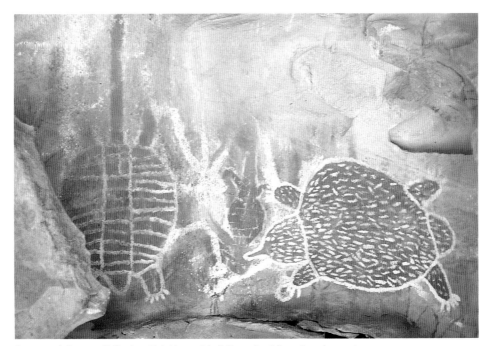

Scattered Group Galleries. Echidna with frill-necked lizard and tortoise.

Scattered Group Galleries. Dick Roughsey looking at Gaiya the dingo.

Bull Creek. Ceremonial men and an echidna, showing an incipient X-ray technique.

View of Emu Gallery.

Sorcery figures of Black Police troopers in the Emu Gallery.

Dick examines paintings in the Pig Gallery.

Central figures in the Pig Gallery include large red bush cockroaches.

Mornington Island. Lardil corroboree dancers performing Warrenby dance.

Mornington Island. Warrabudgera, the
law carrier.

Bloodwood ridge in the Kennedy Creek area.

Dick in Hell's Gate Passage.

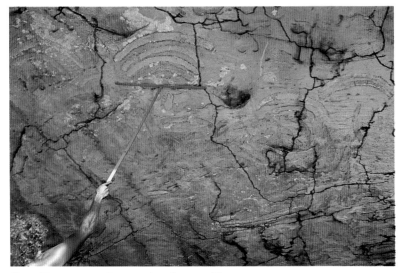

Hann River region. Engraved and painted boomerangs.

Giant Horse Gallery. The giant horse, over five metres long and three metres high.

View of the Giant Horse Gallery.

Giant Horse Gallery. Close-up of Quinkin and stingray at the head of the
giant horse, and a horse throwing a man with a rifle.

The Quinkin sites. *Top*: Dick in the Yellow Crocodile Gallery, *middle*: Ancestral dingo man with dingo, *bottom*: Ibis Gallery with spirit figures, snakes and shrimp.

The Quinkin sites. Flying foxes guard the entrance to the Quinkin cave.

Dick Roughsey, Willy Long and Caesar Le Chu stand at the entry chasm to the Quinkin cave.

The Deighton Lady.

The Deighton Lady site.

A panel of very old red figures at Sandy Creek.

Deighton River sites. The faded
head of a ten-metre long
Rainbow Serpent.

Deighton River sites. A yellow
pig was the last figure added.

The author and Dick in a Ginger Creek Gallery.

Coamey Creek. A beehive surrounded by tracks of animals.

Coamey Creek. Dick at Beehive Dreaming.

Early Man Creek, Goanna Gallery. An emu turning over its eggs.

Goanna Gallery. Two emus with an owl.

Perhaps the spread of Cook's pigs may have been inhibited by similar domestication by the tribes around Cooktown. As children we had a pig which went everywhere with us and the dogs; it obviously thought it was a dog.

An examination of the immediate surroundings soon revealed the reason why the shelters had been extensively occupied and painted. The gully between the two shelters contained a permanent spring. We cleaned out a small hole and enjoyed a drink of cool sweet sandstone water. Because of the spring I decided to defer recording Woolston Gallery and concentrate on the new discovery.

Dick Roughsey and Caesar LeChu returned with me to complete recording the sites. We had picked up Caesar at the Palmer River, where he lived with his wife and seven children. Grey-haired and of medium height, he was in his middle-fifties. Although as dark as any full blood, Caesar's name and slightly almond eyes, hinted at the Chinese presence in the Palmer gold rush.

Caesar's tribe was the Oco-Carnigal, apparently a sub-tribe of the Gugu-Warra, which once lived in the country north-west of Laura. At birth he had been given the name of Awanindinbun, with totems of freshwater shrimp, and porgor, the tommy-roundhead lizard. Caesar's first twelve years or so had been spent living a traditional life in the rough country of the Palmer, successfully eluding troops of Black Police trying to round them up. He proved to be an energetic, willing and humorous companion, a great raconteur with an intimate knowledge of the bush and old traditions.

On the way in we took Caesar to see the dark red figures in the Crocodile Gallery. He immediately identified them as the Black Police, the hated 'Bullymen', which is an Aboriginal corruption of the word 'policeman'; but when they learned English they decided it was an apt name anyway. The two horizontal male figures on the outer wall were also Black Police, identified by red half-ovals on the top of their heads, which he said represented the peaked caps of the Black Police. He said the five-metre-long snake had been repainted, and lines drawn from its head to the foot of one policeman was to put the poison in him.

There were seven white hand stencils along the snake, the signatures of the small guerilla band harrying the Black Police. Caesar said the sign language signal for black police was to cup a hand above the eyes, indicating the peaked cap, followed by a swift gesture which meant 'run that way quick'.

Dick and Caesar were even more impressed in the Emu Gallery. The huge, dark red, horizontal figures of the Black Police had glaring white eyes, and from them emanated an atmosphere of intense hatred. Caesar pointed to a sharp bulge on the thigh of one of the figures and said, 'That would be his revolver holster. I wonder how many kids he shot with that.'

51

Parts of the lower wall and floor were engraved with emu and scrub turkey tracks, ancient and glazed with the silicas of time. High out of reach on the northern end of the back wall was a large faded painting; only the head, shoulders and front legs remained and it was not possible to discern whether it was a dingo or kangaroo. How did they get up there to paint it, and how many thousands of years ago? How many generations of peaceful living were blown away by the shattering roar of Snider rifles?

In the Pig Gallery Caesar identified four of the figures as Black Police. One was very similar to those in the Emu Gallery, but it was upside down. A long-necked bird sat on his arm and pecked into his armpit. It had been stroked in with such passionate hatred that the paint had run from its neck. Horizontal beside the inverted figure was a two-metre-long man in khaki-brown; he, like all the others, was booted, and had wide-flung arms. An unmistakable rifle shape was painted alongside his body; a long-legged bird stood on his body and pecked into his armpit.

Dick said his old people spoke of a black bird which steals the bones of the dead. It flew about at night and when its screech was heard the old people would call out, 'Get away, you rotten black thief; you won't get my bones for a long time yet.'

The other two were painted in bright yellow ochre with white outline and interior decoration. One was inverted and both were booted, with glaring white eyes, but they had no guns. Caesar thought they might represent white leaders of the Black Police.

Caesar stood in front of the inverted dark red policeman and said, 'You're dead, bullyman, and you're going into the ground head down and you won't ever get up—and that's good.'

We camped under bloodwoods outside the Emu Gallery. It was a sad haunted place for each of us. We felt the presence of those desperate people who had fled here to their stronghold to employ bitter sorcery against the invaders, after they had found their spears useless against Snider rifles. The silence of the bush around the long-abandoned sites was mute evidence that sorcery had failed.

Dick and Caesar went hunting while I made scaled drawings of the figures. One day they got a scrub trukey, which provided a tough but tasty dinner. Next day they returned with a pretty little rock wallaby. Caesar removed all the long thin sinews from its tail and hind legs before cooking it in a ground oven. I thought it would be good eating like the agile wallaby, but it was like chewing a rubber inner tube, and I concluded that you wouldn't travel far on a feed of rock wallaby.

I knew vaguely that the British had endeavoured to exploit inter-tribal enmity in order to subjugate the Aboriginal tribes, just as they had done earlier in America and Africa, so I commenced researching the origins and activities of the Black Police.

The first attempt at the formation of a Native Corps was made in 1836 or 1837, soon after the opening of Port Phillip (Melbourne) under an officer named De Villiers, but it led to no satisfactory results, and the scheme was abandoned, or rather, remained in abeyance for some years.

The New South Wales Government revived the Native Mounted Police in 1842. The Native Police were to be employed in the pursuit and apprehension of Aboriginal offenders. The depression of the 1840s made things difficult for the squatters. It made their livelihood more precarious and many were unable to withstand the attacks of the Aborigines. The Native Police were thus expected to give protection to the squatters.

In 1848 the first Native Mounted Police detachment commenced operations in the Northern Districts of New South Wales, which became the colony of Queensland after 1859. The force was under the command of Commandant Frederick Walker who established the first headquarters at Callandoon, approximately fourteen kilometres west of Goondiwindi. As a result it was possible for settlers to spread quickly into new areas without heavy stock losses.

There was subsequently much criticism of the Native Police by various members of the public, and in 1861, a Select Committee of the Assembly (Queensland) conducted an inquiry into the workings of the Native Police Force, and the conditions of the Aborigines generally.

It was decided that the Native Mounted Police of Queensland was to be retained. The Select Committee of 1861 reported that any change in the organisation of the Native Mounted Police by the substitution of white troops for Aborigines would, in fact, lower the efficiency of the Force; that since the establishment of the Force, the loss of life and the destruction of property on either side had considerably diminished; and that any attempt to disband it would lead to disastrous results. Should the composition of the Force be changed so that there were white troopers instead of Aborigines, the running costs would be considerably increased. The fact that the Aborigines were better and cheaper troopers no doubt lent considerable weight to the retention of the Force.

The first detachment of Native Police arrived in Cape York peninsula on 25 October, 1873, when the steamer *Leichhardt* landed a government party of Native Police in charge of Mr Howard St George, Gold Commissioner, and a group of Engineers of Roads under the leadership of Mr A.C. Macmillan, charged with the duty of finding and blazing a track to the newly discovered Palmer Goldfield. They went ashore at the mouth of the Endeavour River and founded Cooktown. Macmillan had secured the services of Jerry, one of the Aboriginal guides who had been with William Hann's exploring expedition the year before, and so had some knowledge of the intervening country.

On 28 October 1873, Jerry led the official party under Macmillan and St George, with thirty Native Police, and with about seventy accompanying armed miners laden with gear and swags. Jerry was aware of the very rugged sandstone country which lay directly between the Endeavour and Palmer rivers and led the party in a wide semi-circle, first west then swinging south-west to skirt the sheer cliffs of the sandstone plateaux.

The party crossed a low divide and followed the Normanby River, where they had sharp and seemingly unnecessary clashes with the local Aborigines. Perhaps Jerry was following Hann's behaviour of the year before and shooting at any black skin on sight. The events which followed indicated that the tribes of the regions traversed by Hann had been so incensed by the needless killings that they subsequently had meetings where it was resolved that if the murderous 'migola' (white men) returned, smoke signals would be sent up to gather all the warriors together and overwhelm the invaders.

Among the miners was William J. Webb, who had arrived from England as a boy in 1855, and he wrote eyewitness accounts of the events (reproduced here from Hector Holthouse's book, *River of Gold*):

> The command left the Endeavour some 108 strong, about 70 of them being on foot with swags from 70 pounds to 90 pounds weight, the supposed distance being about 80 miles, we thought we could not overload ourselves. Some humped swags with a pick, shovel and dish strapped to them, some pushed wheelbarrows, two men who had no horse pulled a cart loaded with food and tools. Most of the miners were armed with breech-loading Sniders.
>
> A troop of native police under Sub-Inspector Dyas rode ahead of them, and in the rear came about 20 Chinese miners. The Chinese kept as close as they could to the main party, but were not allowed to join it.

On 3 November Webb wrote on the Normanby River:

> Some blacks were shot here, I do not know why, as they had not interfered with us. Later a number of blacks appeared and seemed to want to parley. They made no threatening moves but leant their spears up against rocks and trees and stood with their arms at their sides.

Macmillan was either stupid or bloodthirsty, possibly both. He called all the mounted men to him and led them, yelling, straight at the party of blacks, who grabbed their spears and ran. And so the stage was set—the migola didn't want to parley. A war of attrition that would cost the lives of hundreds of whites and thousands of blacks was about to commence.

On 4 November they camped near the end of a range, where, Jerry warned, the Hann expedition had been attacked the year before. They decided to form a barricade by placing saddles and gear in a circle. When a miner went to get water from the creek just before dark and saw fresh tracks of hundreds of bare feet, he rushed back to warn them they were surrounded. They ordered the Chinese miners out to cut logs and help strengthen the barricade.

Without the warning and the barricade, it would have been another 'Custer's Last Stand', for they had been trailed by more than five hundred warriors since reaching the Normanby. Guards were posted but few slept that night.

At dawn between five and six hundred painted warriors attacked. They came in waves, probably composed of separate tribal groups, their war cry the eerie screech of the black cockatoo. They seemed absolutely fearless of the crashing roar of Snider rifles fired by the Black Police and miners, and the first two waves almost breached the barricade. But growing light enabled the Sniders to be sighted on targets, and the Snider bullets, each a solid ounce of lead, tore gaps in their ranks. But as they fell other waves came in over the top of them, and they in turn fell to the Sniders.

The barricade was soon ringed with scores of dead and dying warriors. Others could not understand why their comrades had fallen; they tried to stand them up and staunch their wounds with handfuls of grass. The Aborigines' tactical error was that each warrior could carry only seven or eight spears, and once they were thrown they were helpless. In disputes among themselves they hurled spears at each other, and when their own spears were gone they could pick up spears thrown at them and fight on.

When they had thrown all their spears at the barricade some of the warriors tried to run off the horses—but they were still hobbled; others took cover behind trees and flung the last of their spears. The surviving spearless warriors ran for cover in a nearby swamp, but the Black Police recovered their horses and rode in after them—and as Webb wrote, 'All that went there, stayed there'. Only one miner was wounded.

The place of the attack was called Battle Camp, the scene of one of the bloodiest battles fought in the long war the Aborigines were fighting for the country their forebears had enjoyed unmolested for many thousands of years.

In his book, *The Other Side of the Frontier*, Professor Henry Reynolds concluded that as many as 10 000 blacks were killed in skirmishes with Europeans in north Australia.

The Luraga ceremony.

6

Dream roads

The Pig and Emu galleries recording trip was to be the last to Quinkin country for that year. I took the recordings to Canberra to lodge in the archives of the Australian Institute of Aboriginal Studies, and attend the biennial meeting of its members. There was much discussion by leading anthropologists on the urgent need to record much of the still-living Aboriginal culture before it vanished forever.

For some years Dick had been urging me to return to Mornington Island and continue recording among his people, especially his own group, the Lurrumbanda. I suggested to the Institute that it would be worthwhile making a series of documentary films of such Lardil activities as raftbuilding, dugong and turtle hunting, as well as recording sign language, sacred ceremonies and sites, including the great flood-making ceremony left behind by the ancestral being, Marnbil. Dick had also mentioned a secret language called 'Damin', which intrigued me because he said it contained clicks, glops, whistles and nasal ingressives, apparently similar to the African Bushmen language.

I eventually received a small grant from the Institute for the filming. All I had to do was double it myself and I would have sufficient funds to raise a four-week expedition to Mornington Island, in the Wellesley archipelago in the south-east corner of the Gulf of Carpentaria. The Institute also supplied a 16 mm Bolex camera with lots of black and white film, and a tape-recorder.

I had discussed the project with Warrabudgera, Bunbudgee and other elders when they were in Cairns for the Dance Festival. They advised that July would be a good time, and that they would select a group of men to go to Sydney Island. It was a small island just off the coast of Mornington and called Langu Narnji, their own Larrumbanda clan country, centre of the flood-making ceremony and many Dreaming sites. It was also an important part of the Dream road of Marnbil, the ancestral creator.

When considering logistics of the expedition I asked Dick about hunting the local game to supplement food supplies. He was eloquently enthusiastic: 'Too much Warrenby, too much, dugong, turtle, fish, mud crabs, oysters, too much! Nobody hunts that country now, it's undisturbed, there's too much.' His mouth was obviously watering at the thought of it, so I decided not to take much tinned meat, just the basics of flour, tea, sugar, potatoes and onions etc.

With limited funding I purchased second-hand dinghies, outboard motors, tents, canvas flies, bedding, and lots of fishing gear, including a special bait net, over a hundred metres long and four metres deep. It was all sent around Cape York by coastal shipping, arriving a few days before we flew in.

I had recruited Frank Woolston as cameraman, fellow airline pilot, Tony Ellen, as his assistant, and artist Ray Crooke as general handyman. Ray contributed to funding and hoped for artistic inspiration from the trip.

We flew out of Cairns on a cool July morning, on Ansett's regular Gulf run, landing at Normanton in the rolling Gulf country savannah, before flying out over broad saltpans, serpentine, mangrove-fringed rivers and on over the grey Gulf waters.

The direct route went close to Langu Narnji so I went up to the cockpit to see it come up on the horizon. The highest point on Mornington was a mere one hundred and fifty metres, and Larngu Narnji was low and flat, except for a few large stabilised sand-dunes. The surrounding sea was in delicate shades of azure and aquamarine. It was obvious that it would be possible to cross the mudflats between the two islands at low tide.

The entire village of about five hundred turned out to meet the plane. There was a guard of honour composed of Warrabudgera, Dick, and his three brothers, Kenny, Burrud and Timmy. They were in traditional dress of wallaby fur-string sporrans, hair-belts and war paint, and were carrying spears and boomerangs. I learned later that the intense interest in our visit stemmed from concern that the re-enactment of the flood-making ceremony might unleash a terrible cyclone and tidal surge the following wet season.

I introduced my colleagues to Rev. Doug Belcher and his wife Doreen. They had come to the Presbyterian Mission just after World War II and stayed on to raise a family and become loved and respected members of the Lardil. The people called him Guntha (father). Doug told us we could be delayed a day or so as the mission launch which was to take us to Langu Narnji, had gone on a dugong-hunting trip and was apparently sheltering somewhere from a strong south-easter, which could last another two days.

Most of the nineteen men going with us were from Langu Narnji, but there were three northwind men, and three Kiadilt from Bentinck

Island. There was great excitement as the men arrived with swags, accompanied by their families, who were envious and longing to see their own country again and enjoy its rich harvest of dugong, turtle, fish, crabs and oysters.

All the village turned out to see us off, including Robert, a mad, semi-tame corella cockatoo, which turned up at every gathering to entertain the crowd with aerobatics. They waved and cheered as we chugged away from the little wharf; some of the older people called out, 'Don't you put that clay in the water.' Warrabudgera reassured them, 'No clay from Mundawa, don't you worry.' Some of the children ran along the beach waving until they were stopped by a mangrove creek.

We were passing the mouth of the Minya-darga (Dugong) River when Warrabudgera pointed it out as being one of the story places made by Marnbil, so I got my tape-recorder and everybody sat around to hear the ancient saga of the Balambanda people:

Marnbil and his son-in-law, Dewallewul, travelled across the country from the west. They had no women. The chain of islands did not exist then, it was still a peninsula running out from the mainland. Much later the islands were made by Garngurr, the seagull woman. She dragged a walpa (raft) back and forth over the peninsula, looking for her husband, who had run away with another woman. The walpa dug the channels and the water followed.

As they travelled they dug wells and made springwater; they were naming all the kinds of animals and plant foods. They reached the coast near Point Piper and travelled along it until they came to Bayley Point. Marnbil made a big stone fish trap on a large sandbar called Moonbururu.

They travelled along the peninsula to a place called Mildidji (Robert Island), and made another fish trap, then on to Jalda-ganabul (Francis Island) where they made another. The fish traps can still be seen from the air. They went on to Langunary, a place on Forsythe Island, where they made a big well and camped.

Next day they went to Gwagin; here Marnbil decided to make a story place. He made the law that no one was allowed to talk, whistle or sing at Gwagin; if people caught fish or speared dugong there, the flesh must be cleaned and cut up under water. If fish or dugong flesh was cleaned out of water a great flood would come; the tide would come up and cover all the low-lying country and spoil the sand-wells. Any person eating such fish would be attacked by the Mulgri spirit of that place; the Mulgri would sink its teeth into his throat from the inside as though he had swallowed a fish bone.

On the south-east side of Forsythe, at Moongoolburu, Marnbil and Dewallewul made another big stone trap to catch dugong. Here they also made the mosquito Dreaming; they were still naming all the animals, insects, everything. Marnbil found a woman here; her name was Gin-gin, and he made her his wife. He told Dewallewul that he could have their first girl-child for a wife, saying, 'You are now my son-in-law. From now on we cannot speak to each other; we will speak through Gin-gin, your mother-in-law. That is the law.'

On Forsythe they also made a big sandbank called Girrada-doonguwa, which is still there; at that place Marnbil made a fishing line from the inner bark of the beach hibiscus, mudud, and Dewallewul speared butterfish.

Next day they travelled on to what is now Andrew Island, and from there on to Denham Island. As they went they speared or caught fish with lines, and rocks mark the places where they stood up. They travelled on to Dardidin and made a fish trap, and on to Gunana where they dug a big well. They used their sacred implements, a stick called darrawul, and baler shell called lowalan, to dig three big wells at Gunana, where the mission now stands, and made and camped on a big sandhill, Didjingeer.

Next morning Marnbil said to Gin-gin, 'Tell son-in-law to go and spear fish on the sandspit around to the west. Tell him to make a Dreaming place there for Woorabud, the bone-fish, Galtharr the yellow trevally, and barracoutta.'

Next day Marnbil spoke again to Gin-gin. 'Tell your son-in-law that tomorrow he is to go along the north side of the peninsula. Tell him that we'll meet him somewhere at the top end of this place. He will do all the work that way while I do all the work to the east. He will see our camp smokes as we travel.'

As they travelled they stood up and speared fish and made fish traps. Marnbil stood up and speared fish where later on Thuwathu, the Rainbow Serpent made the Minya-darga River. He made a fish trap at Nyalga on Timber Point, and went to Ja-gwaga to make a grass-string fish net. Next day Marnbil went on to Gunda-woodgin to make a fish trap with bushes to catch bream.

Marnbil and Gin-gin travelled on. Marnbil began hunting fish at night. He could see by smokes that Dewallewul, who was in the Sandalwood country, was also catching fish by night. They made torches from long rolls of paperbark.

At Goobirah Point, Marnbil made a story place for Yarran, the red-backed sea eagle, Bullebul, the spotted stingray, and Wongabel, the honey bee. He caught fish by night at Ewar Point. Next morning he put up bushes and blocked fish in Budulbee-thulba, the lagoon at Jardunga; his footprints are still there in the beach rock. He made a big fire there and also made the rain-making ceremony at Bahudgun Bay.

Next day Marnbil decided to made the Flood ceremony. He went to Mundawah and dug kial (white clay). Then he went to Birriwogah Point and made the Dreaming for Margara, the coastal wallaby. At Wang-guh he made the Dreaming place of Ngarrawun, the blue-fish; he stood up and hit two stones together to bring the fish to the surface. He and Gin-gin then travelled on to Doogooray to make a spring and camp there.

Later on they travelled on to Binburragan and made a fish trap; then on to Linga-wadngala, and made the Black Snake Dreaming, then on to Lil-lil-tuh, white heron Dreaming. Here Marnbil decided to complete the flood-making ceremony. He took the clay he had gathered at Mundawah and wet it, packing it around the end of a long stick, tying it up with paperbark and string. He named the flood-making stick, Doomidjul.

Leaving Gin-gin at the sandy camping place on Woonunyeah, at low tide he went out along an exposed reef to Bidjin-yea-narwe (bad-smell place), to make the big flood.

After carrying out the first flood-making ceremony, Marnbil took Gin-gin to a high camp at Dingelma to await the flood.

A great storm gathered and for three days the water rose higher and higher until it covered all the low country. Then Marnbil made a ceremony to made the flood recede. He gathered large stones and heated them in the fire. Picking up the hot stones in bark he ran down the beach and hurled them into the tunnel of the waves as they curled over to break on the shore. The waters receded.

Marnbil left the flood-making ceremony so we could frighten and punish our enemies with it.

Marnbil and Gin-gin went on to Gundah and waited there to spear dugong. Still making his Dream road he went on to Warrul, then on to Baluyin, where he dug a well for water and waited to spear moonfish, (salmon). Travelling on, he made another fish trap, then a big circular reef where turtle could always be caught in the lagoon. Then on to Gu-oom-buargan, Jubu, and Balwaldu, until Marnbil and Gin-gin came to Baralkea, on Cape Van Dieman.

Baralkea became Marnbil's main camp, and from here he set out to make fish, turtle and dugong traps all over the region. One day he saw bushfire smoke curling up into the sky and said to Gin-gin, 'Your son-in-law will soon be here. We'll be together again after all our big work.'

They met Dewallewul at Bangubella Bay, just north of Baralkea, and made camp there for some time. One day Marnbil said to Gin-gin, 'You stay here. I've two more big works to do and then I'll come back.' He went off to Maldon on Jilkirrie (Turtle Island) and dug a well, but the water was brackish. He made a turtle trap, then went on to Gungoda (Bountiful Island) and dug a well which had sweet water. He made a turtle trap there. The islands were all part of the mainland then.

Gin-gin was in camp preparing pandanus nuts for cooking. She was sitting in shade of pandanus palms smashing the big orange fruit with a thubun (food pounder). Dewallewul heard the pounding, and came over and asked, 'Where is your banyan (husband)?'

'He's a long way off making turtle traps—to the west or south. I don't know when he'll be back.'

Dewallewul sat opposite Gin-gin as she pounded the nuts. 'Oh, my eye!' he cried out suddenly, clapping his hand over his eyes. This was a warning to Gin-gin that she was not sitting properly with her heel into her crutch, and was thus exposing herself. Three times Dewallewul cried out, 'Oh, my eye, it's too red.' But Gin-gin took no notice.

A great temptation came upon Dewallewul. 'My girl,' he said, 'give me a little bit please. Your banyan is away, so give me a little bit. I have no woman.'

'No, son-in-law. It would be wrong; it belongs to my banyan.'

Dewallewul again said, 'Come on, give me a little bit.'

He kept on pleading until Gin-gin also was tempted. 'All right, you can have some. Come on, here it is.'

She shuffled towards Dewallewul.

When Marnbil returned from his work he saw the two together under the pandanus palms. 'Ah, so this is what you do with your mother-in-law.'

Marnbil sat in shade and thought about it. He thought for a long time, then decided he must kill Dewallewul.

Marnbil said to Gin-gin, 'You tell son-in-law that I need water, I am thirsty after my big work. Tell him to come with me and we'll dig a well.'

Marnbil, Gin-gin and Dewallewul went to the base of the sand-dunes and began to dig a well with sticks and baler shells. When water began to flow into the bottom of the well Marnbil said to Gin-gin, 'You tell son-in-law to get down and taste the water to see if it's good.'

Dewallewul bent down into the well but could not reach the water.

'Tell son-in-law to spread his legs and get down really low.'

When Dewallewul was bending right down into the well Marnbil thrust his spear into his anus and through his body. Dewallewul spun round and round on the ground, making rings around the well, which remain to this day.

As Dewallewul lay dying Marnbil said, 'From now on, no man shall ever look at, or speak directly to, his mother-in-law. That is the law.'

Dewallewul suffered and groaned before, body and spirit, he rose straight up into the sky.

At that time all people were immortal, but then Dewallewul shouted down a curse on all mankind, calling out all ways that people would meet with death.

'Marm mahn garuyu—Man will die from the spear.'
'Barwagan mahn garuyu—Man will be strangled by rope.'
'Moogara mahn garuyu—Man will die by nulla-nulla.'
'Wongul mahn garuyu—Man will die from the boomerang.'
'Buraboodi mahn garuyu—Man will die from sorcery.'
'Bulimba mahn garuyu—Man will die from a blow on the nape of the neck.'
'Bola mahn garuyu—Man will die from a blow on the top of the head.'
'Marragu mahn garuyu—Man will die at the hands of a big mob.'
'Turra dubberu mahn garuyu—Man will take fits and die.'
'Juderu mahn garuyu—Man will die from sorcery of an emu feather.'
'Bulleri mahn garuyu—Man will die from hot stones.'
'Juriban mahn garuyu—Man will die from poison food.'

Dewallewul remains in the sky and controls the weather. If people break the laws he can send a cyclone to punish them.

Marnbil and Gin-gin were very frightened by the curses of Dewallewul, and ran far away until they came to a big scrubby country called Birra-barartnga. Gin-gin had a daughter named Yegi. When they died long after, they turned into a stone which can be seen at low tide in the sea between Baralkea and Wallaby Island. Yegi is the one in the middle.

The engine of the old launch stopped a couple of times and we had to let it cool off before Scotty Wilson, one of the northwind Lardil, could coax it back to life again. It was a very pleasant trip and it seemed that every feature of the coastline had a story. It was late afternoon when we anchored in the channel between Langu Narnji and Mornington Island.

We set up our base camp on Doolgarnun Beach, where, according to Dick, Warrenby had fought a great battle with Yanggarl warriors from Forsythe Island. We put up tents, dug pit toilets, and arranged camping gear while Warrabudgera and Burrud took a party to clean out one of Marbil's old wells. I went to help later and found the well among big sand-dunes, which hold the fresh water. It was very similar to the old well on Mornington, and was also full of sand. The past wet season had been very light so we had to go down about three metres to get a metre of water in the bottom. We dug out three baler shells left by the old people. Two big drums with the ends removed were used to line the well. The water was a bit brackish, but we found at high tide we could get enough water to keep the camp going.

We ate bully beef and potatoes that night, while the hunters planned next day's operations. With a water supply secured, a red meat supply had top priority. Dick was hungry for mud crab and suggested to older brother Kenny that we should hunt them in mangroves tomorrow, then go out to the oyster reefs.

Our camp was set among sighing casuarinas on a long golden beach, tall yellow bindi grass, low scrub and clumps of pandanus were behind us. In front the still waters of the channel mirrored the dying colours of sunset, and above a half-full, waxing Gidegal the moon. Around us sat the dark-skinned, proud, true men of the wilderness, who were to be our mentors for the next three weeks. It would be an absorbing education.

Dawn next morning saw all of us preparing the long bait net for the first drag to get our breakfast. It was heaped in a dinghy with two men, and one end of the net held on the beach while they rowed in a big semi-circle paying out the net. When the other end was back on the beach, both ends were slowly retrieved until we could see lots of silver flashes in the water and the belly of the net came ashore full of fish. There were about ten different species and everybody rushed in to select a fish for breakfast. The remainder were pushed back in the water.

Warrabudgera took Frank and Tony in the largest dinghy to film the dugong and turtle hunting. There were four oarsmen and Burrud was the harpooner. The other dinghy had Fred Binjari, a Kiadilt, as harpooner. The three-metre harpoon pole had a detachable head, called a wop, a steel spike about twelve centimetres long, with a long, strong rope attached to it. The dugong herd was located by the streams of white mud coming from where they were bottom-feeding on seagrass.

Once the herd was located the outboard motor was shut down and they approached the dugong quietly by rowing. When a dugong came up to breathe it was stalked until the harpooner on the bow judged it to be in range, and lunged at it with the harpoon, using all his body weight to drive the wop in. He then scrambled quickly back into the boat before the rope ran out and the dugong towed the boat away. When the dugong tired, it was hauled to the boat and its tail was lassoed and lifted over the side of the boat, thus forcing its head underwater till it drowned.

One major project was to build a walpa (raft) out of bush materials, film its making, then use it in turtle and dugong-hunting sequences. So a group of men set off for the seaward side of the island with Kiadilt expert raftbuilders, Dougal Goonara and Pat Gabori, to select driftwood logs from among mangroves and collect hibiscus bark for ropemaking.

About mid-afternoon we heard outboard motors and singing, and Dick went to the top of the beach to shade his eyes and look out over the water. He said the boats were low in the water and must have something. They brought in two green turtles and a big dugong. There would be feasting.

We wished to film the traditional cutting up and sharing out of a dugong, so instead of using steel knives Pat Gabori got a medium-sized baler shell, and using a wad of paperbark to cushion his teeth, took small bites out of the edge of the shell to turn it into a saw-knife. It was very effective.

There was a great 'joking time' around the cooking fires that evening. Men who had been shy and reticent back at the mission, were now self-assured, confident hunters in their traditional clan country. The moonlight and smell of cooking meat brought Wadoon, the dingo, howling mournfully round our camp.

There were three high-degree Warama men in our party, Warrabudgera, Bunbudji, and the Kiadilt, Gabori, so when we were all comfortably full of roast dugong and turtle, I got the tape-recorder and asked about the man-making ceremonies. Warrabudgera took the lead to tell us of the first ceremony, called Luraga:

The first ceremony was held away back in the time when all animals, fishes, reptiles, birds, insects, were still people. Even the trees and all plants were human and ran about. They all changed to their present forms after the ceremony, and went to live in different parts of the country. Those animals, fish, birds, plants, became the bosses of the initiation ceremonies in their part of the country. The main dancer around here is Gather-gool, or Red Bill the oyster-catcher, she's running about down the beach there now, singing her story—girri girri, girri girri girri.

The people gathered together from all over the country to have a meeting and decide which boys to initiate. They met in a country called Gadagarlpa. Gidegal the moon man was the main boss and Lolngurri the white egret was the big song man.

They decided to initiate Galthar the yellow trevally. Gidegal told the other men to grab him and put a hair-belt round his waist in preparation to make him a man. They took the boy to the dancing ground to sit with the big men while all the men and women practised dancing.

Lolngurri never stopped singing. He was father-in-law to Galthar and was to give him a daughter for his wife.

Boss of ceremonies, Gidegal, stood up and called out, 'Ningula walana—who is first?' Barracoutta was the first to get up to practise Bundaree, the sacred shake-a-leg dance. He danced while Gidegal and the others watched.

Gidegal laughed and said, 'Your legs are too short and your body too long—go away and practise.' Lolngurri kept singing and Rock Cod got up and danced. They all laughed and Gidegal said, 'No, Rock Cod—your legs are too short and your body too fat—go away and practise.'

Next to get up was Red Bill. She danced hard and fast, but they all laughed and Gidegal said, 'No good, Red Bill—your legs are too skinny and long—go away and practise.'

Pelican was next, but again the people laughed and Gidegal said, 'No, Pelican, your legs are too short and you have that no-good-foot, go away and practise.'

One after another Gidegal called the people up while Lolngurri kept singing. For two days and nights they practised dancing and singing, men and women together, and they finished on the second night.

Early next morning they circumcised Galthar. Three of his brothers-in-law lay face down, side by side on the ground, to make a table, and Galthar was laid across them on his back. His father-in-law Lolngurri, used the knife, a barb from the mangrove stingray, and cut off the foreskin. He took the foreskin away to wrap it in paperbark. It would be given back to the boy later. All the women then got bushes and brushed the boy all over. They brushed away the smell of blood so the boy's sisters could not smell it.

They had just finished when Bin Bun, the thunderstorm, came along. He wanted to dance but the people told him it was all finished. Bin Bun was very angry because they had not waited for him. He commenced hurling thunderbolts everywhere. The thunder, lightning and heavy rain so frightened the people that they ran away and hid all over the country. They changed from people into all the other life forms.

A few weeks earlier there had been an eclipse of the full moon and I asked Warrabudgera what was the traditional belief about that event. He giggled and said, 'Gidegal been go to get young girl. He likes woman—plenty woman, old Gidegal. He made love songs to sing women to his blanket. He left the big ceremony of Jarrada for us.'

Mother's brother is responsible for the proper raising of children. A young boy is called 'tharabai', uncircumcised, and his uncle arranges his Luraga ceremony of circumcision when he is nine to twelve, and oversees the ensuing teaching of sign language, and food restriction laws. The Luraga boys are secluded from women, and confined to communicating only by sign language. They are not permitted to eat 'big meat', which includes dugong, turtle stingrays, echidna, flying fox, emu, kangaroo and wallaby.

Sign language is very important in the silent business of hunting, and Luraga boys are confined to using it for at least six months to ensure they learn it properly.

The kinship system of the Lardil was more complex than in most of Cape York peninsula. The two moieties were symbolised by a creature from the sea, Thanba, the shovel-nosed shark, and Gurngin, the wallaby, from the land. Each moiety was divided into four subsections, and a subsection could marry across to only two of the subsections in the opposite moiety. The rigid division of the moieties was emphasised by some food laws—land food must never be taken into the sea, and land food and sea food must never be cooked together on the same fire.

Mother's brother was also responsible in seeing that the young man makes a straight marriage according to the kinship laws. When he is ready for marriage, either to a girl already promised or to one selected, the success of the marriage is ensured by carrying out the ceremony of Jarrada.

All the mature male relatives of the man go out and prepare the ground. They use the blades of boomerangs to clear and scrape smooth a large circle. In the centre a shallow, oval hole is dug and lined with small balls of bird down coloured by rolling in red ochre or white clay. It has a red centre and symbolises a vulva.

A two-metre-tall pole is stuck in the ground in front of the oval. The pole is decorated with paint and feathers and represents a penis. Strings of white bird down hang from the top of the poles to symbolises the seminal flow. Oval holes are dug each side of the central symbol and their edges lined with red-ochred feathers.

The men decorate their bodies with red and white paint and ochred bird down. Each paints his own 'mulgri' on his chest and shoulders. On the front of their thighs they paint ovals which symbolise women.

The song man who sings the Jarrada stands before the feathered pole with legs spread, knees bent, and hands on thighs. Two relatives, either uncles, or uncle and grandfather, kneel over the holes at the side, and they begin singing the cycle of love songs. As they sing they swing their hips back and forth in the rhythmic motions of love-making.

The Jarrada songs are said to be infallible. Men put the songs in the feathers of a bird being plucked, and let the feathers blow to where the woman is sitting, so they stick to her skin and hair. A man would get a woman's dillybag or digging-stick, put the Jarrada songs in it and next day it would lead her to an assignation.

With plenty of meat preserved in the ground ovens we decided to spend a couple of days filming the making of ropes from hibiscus bark. They were to make a big dugong and turtle net, and for lashing the walpa together. The older men set about doing that while the younger men took tomahawks and crossed to the mainland to get craft-work material, hollow saplings for didjeridoos, bent gidji roots for boomerangs, ironwood for spears, womeras and foodpounders.

Selling fine craft work was the main industry on Mornington Island, amd material was scarce within walking distance of the mission.

The inner bark was stripped from the outer, and shredded very fine, the tangled mass of fibre growing larger at a surprising rate. When it was large the two rope-making experts, Bunbudji and Gabori, sat down and teased it out in long strands which they rolled rapidly back and forth on their thighs. They used powdered dry clay to ease the friction on skin of hand and thigh, winding the string on a stick held in the left hand.

They soon had a production line going, some stripping and shredding, two spinning string, and Warrabudgera plaiting string into rope of varying diameters, according to its future use. The rope for the turtle net was as thick as a finger and probably stronger than machine-made rope.

By the time the craft-wood getters arrived back in late afternoon, laden with goodies, the ropemakers had made all the rope that would be required for our projects.

Next morning Warrabudgera and Bunbudji looked at the sea and announced that the coming high tide would be full of moon fish, the big silver salmon that came about the time of the full moon. Earlier in the year Frank Woolston had discussed with Dick the problems of preserving fish when there was a glut of them, as the mission had little refrigeration. Frank had investigated the brining of fish as a solution, and we had brought a lot of salt and big drums for brine tanks, to show the Lardil the process. All we needed were a lot of fish, and had asked the old men to let us know when such an opportunity might occur.

Warrabudgera pointed to the narrow channel between Bargu and Doomanu, the small mangrove islands in the channel. He told us how in the old days the people used to catch a lot of salmon there by building barriers with bushes at each end of the channel at high tide. When the tide went out salmon and other fish were stranded in shallow pools in the channel.

At high tide we launched the dinghies and put our big nets across each end of the channel, then returned to Doolgarnum Beach to film the making of the walpa.

The logs they had gathered were mainly about three metres long, the largest being about the thickness of a man's thigh. The logs were almost as light as balsa wood and were obviously driftwood washed into the mangroves at high tide.

I had envisaged a small square raft, but they selected two of the thickest logs which were curved and placed them on the ground to form the outline of a dinghy, then they selected and placed suitable logs to fill in between the first two, putting the smallest end to the front of the walpa. Logs of smaller diameter formed a top layer, then they commenced to lash the logs tightly together. A layer of bindi grass to soften and level the top and the walpa was complete. It had taken less than an hour to put together.

Bunbudji had selected the logs and generally overseen the making of the raft, and had cut two flanged mangrove roots for oars. He claimed the walpa as his and would carry it, as tradition demanded, into the sea on his own; all the others had to do was place it on his back. He bent over to take the load, and they heaved it up on his back. Poor old Bunbudji's knees buckled and he went down under it like a stranded turtle. When the other four helpers had stopped falling about laughing they dispensed with tradition and helped him to launch it. Then they all took turns at riding on it and throwing spears from it. Dick got on it and immediately became a wild myall, shaking his spear and threatening in Lardil that he was going to come ashore and spear them for causing the last big flood.

We returned to the nets in late afternoon to find them sagging under the weight of fish, and the shallow water in the channel boiling with trapped fish. The dinghies were dragged into shallow water and there was much splashing, yelling and excitement as the fish were untangled from the net and thrown into the dinghies. Other men took fish spears and womeras and waded in to spear fish in the pool, yelling warnings to each other about Bul-le-bul, the big spotted stingrays, threshing wildly about in the shallow water. Many large fish either hurdled the net or escaped round the end of it, but we had about a hundred salmon weighing about three or four kilograms each.

While gathering in the nets Warrabudgera saw young men urinating on the mudflats. He immediately began haranguing them in Lardil, waving his womera and saying they had spoilt the fishing, tomorrow there would be nothing—they smell that piss and clear out, they know when they are being hunted. The young men did not believe old Jamba—they put the nets in next day, and got nothing.

The salmon were filleted, washed free of blood and soaked in strong brine overnight, then next day laid out on bushes in the sun for two days until they were properly cured. The Lardil were delighted when they cooked and ate some of it, realising they would be able to take it home to their families.

We had used all our salt but fortunately had a transceiver radio and when we called the mission that evening, they said the Flying Doctor was overnighting there. Next morning he flew over in a Drover aircraft and dropped us a bag of salt to enable us to continue catching fish.

The making of the walpa (raft), at Langu Narnji.

Thundulmindidja retrieves the doolmidjal (flood-stick) from Woonoonyea.

7

The floodmakers of Langu Narnji

The flood-making ceremony created by Marnbil had been under investigation by Dick and myself for some years. As a child, Dick remembered seeing gifts arrive from tribes living in low-lying country to the south, especially the Jungarl of Forsythe Island and the Jangaru from the Gulf. With the gifts was a message-stick, a plea not to cause any great floods during the ensuing monsoon season.

Mornington, Denham and Langu Narnji islands were occupied by the Lardil tribe, and the smaller islands of the North Wellesley group by the Jungarl tribe. The low-lying South Wellesley group, mainly Bentinck; Sweers and Allen islands were inhabited by the Kiadilt tribe. All these people now live at Gununa on Mornington Island.

The Lardil were divided into four groups by direction: to the north the Gidgurumbanda, east the Leelumbanda, west the Balambanda, and south the Lurrumbanda. The Lurrumbanda owned Langu Narnji and the adjacent part of Mornington Island, connected by tidal flats which are completely exposed at low tide. It was the Lurrumbanda who were the flood masters, and the flood-making ceremony was carried out on the north-east tip of Langu Narnji.

The tidal influences in the Gulf of Carpentaria are similar to those in the Gulf of Mexico, there being usually only one high and one low tide in each twenty-four hours. During certain phases of the moon the tide may 'double', and may also remain high or low for longer than the average period. Strong winds also have a marked effect on the tides; a strong persistent south-easter may create an abnormally low tide in southern reaches, whereas a strong northerly wind, usually associated with a cyclonic disturbance, may cause the tide to back up in southern reaches and cause extensive flooding in low-lying areas.

During January of 1964 I was on Mornington Island when a small cyclone, codenamed 'Little Audrey', came down the central Gulf from the north and passed just west of Mornington. On that occasion a tidal surge rose about 1.3 metres above normal king tide mark.

The Lardil have many legends of great floods that occurred in the past. One story relates that during one great flood only the trees on low ridges of Forsythe Island remained above water, and the Jungarl people survived by tying their rafts to the trees. On Langu Narnji only the top of a twenty-metre-high sand ridge could be seen.

In 1948 a tidal surge which rose three metres above king tide level was said to have been caused by Shilling, a Lurrumbanda man, who, after a quarrel with the missionary, had gone to Langu Narnji to make a flood in revenge. That flood also spoiled the dune-wells on Bentinck Island and was instrumental in the decision of the Kiadilt people to move to the mission on Mornington.

The Lurrumbanda say they were blamed by surrounding people for every flood which occurred, whether they had made the flood ceremony or not, and united war parties often came to attack the Lurrumbanda after disastrous floods. The Lurrumbanda exacted tribute from adjacent island and mainland clans by promising not to cause any more floods. One reason for the performing of the flood ceremony was fighting or dispute between Lurrumbanda people and people they were visiting in other regions. The offended Lurrumbanda would have a message-stick passed around the circle of elders who would decide whether or not to carry out the flood ceremony.

During January 1964 I was invited to attend one such meeting. An old Lurrumbanda man living on the mainland at Doomadgee Mission had sent a message-stick by courier on the weekly air service. The courier interpreted the message-stick as a request from the old men at Doomadgee for a flood to punish six young girls who would not marry the men to whom they had been promised. However, between the arrival of the message-stick and the meeting, cyclone 'Little Audrey' had passed by Mornington and on to Doomadgee. After some discussion the elder spokesman of the Lurrumbanda, Warrabudgera, asked if there was any high ground around Doomadgee, and when informed there was not, he said, 'No good, we might drown all the good people too—might be that cyclone bin frighten 'em enough.' It had been a very fortuitous cyclone.

Warrabudgera detailed the sequence of events in the flood-making ceremony:

> First we had to go to high ground at Dingelma, across on Mornington Island and build strong wet-weather shelters. The huts were made with a round sapling framework forming a dome, covered with thick sheets of paperback and bindi grass. Food, firewood and water would be stored in them, the water being held in large baler shells.

When that was complete we would get paperbark, string, and two sticks to hold the clay, then go to Mundawah where Marnbil dug the magic kial (white clay). Then we would follow Marnbil's road down to the coast at Binburragun Creek, then along the coast to Lil-liltuh Point, where the clay and sticks would be left until the next day.

It was decided that Thundulmindidja would be the flood master and Burrud would carry the clay. We would leave the Dingelma sequence until later and go to Mundawah next day. They thought a tide low enough to do the final flood ceremony might occur in a few days, as a strong south-easter had just commenced, and would shift the Gulf waters north.

There was an air of suppressed excitement next morning, and I realised that a ritual, feared by all the people of the southern Gulf, and held in awe by the Lardil, had been seen by only a handful of the old men present. All the younger men were agog to witness a ceremony talked about every monsoon.

The floodmakers, following tradition, did not speak to each other as they cut out two-metre-long sticks of beach-hibiscus which had been stripped of bark to make rope, then collected string and a bark container each, and picked up spears and womeras. The floodmaker, followed by Burrud, led a single file of silent men inland to get paperbark on the way to Mundawah.

Mundawah was located in a low open forest of eucalypts near the middle of the island; it was the head of a small gravelly creek and the clay was exposed in its low banks. All watched silently as Burrud used his womera to dig clay and fill both baskets with dry lumps of it. Then, still in single file, we set out along Marnbil's ancient road to Binburragun and on to Lil-liltuh. I wondered how many hundreds of generations had followed Marnbil.

The flood-making materials were hidden among coralite rocks and bushes at Lil-liltuh, and we returned to Doolgarnan.

It was approaching low tide next day when the floodmakers decided it was time to return to Lil-liltuh Point to continue the ritual. They retrieved the hidden materials and sat down to make the clay wet and pack it around one end of the stick, until it formed an oval mass about fifteen centimetres thick and twenty-five centimetres long. While doing that they also painted transverse bands of white clay across their faces, bodies, arms and legs, to represent rows of white-topped storm waves. They wrapped the clay end of the stick in paperbark and bound it up with mud and string. The doolmidjal was complete. They made another one but substituted a mixture of flour and sand for the clay; that was the one to be taken into the water, and would not cause a flood.

The low tide had exposed a reef joining Langu Narnji to a small islet called Woonoonyea, about two hundred metres east off the coast.

The floodmakers went out along the reef and climbed the northern outcrop to hide the doolmidjals among the low bushes. From Woonoonyea the reef extended in an arc westward then north for about a kilometre. Near the middle there were five low archways under the reef, the flood-making site. They returned to await the very low tide.

Two days later it was decided the tide would be low enough to get out to the underwater arches, so the flood men returned to Woonoonyea and retrieved the doolmidjal. They used more clay to re-paint the storm waves on their bodies, maintaining a sharp watch to prevent a surprise attack by people who would want to prevent the flood-making ceremony.

Taking only the dummy doolmidjal, the flood men walked eastward along the exposed reef until they came to the archways, called Bidjinyea-narwee, or bad smell country—meaning a place where evil deeds were performed.

The five archways were always under water. Burrud took the doolmidjal, tore away some of the bark wrapping, and dived down through the first archway, breaking off fake clay and spreading it through the water as he swam. He came up for air and then dived down through the second archway. The clay turns the water white to symbolise boiling surf, or floodwater.

While the swimmer dives and spreads the clay the flood master stands on a coral-head knee-deep in water and chants, 'Wah, wah, wah' in a loud voice. Usually only three of the archways were used, unless a very big flood was sought. The old people said such a flood might cover all the land and drown everybody. After going through the three arches, the flood men returned along the reef until they reached a small sand cay called Gwa-argan.

At Gwa-argan the final act of the flood-making ritual took place. They waded through shallow water to the beach calling out, 'Wah, wah wah! Tu, tu, tu, tu!' imitating the noise of a big sea. Still calling out they lay down and rolled over and over up the beach, miming big waves rolling up and crashing on the shore.

The men got up from the beach, and with arms held high and wide, danced and high-stepped along, invoking Dewallewul. They passed Woonoonyea and on to Lil-liltuh. As they danced they called out, 'Wah, wah, wah. Now these people, our enemies, will die. All fish, dugong, turtle, shark, will die. The big flood will come and wash them all up on the land. All things must die.'

From Lil-liltuh the men cross Langu Narnji to Doolgarnan Point and cross the tidal flats to join the rest of the people at Dingelma. The people see the flood men coming and know the ceremony has been completed because the flood marks have been washed from their bodies.

74

The floodmakers do not speak as they rejoin their families to prepare for the coming flood.

The flood may come in different ways. It may come as a giant tidal wave in clear weather, or as a series of tides, each mounting higher and higher; but it usually comes with a cyclone. The first sign from Dewallewul may be a large ring around the sun by day, and the moon at night.

Then the air becomes hot and still. The clouds become denser and darker, and the wind begins, soft and sighing at first, then becoming stronger and more gusty by the hour. The rain commences and increases to a steady downpour. Gusting winds get stronger, then cease abruptly and the moaning roar of the next gust can be heard coming far off. Finally a distant roaring is heard, getting louder and louder until a powerful wind engulfs the whole island with horizontal rain and a thunderstorm roaring as it smashes all the trees. It may last for many hours and all the people can do is roll up in paperbark and huddle together on the ground until it is over.

Due to a much lower barometric pressure, the main flood surge is contained within the central eye of the cyclone, and if its arrival co-incides with a king tide it produces a flood from which nightmares and legends stem.

When the people consider they have caused enough trouble they have a meeting and ask the flood men to stop the storm. They gather up stones on the beach, make a big fire and heat them. When the stones are very hot the flood men rake them out, and using bark to protect their hands, pick up the stones one at a time and run down the beach to cast it into the tunnel of a wave as it curls over to crash on the beach. They continue until all the stones are gone and the waves know they must go back.

Dick and Burrud were preparing ceremonial gear for dances and song cycles of the Rainbow Serpent, and needed a large quantity of white feathers. Some of the men said they had seen big flocks of corella cockatoos near Gadmanjilla Point, the refuge from storm surges. Dick suggested we take the shotgun over there and get a lot, and when the rest of the men heard the shots they should come over to pluck and roast the corellas for lunch.

We came on a large flock feeding on the ground and I wandered about at a distance as decoy, while Dick circled around and came in behind a low sand dune to get close. His first shot got three or four, but the second shot came just after they flew up and it cut a swathe through them. When the flock circled over their downed mates another two shots brought down many more; we had more than thirty birds. We gathered the birds into a heap and left most of them for the others, then went up to see the small rock shelter on the nearby peak.

There was a low wall of coralite rock on top of the ridge. It curved out over a rock pavement to form a low shallow shelter. It was about thirty metres above the sea level, and one could imagine a couple of families huddled in there, cold and hungry, watching the sea rising relentlessly higher and higher.

We were plucking our birds when the others arrived. Some commenced plucking feathers and putting them in bags, while others got wood and made a big fire on the coralite pavement to cook the birds. It was blazing fiercely when old Bunbudji came along and looked in horror at it. 'Yackai! Marnbil said you can't light fire over there, it must be on the ground.' The young men looked a bit discomfited, but decided maybe Marnbil didn't know everything.

We put our plucked birds on to cook, then lay about talking while someone turned them over with a long stick. They were almost done when there was a shattering explosion, followed by more loud bangs. We fled to a safe distance and turned to see that layers of the coralite pavement had contained air pockets, which exploded under the intense heat of the fire, scattering rock, fire and birds everywhere. Bunbudji was falling about laughing, and that night he and Dick made great mime of it. Marnbil would have enjoyed it.

During the night, Yalmeal, the south-east wind, dwindled to a light breeze and we woke to a sparkling morning and a flat silver sea. Hunter Burrud decided conditions were perfect for a dugong and turtle hunt, and commenced seeing to harpoons, wops, lines and ropes, while two young men trotted off to climb Gadmanjilla to look for streaky white water made by dugong feeding on seagrass. Warrabudgera decided that oldest brother, Thundulimidja, should take me on Marnbil's road round the island, with Dick to go as interpreter. I got ready with alacrity and was putting my boots on when Dick came along. He was full of suppressed excitement as he borrowed my tobacco tin to roll a smoke. He spoke almost in a whisper. 'You know, Warrenby, we're going to see something very special today, that wallaby story place belonging to Gurngin and Margura, the coastal wallaby. I've never been game to even sneak a look at it, it's such a big law. When I was a kid we had to go past it down on the beach, holding a bush alongside our face so we couldn't look. Old Thabu Kenny is going to tell us all about it.'

I knew the wallaby Dreaming, like the others in the area, had been made by Marnbil but had not realised it was secret and sacred, and now understood why only I was going and why Warrabudgera had requested no cameras.

It was about a ten-kilometre walk around the island, so we carried food and water for the day. We set off heading south-west along

Doolgarnun beach. Near the end of it Kenny held both arms up in salute to sand-dunes behind the beach and said something in Lardil which included Warrenby. Dick translated it to 'poor old fellow Warrenby' because he was buried somewhere along the dunes. He went on to tell of how, sometime after the great flood, Warrenby had been killed by a northwind Lardil revenge party, after some trouble about women. His body had been found floating in the sea off Gadmanjilla Point. He must have been spearing fish alone, when they sneaked up on him. He had died hard because there were four dead men around him

The first story place was Jardunga. It was a large area of flat sandstone, which Marnbil had made for a big fireplace and left his footprint on the rock. Dick translated it as jar-foot, dunga-man, and pointed out the track. A mangrove-lined inlet just past it was called Budulbee-thulba, 'prawn place' where, after the wet season, people formed a line with big scoop nets and waded up it catching lots of prawn (booya). They chant as they go: 'Girdi jili barngan jilaru' (The prawn is small but can hurt you with his spear.)

On the other side of the inlet was Gadmanjilla Point, its highest point being Darbung, the flood refuge. We climbed up and looked out to see the hunting dinghies heading north for Charlie Busch Bay.

Opposite on the main island was Bahudgun Bay, where Marnbil had left a rain-making ceremony, the chants that went with it being sung softly by our songman as we went along:

'Birri yawu layarra.' (There is a big rain coming but we are sheltered.)
'Dalia ranba bolin biyu.' (The storm is coming.)

About a kilometre along the coast we came to Birriwaga Point, and in the dunes behind it was the biggest well that Marnbil had dug on the island. Across the channel were the pink and white cliffs of Goobirah Point, where two brothers, Bul-lebul, the spotted stingray, and Yarran, the red-backed sea eagle, had taken a big catch of fish to cook and eat. They were greedy and ate too much and were rolling about groaning in pain, when a great swarm of tiny bees, Wongabel, came along and got tangled in their hair and beards. The Wongabel could smell the sweet blossom of the ti-tree on the island and wanted to fly over to it, but Bul-lebul told them it was too far and they would fall in the water. They continued to annoy Bul-lebul and he jumped into the sea to escape them. When the Wongabel tried to fly over he splashed water over them and they drowned. Yarran told them to go back and warn all other Wongabel that they could never cross the channel. So there are no bees on the island, and Yarran still sits on Goobirah Point to warn bees, and Bul-lebul, the spotted stingray, jumps and splashes in the channel.

The moral of the story was about greed and sharing, especially of honey, the much-coveted sweetness. Like every living thing, the Wongabel were, in the beginning, people. Parts of the hive were named after relevant parts of the human body. The entrance tunnel was the nose, and the streams of bees coming and going, were the arms of the ancestral being reaching out to gather food. The main law about honey was that the person who finds the hive cannot eat any of the honey. They must call all the other people nearby to eat it, and depend on their share from other people's finds.

We walked around Birribella Bay and were told the country inland from it was Judurugan (garfish) country, and he was boss of fire-sticks, which were made from beach-hibiscus growing there. To get fire quickly you twist your sticks together and call out: 'Shooooo Didmunja Shooooooooooo.'

We turned and I soon noticed a change come over Dick and Kenny. They were silent and walking carefully so as not to make any noise. We approached an outcrop of pink and white sandstone like the cliffs of Goobirrah. In the middle of outcrop was a natural amphitheatre with walls about two metres high; it was Boogar Nilwa Jarjijga, the Dreaming of the wallabies. There were curious natural formations and Thundulmindidja pointed them out, naming them in a low voice, Warama, Tharabai, (the men) Gurnjin, Margura (the women). Older brother was becoming increasingly nervous and was whispering when he pointed out the last place, four round holes at the base of a low wall; water seeping from them had left white stains. Dick interpreted it as semen running out of the wallaby girls after ritual sex. When I looked around to ask a question a minute later they had both silently and swiftly departed.

Dick was waiting down on the beach. He grinned and said, 'Old Thabu couldn't stay—the old people are really scared of those places. He's waiting on the point.' Dick's air of relief indicated it wasn't just the old people who were scared of the Dreaming places.

The next place was Thundulgan Point and behind it the raft-making place, Walpa-Gunduwin. The light driftwood was collected from among the mangroves and brought up on flat ground for assembly. Thabu was singing a walpa song: 'Yakinba rangui—biyarra rama.' (Laden with fish—which way home.)

In the little bay in front was Wanguh, the Dreaming place of Ngarrawun, the blue-fish. It was just off shore where Marnbil had made a freshwater spring. He stood up there and struck two stones together and all the blue-fish rose to the surface. After a good wet season the water bubbled up and was good to drink. It bubbles up because of the pulsing of the gills (wunguh) of Ngarrawun, the ancestral being.

We walked along Lilungla beach and up on to Gurrdungea Point. It was about fifteen metres above sea level and was a wet season camp. Behind it were big stands of ti-tree to make frames of wet season shelters.

Burugun was next; it meant fish net stick. Shrubs which grew along a small creek yielded long, pliable sticks which were strong and could be bent into a circle for the frames of a scoopnet. We followed the creek up to its source, where water trickled from a spring. Marnbil and Gin-gin had camped there while he made the spring which fed Dooguray Creek (semen creek). It was part of the wallaby Dreaming but not as secret, and old Thubu was relaxed. The secret names of the ancestral beings were whispered only at the main Dreaming centres.

We followed Bangeega Bay around to a creek called Baranda Dubulan, which flowed out of Yarbargun country, the place of Bunji (brother-in-law) yams. It was associated with the next story place on Mudu-mudugun Bay which means 'long penis.' Just inland was Linga-wadngala, the big sub-incision place. Warrabudgera was going to show that place to me later on, so we continued around Goonbulgan Bay, past the flood-making place of Lil-liltuh and up along the coast to Yarwalla Bay. The name meant windbreak and was used for cold, dry season camps.

We were nearing Windbreak when Thundulmindidja almost stepped on a large frilled-neck lizard. Mukaji had been dozing in the afternoon sun and thought he was a goner, as indeed he would have been if we had not been anticipating roast dugong or turtle for dinner. Mukaji got up on his back legs and sprinted, frill flared, for his favourite tree. Instead of cutting him down with a boomerang old Thubu commenced chanting Mukaji's song. The lizard hit the tree flat out and in an instant was going up the far side of it like greased lightning, and from then on keeping the tree between us at all times, to avoid spear or boomerang. Dick explained that was what the chant of Mukaji was all about; it was the song you put in your nulla-nulla when going into battle with it, telling it to always keep its wood between you and your enemy, just as the tree does for Mukaji.

As we approached Doolgarnun we heard distant singing and looked up the channel to see the dinghies returning. The timeless refrain came wafting across the sea:

'Wirri birabi laman buru-wirra birabi laman buru
Wirra birabi garka manga-wirra birabi garka manga.'

(We have been hunting—the fish were here and there.
We have had good hunting.)

Dick said it was one of his favourite songs. They had a large dugong and a turtle.

Back at camp I found Dick busy chipping and chopping at a section of tree trunk. He told me he had been out in the bush looking for the curved roots of gidji to make boomerangs, when he noticed a broken dead limb with an almost right angle bend. A hole in the bend was the eye of Thuwathu, the Rainbow Serpent, watching him. He looked and saw a similar eye in the other side. The limb was hollow and the gaping jaws needed only a little sculpting with a tomahawk to turn it into Thuwathu, so he chopped it off and brought the head home. When red-ochred and painted with wavy white bands to represent white wave caps, he had the head of roaring, gaping, suffering Rainbow Serpent for the centrepiece in the ceremony they were to perform next day.

The preparation of ceremonial gear and bodypainting for an important ritual takes many hours. The half-metre tall, peaked headdresses were made of bark bound and covered with human-hair string, with plumes of emu or cockatoo feathers on top; balls of bird down were stuck on to form Dreaming designs. Warrabudgera's headdress had a metre-long wand stuck through it near the top, with a plume of emu feathers on each end. It represented the big ears of Thuwathu.

Some of the snake-like body designs represented the serpentine tracks of Thuwathu, others the waves created by his passage. Bunches of stiff eucalypt leaves tied below the knees hiss like waves coming ashore as the dancers stamp their feet.

The dancers form up and dance in two serpentine lines to represent the wake left by Thuwathu as he travelled; the didjeridoo mimes the sound of his going, and a booming conch shell the mournful moaning of the suffering serpent.

The songs of the latter part of the song cycle, where Thuwathu worries about his sister and her child are haunting and ineffably sad, expressing the universal sadness inherent in all humanity:

'Jararma ami jaram abu
Jararma ami jarama abu.'

The last dance and song is about the shooting star, the eye of Thuwathu racing across the sky. The string and feathers held by the dancers represent the trail of fire. They watch it in awe and fall back in fear when the clash of clap-sticks signals the fall of the star. They sing:

'Birin jalan jalu rungu
Birin jalun jalu rungu.'
(Sparks from the eye.)

The painted head of Thuwathu, jaws agape and hollow-eyed, listened to his ancient evocative songs. Dry white clay on the ground around the base of his neck was the foaming sea from which he had arisen.

Beside the head of Thuwathu stood a more abstract symbol of his presence. A wooden cross stood in the ground, the three upper points bore plumes of waving emu feathers to represent his head and big ears. Strings from the top, to the outer arms, and back to halfway down the centre pole, formed a square, and bunches of white feathers along the strings symbolised white wave caps; two ovals of polished baler shell hung from the cross to symbolise the awful power and magic of Thuwathu.

It was powerful drama to impress upon the boys who were about to be initiated, the responsibility of being mother's brother, and looking after sisters and their children.

Having no training in linguistics I had made some preparations to record the Damin language before commencing the expedition, the most important being a list of four hundred words and phrases drawn up by Dr. Lamont West, an American anthropologist then working with the Yao people in Cape York Peninsula.

I planned to highlight the difference between the ordinary Lardil and Damin, by stating the word or phrase in English myself, then having Burrud, fluent in English and Lardil, repeat it in Lardil, and Warrabudgera to state it in Damin.

It was an astonishing language; some words and phrases sounded like ordinary Lardil, but the clicks, glops, sniffles, grunts, whistles and other natural sounds in Damin, made it sound like no other language on earth. There was a 'small fish way of talking' and a 'big fish way of talking.' The small fish language was learned first; I soon realised that it contained natural sounds one would expect to hear when hunting fish and other game along the shore and in the mangroves, the glop of bursting mud bubbles, the clicks of insects and the calling of birds like the pied oyster-catcher—giri, giri, giri, which meant 'form a circle with fish nets quickly'. The big fish way of talking contained sounds which would be heard when hunting along the outer edge of the reef at low tide, the slap and slop of the waves and other natural sounds.

I learned that a top linguist, Dr Ken Hale, an American, had recorded the Lardil language about six years previously and was working near Alice Springs, so sent the tapes to the Institute to forward to him. His reply was prompt.

Ken Hale had been recording ordinary Lardil and had got a few words in Damin, but having recorded many auxiliary languages used as mother-in-law or brother-in-law 'respect' languages in many groups, had taken little notice. He wrote, 'Your tapes make it very clear that Damin is very special indeed in Australia. What is of particular interest is the fact that Damin appears to have click consonants, heretofore known only from Africa, and another consonant (nasal ingressive) not known in any other language.' Enclosed in Ken Hale's letter was a long list of short sentences to be recorded in Damin, and sent on to him as soon as possible. He hoped to go to Mornington Island after a brief visit to America. I duly taped the Damin and sent it off to him, but chronic illness kept him in America for some years.

I was unable to interest any Australian linguist in Damin and was left to ponder it alone. It provided many more questions than answers. It was obviously a hunting language, but why was it needed when they had sign language for hunting? Perhaps it was merely a fossil language of some earlier *Homo sapiens* hunter group which had been retained and adapted as a respect language for brother-in-law. The Lardil had no answers to my questions; Damin had been in use since its creation by Marnbil.

The answer, as usual, lay within the wisdom left behind by Marnbil. Retracing Marnbil's Road looking for other esoteric information, I came across Ewar Point, where Marnbil had commenced fishing at night, and next day he had looked across to Sandalwood country and observed that Dewallewul was also fishing at night; surely not a coincidence; everything that Marnbil did or said had significance. What had happened at Ewar Point?

Understanding came like a bolt from the blue. Reef-living people like the Lardil do their main hunting at low tide. Elsewhere in the world, except the Gulf of Mexico, the tide regularly ebbed and flowed twice in the twenty-four hours, tugged back and forth by the moon's gravitational pull, except also in the Gulf of Carpentaria, where there is also but one low tide in each twenty-four hours. The twenty-eight day moon cycle meant that in the Gulf about fourteen low tides would occur at night. If Marnbil wanted to eat, Marnbil would have to get out of the sack, at whatever hour, to fish: the narrow, impoverished land behind him would provide little on a long-term basis.

Warrabudgera knew of no other people around the Gulf who had any kind of Damin language; however, he had no knowledge about the people on Vanderbilt Island, or Groote Island, and it's possible that they may have needed a similar hunting language. The coastal tribes on the mainland had the option of living off the low tides in daylight, and hunting possum, wallaby and emu when the low tides came at night. Dick had told me of low tide hunting at night when he was living a tribal life.

During the afternoon the men went to the swamp or creeks where melaleucas grew, and pulled off long strips of paperback to roll into bundles up to four metres long, bound up with green vines to make large durable torches. Sign language was of no use in the dark, or when the hands are full of torches, fishnets, spears etc. Sound was essential but had to be natural to the environment so as not to alarm the quarry of fish, turtle or dugong.

The making of Warrabudgera's headdress for the dance of Thuwathu, the Rainbow Serpent. Warrabudgera (seated), Thundulmindidja (assisting him).

The main camp on the Hann River.

8

Country of the snake men

The Laura store was next to the Laura pub; they complemented each other by being similar bush structures of rusting, sagging corrugated iron, both run by vigorous bush bred families, and both having blue heeler cattle dogs sleeping in the dust in front, with wheeling kite-hawks overhead. There was a horse hitching rail under mango trees in front of the pub.

Bowie Gostelow ran the store. I stopped the Landrover by the old hand-pump petrol bowser and Bowie soon appeared. He was stocky, sunburned, barefoot and genial, with a cheery greeting and an inquiry into how our search for 'that bloody old blackfella stuff' was going. Bowie's family also owned Koolburra cattle station and he had spent much of his life mustering wild cattle in the bush, living off salt-beef and damper out of pack-saddles. As he pumped the petrol up into the glass tank on top of the bowser he said, 'I saw some old blackfella paintings up on the head of the Hann when we went mustering there once—they must have used some funny kind of paint because it ate into the rock.'

I had heard of paint-infilled engravings being found in other countries, but none had yet been found in Australia. I questioned Bowie about the exact location of the paintings and he assured me it was about a fifty-kilometre horse ride south-west of Koolburra home-stead, and was impossible country for a vehicle. I followed him into the store to get a few supplies. There was only a narrow clear floor space in front of the long counter, the rest was covered with camp ovens, quart pots, carbide lights, tyres and other bush bric-a-brac. Bridles, stirrups and saddle-clothes hung from nails on the wall and cowboy hats were stacked over the counter. Dick was busy selling a bark painting to Bowie's wife Vivienne, and then spent the proceeds on tobacco for our trip.

Dick and I were just beginning a seven-week expedition and were going to Cooktown to pick up Willy, who had mentioned seeing paintings on the headwaters of the Hann, when hunting there with the Tomahawk people, but had not said anything about engravings. Bowie told us to call at Koolburra on the way to the Hann and get further directions from his brother, Miles.

We had established a base camp on the Laura River, and left early next morning for Cooktown. The radiator was leaking, and the rough corrugated road had the steering box rattling loose on the ancient Landrover, so we decided to have those defects fixed and everything else checked before taking on the remote Hann wilderness.

Joe Musgrave was with Willy. Joe's country was that of the Magpie Geese people on the Morehead River, not too far from the Hann, and as he knew all that country we asked him along. Willy told us he was supposed to go to Hopevale Mission to get married again, but decided that at his age (he was in his late seventies) another week or two wouldn't matter.

Back in camp that evening we got out our maps and had a look at the Hann River region. There was a large low plateau of sandstone which was part of the Great Divide; it was called the Desert, and was a hub from which five rivers radiated. Three of these, the King, Alice and Coleman rivers, flowed south-west and west into the Gulf of Carpentaria, while the Hann and Morehead rivers flowed north-east into Princess Charlotte Bay. I asked Willy to show me where the caves were on the map, but he said he couldn't read a map, and didn't need to as he had a map in his head. He used a finger to draw a map of the Desert and its radiating rivers in the dust—and then gave a narration of its creation story:

> The snake men were travelling north and hunting other men; they were killing people and hanging them up in trees to collect later. The snake men became thirsty and changed themselves into kangaroos so they could travel faster to a waterhole.
>
> A group of bird men were also out hunting. They saw the kangaroos and decided to spear some of them. Banana-bird speared the largest kangaroo, who was actually the Taipan snake man.
>
> Taipan pulled the spear out of his side and smelt it to discover who had speared him. He sniffed the air and said, 'Ah, he is hiding in one of the trees over there.'
>
> Taipan began to knock all the trees down, jumping this way and that way. He knocked down tree after tree, but Banana-bird kept shifting to another tree. He got into a big, white lady-apple tree. Taipan was tired by then and he could not knock down the strong lady-apple tree, which saved the life of Banana-bird.
>
> When the snake men found they could not knock the lady-apple tree down, they changed themselves back to snakes and hid in long grass. Taipan hid himself under the lady-apple tree.

Banana bird could not see any of the snake men, but he kept on looking all about. After a long wait he decided to climb down, but first he broke off sticks and threw them into the grass all about the tree. There was still no sign of snakes so he climbed down and cautiously put one foot on the ground, still no sign of snakes; he put the other foot on the ground and straightaway Taipan bit him on the back of the leg.

Now all the snakes came out of hiding and attacked Banana-bird. They tore him to pieces and then ate him. After their big feed the snakes lay down in the grass and went to sleep.

Alpudda the coucal was brother to Banana-bird and came looking for his tracks. Alpudda found the remains of his brother under the lady-apple tree and saw all the snakes sleeping there. He went back to camp and told the bird people what had happened to his brother. The women belonging to Banana-bird cut themselves with stones and wailed. The bird men decided to burn the grass and kill the snakes. Anjimagee the pandanus finch, and Alpudda took magic fire-sticks and lit the dry grass in a big circle around the sleeping snakes.

The snakes did not know the fire was coming because it was a magic fire which burned without smoke or noise, just the flames running swiftly through the grass. The snakes woke up and saw the flames; they looked for a way out but the fire was all around them. Only five snakes escaped—Taipan, Brown Snake, Death Adder, Black Snake and Carpet Snake. They travelled underground and each came up in different parts of the country.

The bird men sang up a rain to put out the magic fire, the water followed the escaping snakes and made rivers.

Grass will not grow where the magic fire burned, and it is now known as the Desert. Banana-bird, the blue-faced honeyeater, still flies from tree to tree to cross the Desert.

We packed up and got away early to get fuel and supplies in Laura, and reached Koolburra station at about noon, to find that Miles and Connie Gostelow were out on a packhorse muster. We had lunch under mango trees, and Willy and Joe were so sure of their ability to navigate across country that we set off following a station track in the general direction until we reached Jones Creek, where we cleared a crossing to pick up an old wagon track that Willy said would take us in a big semicircle to clear swampy country.

We found the wagon track and followed it a long way before losing it in sandy country. Willy then chin-pointed to a low hill where his father was buried and said we had to pass south of it. It was all open forest country of stringy-bark, sprinkled with ironwood, bloodwood and wattles. There were also many lady-apple and nonda fruit trees, the latter laden with a heavy crop of immature fruit. Some of the country had been burnt which made cross-country travel easier. We crossed Paradise Creek just before sunset and decided to camp there.

Dingoes howled along the creek in the early morning, and Dick howled in reply, saying he was imitating a dingo bitch. We were having breakfast when a fine, big orange dog loped past our camp, looking in astonishment at our Landrover.

We struck ti-tree country and had to push through a lot of sand. Using low-range gears continuously caused the spark plugs to foul, but after another gruelling twenty kilometres we chugged on to the Hann and made camp under shady paperbarks. It was a branch of the Hann called Jungle Creek.

On its headwaters the Hann was a curious river. There were no sandy banks, just crystal-clear water flowing through grass, in places so narrow it could easily be jumped. The water was so clear its depth was deceptive, as Dick found when he stepped into it for a wash and found the water suddenly over his ears.

Not far below our camp the river spread out into a big swamp. Dick said afterwards he should have been more careful of a waterway that had been made by old Taipan. I wondered if the other rivers coming out of the Desert plateau also had narrow, deep beginnings, thus lending logic to their mythological origin.

Willy said the main place was over on the western side of the low valley. We walked south along the low scarp but found only a few very small unused shelters. We crossed to the western scarp and travelled back toward the camp, finding three small shelters, each of them containing a few engravings and paintings, but none a major campsite.

Returning to camp around the edge of the swamp we surprised a big mob of pigs; a hasty shot wounded a small one but it escaped into the swamp, much to the disappointment of Willy and Joe when we returned empty-handed. They were anxious to return home with cooked pork, so Dick said he would go pig-hunting before we returned.

That night Willy told us a story about a frightful Quinkin called Ungarr, or Ahbin. The story place was on the other side of the Desert in Willy's country along the Alice River. It concerned Ungarr the Quinkin, Tul-tul the plover and his wife, and their son Minya, the black-faced cuckoo-shrike, which flies from tree to tree calling, 'Minya, minya' which means 'meat' in Olcula language:

> Tul-tul the plover took his spears and went hunting, leaving his wife and son in camp. The wife was smashing up pandanus nuts to prepare for cooking, and Minya played among the trees awaiting the return of his father. Minya went from tree to tree calling out, 'Minya, has my father speared a kangaroo?' or 'Minya, has my father speared an emu?' or 'Minya, has my father speared a plains turkey?'
>
> Ungarr was spying on the camp and saw the woman sitting cross-legged pounding pandanus nuts. She was not sitting properly with a heel in her crotch and was exposing herself. Ungarr crept up, pushed her over and put his long penis into her. It went right through her and came out her mouth, pushing her insides out. The woman died and Ungarr ran away to hide in his home, a tall, hollow, dead tree.

When Tul-tul came home he was carrying a kangaroo on his head. Minya told his father how the Quinkin had killed his mother, and showed him where Ungarr was hiding in the tree. First Tul-tul cut a big piece of meat from the kangaroo and put it inside his wife through her mouth, but it wasn't big enough and fell right through. He then cut bigger piece, pushing it in until it stuck in her chest. Cutting another piece he pushed it up through her vagina. With the pieces of meat he made her insides again, and the woman came back to life. Tul-tul put his arm round his wife, and they both cried. Tul-tul told her she would be all right.

Next, Tul-tul called his son Minya and told him to get fire-sticks and be ready to light a fire quickly. He cut a hole in the bottom of the tree where the Quinkin was hiding, filling it with dry grass and sticks. He then blocked up all the other holes in the tree with pieces of bark.

'What are you doing?' asked Ungarr.

'It's all right, it might rain and I'm covering up all the holes so you won't get wet.'

'That's good. You're very kind to do that for me.'

When Tul-tul had blocked all the holes, he jumped down from the tree and called to Minya to light the fire with his fire-sticks. The fire soon roared up the hollow tree and they could hear Ungarr huffing and puffing as the heat and smoke rose up around him. They saw urine and then dung come down. Ungarr was very frightened.

The tree soon burnt down and Ungarr was burned to ashes. The only thing left was his very long penis, which was too hard to burn. Tul-tul got his stone axe and cut it up; he cut it up into small pieces, then threw the pieces all over the country so that every man and woman got a piece. That was how men and women first got their penises and clitorises.

Dick then told Willy and Joe how Gin-gin had tempted Dewallewul while pounding pandanus nuts and how it stressed the law that women must sit properly so as not to tempt men.

I told of how Eve had tempted Adam.

Willy was keen to see the main camping place so we all set off again next morning to continue along the western scarp. We soon came to a big shelter. It was a high open place shaped like a sound shell, with an easterly aspect; it was fifteen metres wide, five metres deep, and the curved ceiling three to six metres high. The floor was mainly rock with only shallow deposits of sand, and had many axe-grinding grooves in it. There was a litter of stone material on the floor.

There were both engravings and paintings, and most of the fully pecked out engravings of small men, boomerangs and an eel, were outlined in dark red, and a few of them completely infilled with dark red. These were the first painted engravings we found. Most of the paintings portrayed men, some as monochrome dark red silhouettes, others cream silhouettes with dark red outlines and decoration; one of the latter was a female anthropomorph of unknown identity.

Everything appeared to be very old and I was disappointed to find that Willy and Joe knew nothing of what they meant.

Willy said the main living site was further north so we continued along and found two more small shelters, each containing a few faded paintings and more engravings. I was hoping that the main camp would have more recent paintings of which Willy and Joe would have some knowledge. They had said the Desert area was shared by Tomahawk, Possum and Snake language people, who lived along various rivers emanating from it.

In a short side gorge about a kilometre north-west of the first large shelter we came on the main living cave. It was the best shelter in the region, being about twenty metres wide, six metres deep and two to ten metres high over its domed ceiling, and also had an easterly aspect. Once again both paintings and engravings appeared to be very old; two white hand stencils low on the back wall were the only recent additions.

The engravings, mostly fully pecked boomerangs, were placed high on the sloping ceiling, some three or four metres above the present floor, which was a deposit of blackened sand and charcoal at least a metre deep.

High on the sloping ceiling only the hand and arm of a large engraved human figure remained, the rest had disappeared in a small rockfall, a slab now half-buried in the floor. It had happened so long ago there was no difference in colour or patination from the rest of the wall-ceiling, but its limits could be seen by parts of the remaining painted engravings. If the slab fell on charcoal there would be a vital radiocarbon date which would give a minimum age for the engravings.

There was a level mark along the back wall, and the colour of the rock below it suggested that it had been the level of an old floor, over a metre above the present one, from which the engravings had been created. The inward sloping wall would have made climbing poles, or anything but the most sophisticated scaffolding very difficult to erect.

The most logical causes for the disappearance of the old floor would be scouring by wind or water. The situation of the shelter suggested that only a flood of biblical proportions could have provided that water. Climatologists inform us there were thousands of years of searing droughts in Australia, especially from 17 000 to 15 000 years ago, and the winds of those arid times probably blew away the occupational debris of previous thousands of years.

There were parts of engraved eels, and two other engravings which appeared to represent tracks. One looked like the track of the four-toed scrub turkey, and the other a four-toed paw about fifteen centimetres long. If the engravings were of upper Pleistocene Age the large paw could represent the track of one of the extinct species of

marsupial megafauna, all of them bundled into extinction by the sear
ing droughts.

Willy knew nothing of the few old paintings. They were faded
anthropomorphs in yellow, with dark red outlines and interior decoration, or dark red silhouettes of men painted in dry pigment. When
next I met Taipan man Jerry Shepherd in Laura I asked him about the
Hann sites and he said, 'We never knew the people who did those
paintings. The paintings have always been there.'

The Hann sites appear to offer evidence of two occupations, the
first occurring during the late Pleistocene Age, followed by a long
hiatus during severely arid times, and with a reoccupation commencing at the end of the Ice Age, about 10 000 years ago. Archaeological
excavations will probably reveal the secrets.

The return trip through the forest was made easier by having our
wheel tracks to follow, but the heavy going through sand meant a stop
every half-hour to clean the spark plugs.

We were coming down off a stringy-bark ridge when Willy called out,
'Ichamba! My tucker, shootim quick.' About a hundred yards ahead
an old man emu, trailed by five almost fully grown young ones, was
running across our track. I stopped the engine and asked Dick to lean
out the window and whistle shrilly through his teeth. The emus had
been running flat out, necks outstretched as they hurdled logs and
dodged about through trees, but they gradually slowed down and
stopped, looking toward the vehicle. Dick kept up the shrill whistling
and the emus were drawn inexorably toward it by their insatiable curiosity. I slipped out the door and as Willy handed me the rifle I asked
him which one he wanted. 'Any one—just don't miss.'

The emus were approaching the passenger side so I rested the rifle
over the bonnet and we waited motionless as they came to about
thirty metres away and began milling about as they peered at this most
astonishing stranger in their forest.

The young birds looked magnificent and it was hard to squeeze the
trigger, but they belonged to Willy and Joe, so I chose one and shot it
immediately dead. The rest fled at breakneck speed while my companions tumbled excitedly out and ran to the emu.

Dick immediately felt its breast to see if it was fat, and said, 'We
can't eat him—he's proper bony bugger.'

But Willy was feeling the thigh and rump and said, 'No, 'im proper
fat young one, good minya, Ichamba.'

Dick had never hunted emu, as there weren't any on his home
islands and he was feeling for the fat pectoral muscles of a flighted
bird, in accordance with the law of not eating anything poor, unaware
that emus have a horny chest-plate. It took Willy and Joe some time to
convince him, then we tied the big bird on the bonnet and drove
down to Jones Creek to clean it.

While they plucked and cleaned the bird, I used buckets to water and firm a track up the steep bank on the other side of the creek, then hurled the Landrover up and over it.

They wasted nothing of the bird; Dick got all the feathers for corroboree and Willy and Joe left only head, legs and gut.

We reached our camp on the Laura about sundown and commenced cooking the emu, most of it in a ground oven. I roasted a choice piece of rump in the camp oven, while Willy and Joe had a snack of grilled liver and other smalls. The young emu was tender and juicy, very like plains turkey.

Next day, Dick stayed in camp painting on bark while I drove Willy and Joe to Cooktown, stopping at the Lion's Den Hotel to get some beer for them. I went in to King's Plains swamp to try and get a pig for them, and was stalking a mob when the wind changed, and they disappeared rapidly. Joe's wife, Nancy, was disappointed. 'You know the children can't eat Ichamba.' The old laws still persisted.

On flights into Coen airstrip I had noticed white stone arrangements in the foothills of the McIlwraith Ranges. We decided to drive up and investigate. We camped on Lankelly Creek in a shady place, and next day Willy found one of his relatives who could show us some of the bora grounds. He was Johnson Upton, an Olcula man who was employed at Coen as a police tracker. Johnson was a fairly big man, with iron-grey hair and appeared to be in his middle-fifties.

We travelled south-west from Coen, following station tracks until we came to a place where we had to leave the vehicle and walk through the bush to a bora ground about a kilometre across a stony ridge.

It was the bora ground of Goonbudji, the red kangaroo of Cape York peninsula, which was actually the antilopine wallaroo, a gregarious grazer of open forest and savannah woodlands of the monsoonal north. It was located about ten kilometres south-west of Coen, on the west bank of Emily Creek. Johnson located it by sighting on a small conical hill called Yorma-minda, about a kilometre south-south-east of the site.

The bora ground was composed of thin slabs of siltstone arranged in a serpentine line along the banks of the creek. The stones, 227 of them, stood on edge and ranged in height from a few centimetres to half a metre. The line was over eighty metres long, and crossed a small gully near the southern end. Another short line of stones near the gully was placed a metre west of the main line. About ten metres short of the southern end, and also just west of the line, was a small circle of white quartzite rocks with pink stains on them.

Johnson had visited the bora ground with an old Kandju man while mustering cattle. He was told the stones represented spirits of kangaroo people. The kangaroos travel in single file and the varying sizes of stones represented young and old kangaroos of both sexes. At each end of the line there was a very large slab which represented an old man kangaroo leading the way, with another bringing up the rear.

It was the fourth sacred site we had seen along the Dream road of Goonbudji the red kangaroo; another was located where it crossed the Palmer River, another was on a flat by a spring above Kelly St George Creek. The final Dreaming place, where he was called Ngalculli, was on Light House Mountain, south of Mt Carbine. It was a logical end to the Dream road, as that was about the southern limit of the antilopine wallaroo's range.

During the afternoon Johnson took us about twelve kilometres north of Coen to see the bora ground of the tortoise. It was also by a creek and was in the form of rounded tops of granite boulders protruding from the ground. They represented the carapaces of long-necked tortoises.

About a kilometre from Coen, near the foot of Mt White, (called Ilka-Toigu by the Kandju) was the bora ground of the bony bream, represented by three stones in a small clearing. The remaining Kandju knew nothing of the bora stories.

In the sandstone cave areas between Cooktown and the Palmer River, the sacred sites are almost always in rock shelters, with the spirits of ancestral beings embodied in ochre paintings or rock engravings. In areas where there were no rock shelters for paintings, the clan ancestral spirits were embodied in rocks, trees, waterholes, or stone arrangements.

'The most astonishing figure was a giant yellow horse . . . in front of the horse's head was a tall skinny dark red Quinkin, and a dark red, round stingray with long whip tail.'

9

A giant horse and Quinkins

The next expedition was to continue systematic exploration of the Laura valley escarpments for more painted rock shelters. I had two keen explorers—Dick's son Mervyn and my son Matthew—with me. We camped on the Laura River about fifteen kilometres upstream from Laura, and set out for the northern scarp where an aerial survey had revealed a small hidden valley in the top of the plateau.

Steep cliffs of conglomerate isolated the small valley from all but agile hill kangaroos and wallabies, and we gained access by following a kangaroo pad up from the river.

By noon we had found three small galleries, two in the base of the main scarp, and another among scattered slabs on top of the plateau. The two in the base contained a male Quinkin with distorted limbs and genitals, a cluster of yams or fruit in monochrome dark red, 2 two-metre-long snakes with red outlines and dots, traces of faded paintings and many hand stencils. The top gallery contained only one figure; it was on the ceiling of a small low shelter not used for camping and portrayed a man, obviously painted for sorcery purposes. The monochrome dark red figure was about a metre tall. I learned later that hidden sorcery figures indicated a killing within the clan, and were thus secretive to avoid pay-back action.

After lunch we continued along the top of the cliff hemming in the small valley, which was full of luxuriant growth of melaleuca and swamp mahogany trees, all flowering and full of shrieking rainbow lorikeets. We found a way down into the head of the valley and split up to explore among a mass of large slabs on a lower terrace.

I soon found small shelters with a scatter of ochre figures, tortoises and small human figures etc. Four of these appeared very old and faded; a woman was portrayed lying flat on her back with legs wide-spread, and a queue of three men with erect penises stood in front of her. A later figure in solid orange, also with erect penis, had been partly superimposed over the leading man, to 'jump the queue'. It was obviously a portrayal of ritual sex, and when Dick saw it later on, he thought it was 'mungara', meaning 'too much', and explained it was a way of quieting a flighty wife who was causing trouble.

At night time the husband directed the wife 'to go lay belly up' under a certain tree, then sent all the men in turn who were not close relatives, to have sex with her. They each gave the husband a present of a spear, boomerang or fish net etc. It was supposed to quieten a woman down, but when I asked my jamba (grandmother), Nagarra, about it she giggled and said she had been through 'mungara' when young and it had been no great punishment.

Just around the corner from the 'mungara' gallery I looked across a small gully and saw an immense high open shelter with hundreds of bright ochre figures in superimposed layers over an area of its back wall, about thirty metres long by three metres high. My excited whoops brought Matt and Mervyn crashing through the bush to marvel at the sight of it.

The most astonishing figure was a giant yellow horse, which had been outlined and decorated with white. It was almost six metres long and over three metres high and was the top layer of about ten superimposed layers of other small figures. Its front feet trampled the body of a life-size yellow and white woman wearing a pearl-shell pendant of love magic. The head of the horse was very well drawn and it was clearly a male; but the artists had been beaten by the tail, which looked like a long-handled fly-whisk. The yellow body colour was semi-transparent and under it could be seen a big red dillybag, a dark red crocodile, large tortoise, yams, flying foxes, fish, echidna, scrub turkey, a very large ancestral being with rayed headdress, and in lower layers, parts of a huge saw-shark over ten metres long, in dark purple-red with intricate white outline and decoration. It had been super-imposed over an equally long beehive in yellow with dark red outline, and red dots to represent bees. In front of the horse's head was a tall skinny dark red Quinkin, and a dark red, round stingray with long whip tail, plus other animals, human and yam figures.

The mass of ochre figures along the wall behind the horse included humans, snakes, fish, crocodiles, kangaroos, dingoes, emus, echidnas, tortoises, flying foxes, yams and scrub turkeys. One red scrub turkey stood over a clutch of eggs, and another in yellow silhouette was deli-cately and beautifully drawn. Near the western end of the gallery a menacing dark purple-red Quinkin hovered over an equally menacing dark yellow and red snake.

I was looking at what appeared to be a stencilled horse's hoof near the Quinkin when I heard Matt calling around the corner to the west. There were two more large painted areas and each contained a yellow horse about three metres long and two metres high; there was also a dark red pig in the third shelter. The horse in the middle shelter had a horizontal dark red man in front of it, dark red lines (reins) extended from the neck of the horse to the right hand of the man and a red rifle was under his left arm. More sorcery against the hated Black Police.

There was a magnificent vista from the main gallery, which had a sheer drop of about fifteen metres in front. Far below and about two kilometres distant a speeding vehicle raised dust on the Peninsula Development Road, and away beyond were the dusky blue ranges of the Great Divide slumbering in the sun. Scrub turkeys flapped about in the vine forest below, and the gleam of surface water indicated the reason why this was a favoured living place.

The first horses ever in the Cape York peninsula were those of the Edmund Kennedy expedition in 1848. We had found trees marked with a 'K' on the Palmer River just the other side of the Great Divide, and another on the Laura River near Laura. Immediately north of the 'K' tree on the Palmer, the Divide can be easily crossed with horses, and the Laura River then followed down to Princess Charlotte Bay, where a ship had cached more supplies for the expedition. In 1872 the William Hann expedition had also travelled down the Laura, and prior to these expeditions the largest animal to be seen in the region was a red kangaroo, and horses must have been an astonishing sight to the Gugu-Minni, who perhaps linked it with Gaiya, the giant devil dingo, and provided the motivation to create the largest figure in the art body. The smaller horses around the corner may have been painted later, during the guerilla warfare of the gold rush days.

Reports of our discovery of a giant horse in a hidden valley created considerable interest across the nation and soon had a Sydney television station anxious to make a documentary film on it and other sites discovered in the region.

A couple of weeks later our filming expedition left Cairns in three vehicles, Beverley driving a station wagon and Xavier Herbert and myself driving Landrovers. Our heavily laden convoy raised a lot of dust on the day-long journey over the rough dirt road to Laura. We camped on the river below the galleries, and brought Willy out from Laura to stay with us.

Packing heavy camera gear into the steep hills under a blazing October sun took a whole day. It was a day of sweat, toil, thirst, falls and ferocious green ants; a day that will never be erased from the memories of the poor camera crew. Their feelings were reflected in the soundtrack of the completed film, punctuated with words like 'hellish sun', 'hot rocks', 'sheer cliffs', 'dry hills', and so on. Each morning we climbed into the hills and worked, and returned in the evening to the luxury of the cool waterhole.

One morning I was making scaled drawings of the figures when

Xavier came along and asked if I had any other prospects in the vicinity that he could explore. I drew him a rough map of the area and marked a place I had sighted from the air, soon after finding the Giant Horse Galleries. About two kilometres north-west across the plateau another shallow gorge ran due west and I had seen large slabs of sandstone near its eastern end. A darker green in the gorge trees indicated the probability of permanent water and hence habitation.

Three hours later we were having tea in the shaded end of the gallery when we saw Xavier returning. He was excited and bursting with news of a remarkable discovery in the gorge I had marked for him. He spoke of large crocodiles, snakes, emus, dingoes and other masses of paintings, but he was especially impressed by a gloomy cave with awesome Quinkin figures. The silent bush had yielded up another of its long-hidden treasures.

All work came to a halt and I led the rush across the plateau through bloodwoods and grasstrees, to inspect the new-found galleries. There were six major galleries, and they were all spectacular in markedly different ways. The darker green of the trees was due to the presence of permanent water running from a spring under the sandstone; it was fringed with cabbage tree palms and swamp mahogany. A close examination of the galleries revealed them to be the most important yet discovered in Cape York peninsula, and they contained every style of art extant in the region, from the earliest style of rock engravings to the last 'mudman' style of slurry painting.

It took over a year of intensive investigation before we had a good understanding of what the associated group of painted and engraved sites meant to their former owners. As soon as possible I got Willy and Dick to view and discuss the galleries, and Willy questioned the ancient greybeards in Laura, old Sandy and Barney, and had information from an old Gugu-Minni man at Hopevale Mission.

The easternmost shelter housed the ancestral beings, fifteen men wearing two different types of headdress; five had rayed-feather headdresses, made by sticking a lump of beeswax on the back of the head and sticking feathers in it—black cockatoo or white cockatoo, depending on the wearer's moiety. The other ten had 'tree' headdresses, a single vertical trunk from the top of the head, with three short rays at the top to represent a tree with branches, symbolising the tree which contains the beehive.

The main animals represented were dingoes, kangaroos, emus, tortoises, an eel, a scrub turkey, and two different species of yams. Two elongate ovals in dark red with white dots probably represented beehives. There were stencilled and painted boomerangs, and many red hand stencils. All the dark red figures looked very old and most were faded, despite the excellent protection offered by the igloo-shaped shelter.

One dark red and white dingo was under the outstretched arm of one of the ancestral beings; they both wore the same belt of manhood, and both had been retouched, the dingo with white claws, and the man with a new white belt and toes. Five of the rayed-headdress men had a leg raised up to symbolise a dingo marking his territory, the action mimed in the dingo dance associated with the initiation ceremony.

The last addition to the sacred site appeared to be a pale yellow kangaroo, with dark red outline and belt of manhood. The largest figure in the gallery was an eel, in dark red with cream outline and dots, about two metres long. There were more than twenty faded red hand stencils, mostly small hands of youths. Five very small and faded paintings of catfish and eels were located on a large slab in the northern end of the shelter.

A small tunnel under a ledge at the south end of the shelter connected through to another sacred cave on the other side of the large sandstone slab. It was about ten metres long and was a crawl tunnel used in the initiation ceremonies to symbolise the initiates being reborn into an afterlife.

About twenty metres north along the same rock face there was a small, open, mostly rock-floored shelter. It contained three roughly drawn human figures, probably of a sorcery nature, several faded red hand stencils, a child's foot stencil and a gridded linear design in dark red dry pigment. In the northern end wall a band of dark red ochre over four metres long and half a metre wide in the middle, had each end tapering into a natural recess, and probably represented a snake passing from one hole into another. There were five white hand stencils over it, and below it were traces of old red and white figures and some linear and grid drawings in dark red dry pigment.

Around the corner on the west side was a delightful frieze of colourful, well-drawn figures. They were dominated by a large white ibis and the entire composition was laced together by two long dark red and white snakes. It was remarkable for the large number of unique figures it contained: among them were three strange little men, whose leaf-like fingers perhaps indicated they were plant or tree spirits; a large horizontal Livistona palm with a fruiting branch, and three long paddle-shapes representing new fronds before they spread and split into the classic fan shape. Dark red fish had white outlines and a skeletal bone pattern drawn on them, while other fish were dotted and a long white line drawn from the nose portrayed rifle-fish shooting insects with globules of water.

A painting of a giant freshwater shrimp (*Macro Rosenbergi*) was the first portrayal we had seen of a shrimp. In the lower layers were paintings of ancestral beings, men and women, with no facial features drawn.

The Ibis Gallery was at the entrance to a small chasm dividing two very large slabs of sandstone. Opposite it was a small enclave which contained a delightful frieze of thirteen flying foxes, hanging upside down in a row, painted in varied shades of yellow ochre and outlined and decorated with white. They partly obscured an old dark red figure of a man.

The flying foxes were a warning that further up the chasm was a place forbidden to all but the esoteric. Ten metres into the chasm and on the same side as the flying foxes was a very neat painting of a bark coffin, its ends bound up with string; a clear message that further on was a sacred place associated with life after death, in Woolunda.

A further twenty metres up the chasm was the entrance to the Quinkin cave. The cave was about eight metres deep, twelve metres long, with a maximum roof height of about three metres. It offered absolute protection against the rain, wind and sun, and the ancient figures on the sloping back wall were remarkably well preserved.

The cave was perpetually gloomy, and shrubs and vines growing in the chasm reflected an eerie green light into it which heightened the atmosphere of ancient mystery. A thin, three-metre-tall, dark red Quinkin with white eyes, seemed to hover in midair, its long thin arms raised in an attitude of invocation, or greeting. It was surrounded by five other smaller, dark red spirit figures, one of these a woman, with plump breasts and branching-tree headdress.

Willy had walked silently into the cave, eyes rolling about taking everything in; he pointed with his chin at the dominant figure and said, 'That one Timara, big boss belong everybody—white man too.' It was the supreme deity.

At the back of the cave was the metre-high, round exit of the crawl tunnel. Willy said the boys crawled through the tunnel which was a birthing canal into Woolunda and symbolised rebirth. They were then placed on the low, flat, highly polished rock under the overhanging figure of Timara, who watched while an upper front tooth was removed, leaving the hole-in-the-head, the token which ensured admission to Woolunda.

Underneath the solid, dark red figures was a linear painting of a horizontal woman with a small oval headdress. She had interior decorations of lines and dots and was highly stylised. She was a rare example of one of the earliest painting styles in Australia, the meaning of her existence however, was lost in the mists of remote times.

Just across the chasm from Timara's cave was another overhang providing excellent shelter for another ancient Dreaming, that of the platypus. The drawing of it was just under a metre long, originally executed in purple-red dry pigment lines, with very faded white finger dots over most of the body. Most of the tail and upper hind leg had been outlined and dotted with white paint, but the rest of the body had not been outlined. About fifty very faded red hand stencils were over the platypus, and on the wall and ceiling, many of them the smaller hands of youths, and some with abnormally short thumbs.

There were no platypus remaining in the Laura River drainage system, the nearest known populations being in the cool rainforest streams of the Atherton Tablelands. They probably disappeared from the Laura system during the searing droughts of 17000 to 15000 years ago, or even earlier. Once the platypus disappeared from the region its significance as a Dreaming animal would have been lost.

West around the corner of the flying fox panel was a large and excellent camping shelter, and obviously much-used as such. A superimposed mass of ochre paintings on the back wall was dominated by a large, bright, yellow and red freshwater crocodile, almost three metres long. There was a very large yellow and red kangaroo with a big yellow ochre emu partly over it, some parts of which had been repainted with a lighter yellow. The three large animals were superimposed on earlier red monochrome figures of ancestral beings with rayed headdresses. But under all was an astonishing array of ancient engravings; a few were clearly emu tracks, but others were just a maze of meandering grooves, circles and radiate lines giving no clue to their meaning. Comparatively recent paintings of men and women, associated with sorcery, were the latest additions to the gallery.

About fifty metres further west among the tessellated slabs of sandstone was the mortuary site, the final repository of the bark containers. Black termite tunnels going into the main tunnel in the wall ensured there was no trace of bark or bone left; only recent kangaroo bones littered the floor of the huge gloomy shelter. The outer walls and entrance had panels of amorphous spirit figures of men and women, most having no hands or feet, and they were very faded. They had all passed on to Woolunda long ago.

The last gallery was about a hundred metres west down the gorge, but on the north side. The large open shelter of colourful pink sandstone faced south and offered relatively poor protection from the elements. There was little occupational debris on the floor and it appeared to be a ceremonial site. Men had climbed up on a ledge to paint a big fat freshwater crocodile in white with red outline and decoration; a very symmetrical long-necked tortoise in stark white was painted on its faded body, and the lower leg of the crocodile was under the back of a huge dark-red emu, which in turn, had a cream and red man horizontal on its back; the ancestral man was well decorated and wore a pearl-shell pendant, and had been identified as a 'guardian figure', very similar to one found near the Woolston Gallery. There were more engravings but in a different style and obviously more recent than those in the Yellow Crocodile site. The main engraving was a pecked outline of a woman with short arms and legs, but without hands and feet. There were ten fully pecked-out circles about ten to fifteen centimetres in diameter, which may have been eggs associated with four red emus, one of which was over a white kangaroo; there were about ten human figures and most appeared to be ancestral beings.

The newly found Quinkin group were so spectacular that, together with the Giant Horse group, they provided more than adequate material for the documentary film, and the rugged country that housed them provided enough exercise to turn the camera crew into athletes.

By the time we had finished there I realised that the Quinkin group of sites was beautiful and unique, a microcosm of Aboriginal tradition and culture, with virtually every style of art represented, from the ancient and mysterious engravings of remote times, to modern paintings of less than a hundred years ago.

'Around the corner . . . was a delightful frieze of colourful well-drawn
figures . . . dominated by a large white ibis.'

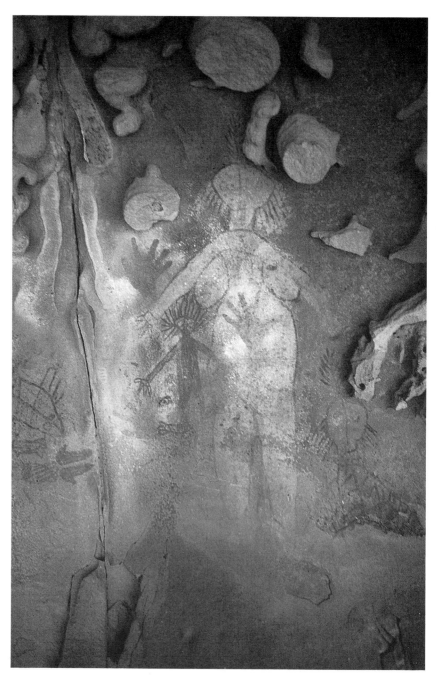

'The most prominent figure was that of a woman . . .' The Deighton Lady.

10

The lady of the Deighton

When we returned to explore more Quinkin country in 1969, a good wet season had arrived after nearly a decade of drought. Dick and I had with us a new companion; he was Eddy Oribin, a Cairns architect with a love for wild places, who had been following our past exploits with great interest, and who joined us with an infectious enthusiasm. Our target area was the Deighton River region to the north-east of Laura, rugged sandstone country which aerial surveys suggested should be full of art sites. We drove the Landrover as far as possible along the lower reaches of the Deighton, then backpacked along it to camp on a bend among shady paperbarks.

A broad gorge ran in from the south just opposite our camp, and in the afternoon Dick and Eddy climbed up to explore along the western scarps while I covered the eastern side. Every small shelter contained a few very faded red figures, mainly of people, but there were no major sites. The others had arrived back before me and were excited about a huge cavern they had found, which contained only a few figures, but one of these was a large woman, painted in white with red outline, which Dick thought was a very special figure that I should see before we left.

Early next morning we climbed east up the steep rocky slope to carry on from where I had left off yesterday. We travelled along the base of the cliff and where it turned east into a small deep gully we found three small but good shelters containing bichrome paintings of humans, animals and of yams, all of which were small and very faded. None of the shelters had been used for a very long time, and the art style was similar to that in Isabella Gorge near Cooktown, in Guju-Imudji country. Willy had told us that their country also extended to the Deighton, and the art style appeared to confirm it.

We walked on in a line to cover all possible shelters in the main scarp and the large outlying slabs scattered down the scrub-covered hillside. At the base of the cliff I found a red lady-apple tree laden with fruit and was sampling some when I heard Eddy cooee from below. He had found an excellent small shelter containing about forty painted figures, some of them very bright.

The most prominent was that of a pig about a metre long. It had a solid body of yellow ochre, outlined and decorated with white, and was clearly the last addition to the gallery, being superimposed on a mass of older figures of kangaroos, emus, large fish and humans. In a small recess there was a large, dark red painting of a phalanger with a long tail. Another fine painting was that of a small kangaroo, well drawn in dark red, with white outline, interior dots and bars.

We were photographing the figures when we heard a muffled shout from Dick, coming from among large outliers ahead. Dick's gallery was in a large gloomy cave, the vaulted ceiling curving down at the outer edge to provide total protection. There were more than a hundred figures, the smoother areas containing superimposed layers of figures. Large emus and kangaroos two to three metres long, dominated the gallery. There were several large dingoes, fish, snakes, men, women, beehives and yams, as well as three little bichrome owls about fifteen centimetres tall, plus two line drawings in dark red of a fruiting vine.

Only thirty metres away there was another large open shelter with a heavily superimposed sequence of paintings high on the back wall. The artists had stood on a narrow ledge to do their work. The most impressive figure was that of an emu, about two metres tall. Its body colour was faded white, outlined and intricately decorated with fine lines and dots of dark red. A large eel-tailed catfish, executed in clay slurry and dark red outline, had been superimposed on the lower parts of the emu. On top of both these figures was a big oval beehive, drawn as the hive would appear inside a hollow tree. The beehive had a projection near one end, representing the wax entrance tunnel, and from it a stream of dots represented bees arriving at or leaving the hive. The interior of the painting was covered with fine dots to represent bees inside the hive. Other figures included two large fresh-water crocodiles, a kangaroo, tortoises, yams and men and women.

Eddy was curious as to why the figures were superimposed in layers, apparently spoiling those underneath. Dick explained that the paintings underneath were not spoiled, they still retained their power, and those in the living sites were not only painted for magical purposes, but also to teach the children the 'outside' version of the great creation myths and so be ready for the secret and sacred revelations about the ancestral beings when undergoing the man-making ceremonies. He pointed to the beehive, 'We call the honey bee Wongabel, which, like every other living thing, was once human. The painting of it is to teach the children about the sharing of the honey and the wax. We name different parts of the hive after parts of the human body, the wax entrance tunnel was called the "nose" of the sugar bag, our name for a beehive, and the "nose" resembles a human nostril. The stream of bees flying away were the arms of the ancestral being reaching out to gather in the food.'

By noon we had found six more smaller galleries, mainly in shelters under detached slabs. Most of the figures were in faded dark red and appeared to be very old, and none was different from thousands of others we had discovered in other areas of Cape York peninsula.

The main cliff was rising steadily higher as we continued north along its base, pushing through vines and low undergrowth. Eddy told us later that he had been greatly excited by some of our finds and was puzzled by our seeming nonchalance about them, wondering what kind of marvel we would have to stumble on to excite us. So when he heard me call out and saw me crashing through a wall of vines screening the cliff face, he knew I had either stepped on a snake or had seen something special.

Through the vines I had seen part of a shelter under a great over-hang of rock, and on the back wall was what appeared to be the head of a huge horizontal man. We all scrambled into the shelter and saw it was an immense painting of a snake. Dick was excited, 'That's old Rainbow, old Thuwathu—they call him Goorialla over here.'

The Rainbow Serpent was over ten metres long and two-thirds of a metre wide over most of its length. The anthropomorphic head was a metre wide, with large round eyes and short projecting rays around the top of the head. The figure was a faded white silhouette with dark red outline and intricate interior decoration. Faded scales could be seen over some of its length, which had been superimposed on a mass of faded red dingoes and other figures, while a few later ones had been placed over parts of him. Goorialla must have been a magnificent sight when his image was first created.

We had lunch in that cool place, sitting with our backs against trees so we could study the marvellous figure while the billy boiled and Dick told Eddy the Gugu-Yalanji version of the Rainbow Serpent story which we had learned from Joogumu. Dick speculated that the rays on the head of the figure before us might represent the rayed feathers he wore when dancing. It seemed that the Rainbow Serpent had its origins in spectacular transits of Halley's Comet, burning across the sky every 76 years, reinforcing stories handed down by law-carriers and custodians. Some of the volcanic activity on the headwaters of the nearby Laura River, about 12 000 years ago, may have added some colour to the Serpent myth, especially the part where Goorialla tore the great mountain apart and hurled it all over the country.

The Rainbow Serpent myth not only occurs right across Australia, but also in South America and southern Africa. In Arnhem Land we saw the serpent with the head of a kangaroo, and in Zimbabwe there is a painting of a huge snake with an antelope head on each end.

The towering red cliff leaned out to provide many large, open shelters along its base. They had not been used for camping and obviously had a ceremonial role. Nearby was a fine life-size, red and white painting of Ngalculli, the red kangaroo. There was a dark purple beehive with two entrance tunnels, and from one of them emerged a swarm of bees, most with wings. On a cliff face ten metres above the beehive were strange faded figures, no longer accessible as a ledge had fallen away in remote times.

A little further north along the cliff we found a recessed shelter containing life-size paintings of several people. They were monochromes of cream and white clay, roughly slathered on the walls and having little artistic merit; but there was no mistaking their purpose—they were sorcery figures, painted and repainted for ritual killing of an enemy, or a runaway wife. An aura of animosity and evil permeated the place, and when I turned to ask Dick a question about them, he was gone.

We found one more large shelter on a point jutting out from the main scarp. It contained about fifty figures, including another large snake, and a horizontal man, three metres long. Like all the other shelters we had found on the Deighton, it exhibited no evidence of having been used as a living place for many centuries. The gallery containing the yellow pig had recent charcoal but was too small for a major camp. Somewhere in the area would be an excellent shelter which had been used annually as a wet season camp for thousands of years. The floor would be dark grey with charcoal and burnt sand, and bright paintings would adorn the walls.

Across the valley we could see large caves in the base of the main cliff and we hoped to find the main camp there. The scarp we were following had turned east and dwindled in height, with no shelters, so we called it a day and went down to follow the river back to camp.

It was always a pleasure to arrive back in a good camp after a hard but successful day in the bush. The sun was setting as we swam in the waterhole, then got the fire going to make a billy of stew. While it was cooking we rewarded ourselves with a large nip of rum and river water, and discussed the new discoveries.

Across from our camp a flock of rainbow lorikeets squabbled noisily over the scarlet blossoms of a tall bean tree. There was a sudden shriek of warning, and silence fell over the lorikeets as they all slipped deeper into the foliage. A falcon shot past the bean tree and streaked away to vanish behind large paperbarks. The lorikeets had just emerged to resume haggling over the blossom when the falcon returned like a brown bullet to hit a hanging lorikeet with his curved wing. Poor Bil-bil fluttered down like a falling blossom and the falcon swooped on him with yellow talons.

We left early to explore the western scarps north of camp. The country was just as rough and steep as the other side, and the green ants equally aggressive. We were soon finding small shelters with faded red paintings, which suggested that every possible shelter had been used in remote times when there must have been better conditions supporting a much larger population.

Soon we found positive signs that a big living site was in the vicinity—big, red lady-apple trees, many bearing fruit. The red lady-apple was one of the most pleasant fruits in the bush and seeds scattered about the main camp sites ensured a good annual supply. The trees grew among large blocks of sandstone and under one of them we found the big, recently occupied shelter. It was an excellent wet season living site for a full family horde. The floor was black with charcoal, and pieces of old green bottles which had been trimmed for knives, and bright paintings adorned the walls.

The shelter had in it several large detached slabs which divided it into many sections suited for camping, as well as offering smooth surfaces for painting. There were about seventy-five painted figures, some superimposed on others and covering most of the range of motifs found in the region.

The major and most recent figures in the gallery were those of women, most of which seemed to have been painted for love-magic purposes. The most outstanding of these was a life-size woman portrayed horizontally on a wall in strong dark red ochre, with thick white outline and interior decoration. Her arms were flung above her head and a pendant hung round her neck. Between her widespread legs was a man, lying horizontally in the opposite direction so their legs crossed, and his attenuated penis was depicted penetrating the woman. The male figure was very faded, only his penis having been repainted in the same strong red as the female. It was a revitalisation of love-magic.

On a low ceiling there was a painting of a strange bird, in dark red with white outline. It was fairly large and emu-like, but had a more upright stance, with six toes on one foot and five on the other, but it did not have the fantail of a scrub turkey. We speculated that it could represent an extinct species. We explored further but the cliff soon petered out and we returned to go up and inspect the White Lady site, found earlier. It was a massive cavern of pink sandstone, more than fifty metres wide, about twenty metres deep, and ranged in height from about two metres at the back to fifteen metres in front. It was gloomy in afternoon light, which deepened its air of mystery. Intensive aeolian and water sculpting had created large honeycomb friezes on the ceiling and back wall, some of them so regular in repetition that it was difficult to believe them natural and not the work of man. Shapes like penises, breasts and clitorises hung from the ceiling to create a unique fertility cult centre. The rock floor was glazed with a thick coating of gleaming dark brown silica, and sloped upwards at an angle of about 25 degrees to meet the low back wall. Exactly in the centre of the back wall was a rounded recess which housed the sacred figures painted there.

The most prominent figure was that of a woman in solid white, with dark red outline and interior decoration of red lines and dots. It was a very striking portrayal of the qualities of womanhood. She had a branched headdress and wore a breast pendant. Round eyes, hair, and the general attitude of the figure conveyed a feeling of benign tranquillity and motherhood. Plump breasts with nipples and a swelling body symbolised fertility and fruitfulness. There was a quaint little red linear man under her right breast, and her feet were partly over a very faded replica of herself. Three neat white hand stencils had been placed carefully on and near her body. To the woman's right a two-metre-long crevice ran up the centre of the recess, and the central part resembled a vulva; sandstone shapes on either side had been broken off to enhance the resemblance. The part that represented the clitoris appeared to have been painted a light orange brown, which matched the body colour of the original faded woman, and white hand stencils had been placed on either side of the vulva.

To the right of the crack was a life-size painting of a dingo, facing toward the woman, with human and kangaroo tracks immediately in front of it. The dingo was faded and executed in exactly the same shades of light brown as the old faded female figure. The dingo and the first woman appeared to be contemporary with each other, and very old, but many millennia before their creation, other artists had been there to leave their marks.

Early man had placed his work on the steeply sloping floor on either side of the recess. Engraved on the left side were strange meandering lines and maze patterns, two of these about half a metre long. The original pecked grooves had not been very deep and dark brown silica had completely filled some parts. One smaller engraving suggested a plant shape and had been engraved very deeply into the indurated sandstone, to a depth of two centimetres. A pair of small kangaroo tracks were the only identifiable shapes, and they appeared to be much more recent additions.

On the right side a pattern of meandering lines, joining circles, oblong and irregular shapes, formed a maze about two metres long and a metre wide. Near it were two emu tracks.

Large slabs of fallen rock littered the front of the shelter, and the floor was all rock. A few very faded figures of men, women, kangaroos, and a dingo, were scattered widely over lower parts of the ceiling. They were all outline figures in dark red. There was not the slightest trace of occupational debris and we felt quite certain that it was a sacred place of great significance, one of the temples of Dreamtime.

It was obvious that the spectacular cavern with the centrally located natural vulva, had been identified by early man as the place where one of the female ancestral beings had turned herself to stone in Dreamtime, her spirit residing there forever, and having with her all the unborn baby spirits to provide the future generations.

The first men who came to revere their women through the hallowed place had been the early engravers, their panels of meandering lines and geometric shapes perhaps symbolising maps of the travels of the ancestral beings, as they travelled about creating the features of the land, a part of one of the many Dream roads which crisscross the continent.

The brown silica coating over the engravings appeared to have come from a deep crack in the sloping floor above them, transported by water during a wet phase of the Pleistocene Age. Climatologists had informed us that any art under the brown silica would be more than 18 000 years old, at present the only clue to their antiquity. The identity of the engravers, how long they lived in the region, and what became of them, is a mystery still to be unravelled. Later men had executed the outline drawings in red ochre paint, of humans and animals, some of which had been covered by the later dingo, and the two portrayals of the woman in solid bichrome ochre paints.

The dingo figure was almost intact, only the base of the tail being indistinct. Below its neck were two red linear human foot tracks, and immediately in front of them red linear drawings of a pair of rear-foot kangaroo tracks. The nose of the dog was just above the kangaroo tracks, as though sniffing them, and illustrating the value of the dingo in tracking game.

Only the head and shoulders of the first portrayal of the white lady remained, the lower part perhaps eroded away by rock wallabies, so later men had repainted her on the wall above, giving her the same branched headdress, which symbolised the tree, in the hollows of which the bees built their hives, and the red dots inside her body represented bees. Perhaps Wongabel, the ancestral bee woman, had been first painted there to celebrate the arrival of the first dingoes to sniff out the location of beehives.

We decided to call her the lady of the Deighton. The cavern was located in the top scarp of a small gorge running into the Deighton from the south, and offered splendid views over the Deighton gorge and away east across the hills toward Cooktown.

We returned the following year to record the sites, but another sixteen years were to elapse before we found more very significant sites on the Deighton River.

Dick Roughsey examines an ancient engraving at Sandy Creek.

11

An ancient axe

The next area for exploration in 1969 was Kennedy Creek, an important tributary of the Laura River, draining about two hundred square kilometres of sandstone plateaux and gorges south of the Laura, and joining with it about fifteen kilometres south-east of Laura township.

Eddy, Dick and I set up a base camp on a little knoll just above a good waterhole, where two big crowfruit trees provided dense shade. We erected an eight-man army tent and furnished it with stretchers, folding tables and chairs, and other gear.

Next morning we climbed up to the foot of the western cliff and found a long open shelter in the base of it. The main figures were five big kangaroos, in white and red, from two to three metres long. There were 26 figures in all, including some of humans and crocodiles. Several of the kangaroos had spears through them and the place appeared to be associated with hunting magic.

From there we could see over much of Kennedy Creek, which had two major branches, and it was on the eastern branch that we had found Hell's Gate the previous year. We followed the western ridge along to a stone arrangement and photographed and mapped it, then went on to a stand of nonda trees. Most of the nondas had only recently dropped a heavy crop of fruit; the ground under the trees was covered with rough seeds where birds and animals had been feeding.

Explorer Ludwig Leichhardt said he called the tree 'nonda' from its likeness to a tree so called by the natives of the Moreton Bay district. It is described in Bailey's *Queensland Flora* under *Parinarium, Juss.* The Kennedy expedition was pleased to come across nonda trees and botanist Carron described them thus: 'a great many trees of moderate size, from fifteen to twenty feet high, of rather pendulous habit, oval lanceolate expistulate leaves, loaded with an oblong yellow fruit, having a rough stone inside; the part covering the stone has, when ripe, a mealy appearance and a very good flavour; we all ate plentifully of it'.

About fifty metres south-east of the stone arrangements the scarp of the upper terrace of Kennedy Creek looked high enough to contain shelters so we went to explore it. Under the edge of the low cliff and within sight of the stone pyramids, was a small shelter which contained many painted figures. There were 38 in all, painted in red or white. The main motifs were men, with a few emus and goannas. There were no paintings of women.

The most important figure was an outline in red of a large emu, about two metres tall and three metres long. The tail of the emu had radiate red lines representing feathers, the horny bump on the chest was clearly defined, and two pecked holes represented the eyes. Most of the men portrayed were small, the largest a metre tall; they were painted as solid silhouettes in dark and light reds, or white with red outlines. All were faded and appeared very old. Many had only three fingers and toes, and probably represented men of emu Dreaming. The shelter was unsuited for camping, but there were huge blocks lying further north on the terrace and we went among them to look for the camping place.

At the head of small dry watercourse we found two immense shelters, their floor dark grey with charcoal and with many bright paintings on the walls. There were traces of much older figures on the places suitable for painting, but these were mostly obscured by bright figures of several species of fish, a fine dark red dingo decorated with white lines and dots, echidnas, men, women, and a few Quinkin figures. Many white hand stencils were scattered about, some having been placed on painted figures.

Eddy and Dick had paused only briefly at the main shelter and were soon calling from further on among the rocks. They had found another long shelter, less suitable for camping, but containing about twenty-five paintings, including two goannas, one bright yellow, the other red. Seven small ibis, each about fifteen centimetres high, marched in single file across the back wall. There were several pot-bellied little Quinkins, and another larger one located on a rock wall opposite the shelter. It was portrayed as though hovering over the entrance to a small dark tunnel which penetrated the rock wall, a typical dwelling place for the little devils.

We found the floor of the main living place thick with seeds of nonda fruit. Willy had told us the Gugu-Minni people had owned that part of the country, and Dick thought it was a main summer camp of the clan. He said the Gugu-Minni would move up there after the first storms in October, to live on a staple diet of nonda fruit, supplemented by the occasional kangaroo, rock wallaby, goanna, and honey.

About a kilometre away on the watershed we found a small isolated rock shelter in the open forest. It contained a lot of small red hand stencils on the walls, and evidence of a stone-flaking industry. Dick believed it to be the place where initiated boy were kept in seclusion while they learned tribal laws, sacred myths, and the making of stone implements and weapons.

Later, in the Deighton region, we found another initiate seclusion shelter located in the midst of a grove of large Burdekin plum trees, which served as the staple food supply. The shelter had panels of small male figures, each holding a boomerang, which was used to harvest the top fruit from the twenty-metre-high trees.

It seemed a pleasant way to spend the wet season, with plenty of food and water, excellent shelter from stormy weather, with cooling breezes to relieve the steamy heat. It was also above the main mosquito level.

The stone arrangement on the rock saddle was probably associated with maintenance rituals, the stacks of small stones symbolising the full baskets or dillybags of the women. The long grey phallic stone projecting from the central pile represented the penis of the Dreamtime ancestor who had become a nonda tree.

The nearby shelter containing the large emu and very faded men with three fingers and toes, hinted at remote times when a wetter climate saw flocks of emus feeding on nonda fruit, and earlier people coming to feast on the big birds. Changing weather conditions, probably drought, back in the Ice Age, had caused the disappearance of the emus and had reduced people to eating the former food of the emu.

Later on we found another small shelter containing a larger-than-life female ancestral being, and other smaller figures. Near a big woman was a fruiting-branch of large nondas, painted in red ochre, thus completing the male and female components of nonda rituals. We named them the Nonda Galleries.

During the next couple of months we found many more galleries on Kennedy Creek, but much of the south-western parts still remained to be explored. There were a number of long low shelters in the base of cliffs on the north side of the creek, containing many different kinds of figures, but the outstanding feature was the panels of hundreds of tiny men figures wearing big headdresses, with hands joined as though in dancing. I was busy drawing a panel when Dick decided he needed a break from bark painting and set off with the dogs to explore further west.

About two hours later the dogs came panting back into the shelter, followed by Dick, who dumped an armful of wood for a fire and said 'Well, Warrenby, you might think you found the best paintings this year—but I've got you beat this time.' While the billy boiled for tea he described three new galleries he had seen two kilometres further west. The main figures were a large crocodile and a kangaroo, each painted in yellow ochre and outlined in purple red. There were many other animals, and strange male spirit figures wearing headdresses.

We shifted camp to the largest of the new caves. It was a very low shelter under the base of a massive detached slab, which was propped up by other slabs to provide an area about ten metres deep and twenty metres long. Other slabs in front made the cave gloomy, but gave it protection from wind and rain. There were about eighty figures in the three galleries and by the time I had made detailed drawings, colour notes and taken photographs, I was weary of recording work and decided to spend the last days of that trip exploring, and leave further recording till later on.

Back in our base we had nocturnal visitors. The first was a northern brush-tailed possum which drove our dogs mad. They seemed to be able to hear the possum the moment it set foot on the ground, and rushed toward it, but it was always metres up another tree when they arrived, and answered Dog's barking and Dingo's moaning with cheeky scolding.

Next morning I woke when the trees about our camp were black silhouettes against the first flush of dawn. It was too early for birds and the only sound was a faint rumbling snore from Dick. I was looking at the black tracery of limbs of a small hakea when what appeared to be a long-tailed bird swooped up and landed on the trunk. I thought it was a species of night parrot until it began scampering about in the tree and I realised it was the dainty little phalanger, a sugar glider. It ran up to the top of the tree and looped off into the gloom with all the aplomb and assurance of a bird.

The eastern side of Kennedy Creek was walled in most places by vertical cliffs of coarse grey conglomerate, which seldom provided shelters suitable for camping or painting. On top of the conglomerate there was a forested terrace which sloped gradually up to a cap of smooth red sandstone, much of it tessellated into huge blocks. We decided to climb up and explore the top layer.

There were many fine big shelters in the top sandstone but only a few had faint traces of occupation. We found some paintings of humans, and what appeared to be portrayals of flowers, probably waterlilies. We covered about ten kilometres of the ridge and found more than a hundred figures. A notable figure was a faded dark red silhouette of a koala, outlined with white. Koalas were extinct in Cape York peninsula and may have been so for a very long time. There were some Quinkins and three large stark white crocodiles. The art on the eastern side of Kennedy Creek was different from the art on the western side, and we thought a clan further east on Earl Creek may have used the ridge for wet season shelters.

A Folker Friendship moaning overhead on the daily flight to Weipa, caused me to remember one of my aerial prospects on the remote headwaters of Coamey Creek. I had mapped the easiest way to walk into it. The hills were dry but we decided to travel light and take enough water for a two-day trip for preliminary exploration. We would go via the Pig and Emu galleries where we also had water stored in plastic containers.

Just after daylight next morning we left the Landrover on the Laura River, and set off with light packs on the long steep climb into the galleries. Along the top of the narrow ridge we found a fairly fresh trail of a herd of wild pigs, travelling in single file down, sure proof the high springs were dry and the pigs had left. The sun was fierce and temperature high when we dropped our packs in the shade of Pig Gallery. The stored water was good so we boiled the billy and enjoyed the colourful gallery while we had lunch.

It was late evening when we stopped to camp among rocks on the nose of a bloodwood ridge. It had been a hard hot day and the dogs were nosing the water containers, asking for their ration. The small plateau we were seeking was about another hour's walk away, and we decided we would leave our gear in the morning and take only water and a camera for a quick survey.

We travelled fast in the cool early morning and before nine o'clock were at the base of the cliff around the plateau. There were several large shelters, most of them about ten metres high in front, ten metres deep and up to thirty metres long, but their floors were spoiled by fallen slabs, and the walls were too rough and eroded for painting. After finding nothing in six such shelters we were rather despondent, then we rounded a corner to enter another vast cavern and saw two long white paintings down the far end.

From a distance they looked like big snakes but as we got closer we recognised them as big beehives, easily the largest we had ever found. They were placed one above the other, the top one about seven metres long and the lower slightly under five metres, both about half a metre wide over most of their length. White barite had been used for the base colour which was then outlined and decorated with dark red. Red dots the size of a fingertip covered the interior of both figures to represent bees in the hive.

The top hive was divided into two parts by a line drawn across it about two metres from the thicker end, which Dick said represented the back of the hive where the best honey was stored. The other end tapered to a fairly fine point to form the entrance tunnel, from which a number of small dots and two larger shapes had emerged.

The smaller hive was divided into three sections. A quaint little man in white and red was portrayed near the base of the hive and poking a stick into it. From the other end a swarm of bees issued forth,

117

accompanying three larger queen bees. The painting illustrated the method of taking honey from a hive, first by locating it precisely by putting an ear against the trunk to hear the hum of the bees, then chopping a small hole just below its base, and then inserting a pliable stick or cane up into the hive and twirling it about to release honey so it would flow down a stick into a bark container. Some bees might then remain to repair the hive, while others swarmed off to make new hives and more honey. It was obviously an important site associated with rituals of honeybee Dreaming.

We continued to where the cliff turned north-east, offering a better protected aspect for camping, and about a hundred metres on we came to another huge shelter which had been a main wet season living site.

The ceiling was low at the back, but rose upward in stepped faces to about six metres in front. It was painted all over with scores of figures of people, animals and implements, all the things that mattered to a hunter-gatherer people. The clan had created a richly endowed home to which they could return with pleasure each wet season, and had returned for thousands of years: now only the rock wallabies camped there.

On the way back we decided to have a look through big outlying blocks of sandstone in the forest below the cliff. Dick took the high level and I went lower down. Most slabs had no shelter, but I found a small one containing a few emu tracks and circles, and was photographing these when I heard muffled shouting from Dick further up the hill.

I found him in a fine, big cool shelter, one of the best natural camp sites we had ever seen. The floor was sand and the high ceiling vaulted over and down to provide total protection against weather. A thick growth of bushes along the front enclosed the cave like a room and cast a green light over it. When my eyes adjusted to the gloom, I saw a partly faded figure of an immense man, painted horizontal on the lower back wall. The body colour of pale orange was outlined with dark red. The figure was rather crudely executed and had no interior decoration, but it was five metres long and almost a metre wide at the hips, so must have had considerable significance.

More interesting was a large array of white and red paintings on a side wall which extended into a shallow tunnel. There were many precise figures of kangaroo tracks, portraying both front and rear feet, human foot tracks, a small oval beehive with a large swarm of bees emanating from it, a delightful little owl, some crescent grub-shapes, and for the first time, paintings of a design resembling the head of a pitchfork, which so far we had seen only as an engraved design of early man.

The white barite paintings exhibited a high quality of drawing, and were finely decorated with red lines and dots. Although the figures were clear and well preserved, they gave the impression of considerable age and I thought they probably belonged to the Great White Phase of about 5000 to 8000 years ago, when rock art reached its peak in Cape York peninsula. The deep shelter afforded them excellent protection, and for some reason they had not been covered with layers of later paintings, as was the case in most other galleries. It was not a living site and perhaps the huge horizontal man had something to do with the avoidance of the site by later generations.

The white pitchfork designs looked like box jellyfish suspended in the sea. There were five of them, each with seven to fifteen lines. Three had a number of short lines radiating from the top, one had only one short line, and the fifth none. The one without any top lines had a series of short red stripes painted down between the white lines, and Dick suggested it looked like falling rain. It then dawned on us that they probably represented thunderstorms, and were painted as part of a rain-making ceremony, the radiate lines portraying the spreading nimbus cloud heads of a mature thunderstorm.

Dick was pleased with his find and commented that now we knew why our eyes had always been drawn to that far hillside while camping at Pig Gallery—it was the spirits in the caves calling for men to come again and visit them.

The next expedition in 1969 was a family affair during school holidays. We set up camp on the Little Laura River, which was at first to be an artists' camp, then the base for an archaeological dig on nearby Sandy Creek. Eddy brought Noel Risley, a noted Cairns sculptor anxious to try the Laura sandstones for his art forms. Dick and I picked up Willy in Laura and took him out to camp with us.

The Little Laura flowed clear shallow water over black bedrock, and we erected two big tents and canvas awnings on top of a high bank. Behind our camp termites had created a painted forest of bright orange by encasing the lower ten metres or so of tall stringy-barks with a thin shell of caked red soil, apparently so they could eat the outer layer of dead bark under shelter of the covering.

After a few days Beverley arrived with our daughters Vicki and Anna, and accompanied by her brother Dick, and his wife Sue. All were volunteer diggers for the dig on Sandy Creek, at a place called Rainbow Snake Rock, which Dick and I had found a few years earlier.

At the base of a low sandstone plateau a ten-metre-high and sixty-metre-long slab of sandstone had split off from the main cliff and weathered into a dark, rounded shape, with two bumps just behind its big head. It looked like a giant snake emerging from a hole in the base of the hill. Near its middle, large slabs had broken away from underneath it to provide an excellent living shelter—as Dick put it, 'right in the guts of old Goorialla, the Rainbow Serpent'.

The shelter was in two parts, with a high open section full of tumbled slabs of sandstone, and under a low ceiling, a sandy area provided an ideal camp site. The low ceiling had many figures painted on it, the most prominent a red and white snake about four metres long. In the high section the ceiling had paintings of humans, fish, and a crocodile.

Most important of all, early man had been there and engraved his mysterious symbols on some of the slabs. A large rounded boulder was jammed in among others and early man had selected it to engrave a maze of interconnected lines and circles which extended over three sides of the irregularly shaped stone. The strange design was covered with a thick layer of smooth dark brown silica, a state which indicated considerable antiquity, and was the reason we had selected the site for excavation. Near the back of the shelter a rounded boulder of sandstone protruding through the floor, also had an engraving which disappeared below the floor.

After a week's solid work we had removed and sieved one and a half metres of fill from a rectangular plot surrounding the partly buried engraved boulder. Each layer removed was incredibly rich in stone implements of every description, from tiny quartz spear barbs, scrapers, knives, chisels, sanders, hammer stones, to large hand choppers, stone axes which had been hafted, and there were many pieces of utilised ochre material. Quartz was a most popular material, along with colourful agate and ribbonstone in the upper layers, but every type of hard lithic material had been used as they were readily available in gravel beds of all streams in the region.

The buried engraving slowly emerged as a very large version of the pitchfork design, very similar to a smaller one engraved on one of the higher rocks. It was badly eroded, perhaps by later generation people sitting on it and using it as a working platform, but it was still possible to see the gothic-shaped, wide outer line with parts of a number of engraved lines extending about a metre down the rock face. No part of the engraving had a silica skin.

Further excavation saw the fairly abrupt disappearance of the colourful, finely made, small artifacts, to be replaced by evidence of a larger type industry which used hard grey stone. These were more utilitarian and less artistic.

At about two metres we encountered a hard gravelly bed of pink sandy material, very difficult to excavate as it was calcified and contained no identifiable artifacts. Richard Wright's excavation at Mushroom Rock suggested that we were probably working at about an 8000-year-old horizon, but the silica-skinned engraving on the high, exposed boulder suggested a possible horizon below at more than 18 000 years. We decided to persist.

Noel Risley made us ironwood crowbars and hand shovels to hack away at the hard pink material. Sieving it yielded only one small piece of white quartz which may have been an artifact, and there was no charcoal. We persisted to three metres, and I was scraping away at the bottom with little enthusiasm when a piece of smooth pink quartzite began to emerge. It was a stone axe.

We continued with great enthusiasm, but a few more centimetres saw the finish of the hard pink material, to be replaced with a pale grey sandy material which appeared to be decomposed sandstone bedrock. There were no more artifacts or charcoal, so we commenced to back fill.

The recovered stone axe had been finely edge-ground, with the edge still sharp and polished, and it had clearly been made for hafting. It was a slight tool when compared to the upper level stone axes, being about fifteen centimetres long by twelve centimetres wide, with a maximum thickness of about three centimetres. It would have been of little use to cut wood or any hard material, and we concluded that it was probably a meat cleaver, used to butcher large animals.

We knew we had the oldest stone axe yet recovered in Australia, but there was no possible means of dating it.

Two other types of stone material excavated had us puzzled as to their possible use, until we showed them to our Aboriginal companions. The first were four, long, rounded pieces of a dark grey slatey material, which bore no obvious marks of any usage. They varied in length from fifteen to twenty centimetres. Dick looked at them and laughed, saying, 'They would have been for joking time in the evening, a young lad would bring it back to camp and placing it in the appropriate place, call out to his grandmother, "Hey, granny, you like this one—it's proper hard, this one," making great fun in the camp.'

The other stones were pieces of many-faceted quartz crystals, which glittered like diamonds when turned in sunlight. They greatly excited Willy, who proclaimed them to be 'for eye belong Quinkin'. Further explanation revealed they were powerful magic stones, which, when placed to catch light from the camp fire, would protect the sleeping owner from Quinkins. The magic, flashing light would blind and knock down the Quinkin, forcing it to beat a hasty retreat back into the darkness.

The lack of charcoal in the lower horizons of our excavation permitted only speculation for a chronological sequence of events in the past. The metre-thick layer of pink gravelly material suggested a very lengthy hiatus between two human populations. The hiatus was probably caused by drought—many thousands of years of drought, as without the addition of human camping debris, the metre-deep layer would have accumulated much more slowly. The first human population would have commenced in very remote times, probably during a humid phase which provided silica skins over the ancient engravings, and ended some time after the onset of severe aridity, perhaps more than 18 000 years ago.

According to climatologist, J.M. Bowler, the severest droughts occurred from 17 000 to 15 000 years ago, then the climate improved slowly to the present condition. Reoccupation of the region would have occurred some time after the end of aridity, with the most likely time being the minor humid phase identified by Kershaw and others, as occurring between about 8500 to 5000 years ago. That wetter phase allowed the re-establishment of rainforests on the Atherton Table-lands, and provided optimum conditions for the return of flora, fauna and human populations to former desert areas.

We had identified the Great White Phase of paintings as being executed within the lesser humid phase, as the figures reflect a time of leisure without stress, made possible by a replenished food supply.

As evidenced by our own, and other excavations across the continent, the stone tool industry reflected a similar improvement in quality about the same time. The implements not only had to be utilitarian, but they also had to look good, and the colourful agates and ribbonstones of a microlithic industry began to appear in the upper horizons, and continued on to the surface as the populations increased.

Future recovery of charcoal from the lower horizons, and examination of the sequence of fossil pollens, will eventually yield a chronological sequence of climates, and human populations fluctuating with the seasons.

The ancient, silica-skinned engravings, suggest that their origins will eventually be dated at well beyond 40 000 years.

Dick and I stayed on to do some more painting and Willy kept us company. We spent a couple of days exploring distant scarps of Sandy Creek, but they contained few shelters and we found only one painting—a fine portrayal of a large wallaroo.

*'We spent a couple of days exploring distant scarps of Sandy Creek,
but . . . we found only one painting—a fine portrayal of a large
wallaroo.'*

'We sat on rocks to examine the largest work of early man yet discovered in Cape York Peninsula.'

12

More of early man

April of 1970 saw the end of one of the heaviest wet seasons for many years. The coastal strip around Cairns received over two and a half metres of rain, much of it the product of a string of cyclones which had spiralled down the coast. One of the fiercest, codenamed Althea, had roared in on Christmas Eve to devastate Townsville, tearing scores of buildings apart and sending cars bowling down the streets like tin cans.

Quinkin country had received over one and a half metres of rain so we knew there would be no shortage of water in the hills when Dick, Eddy and myself set off to record the new-found galleries on Coamey Creek.

We established a base camp on Wattle tree waterhole in Kennedy Creek, and early in May hiked in to complete exploration and record the found galleries. Further exploration of the rugged terrain yielded only two more small galleries, containing about eighty figures between them. Notable figures were beehives, strange yams, and two fierce-looking little yellow Quinkins, a male and a female.

Another aerial prospect lay between two creeks which flowed south into the Laura, just below where Coamey Creek entered it. We crossed the Laura and walked north over a small ridge to come down on the first creek. We crossed it on a bar of black rock, dished by scores of stone axe grinding grooves. The evidence of past occupation boosted our hopes of finding galleries of art in the locality. We named it Stone Axe Creek.

By midday we were not so confident as the northern cliffs of the creek had yielded no suitable shelters. We had reached a saddle on the divide between the two creeks and our main target area was just ahead—a plateau with many large slabs scattered about in the forest clothing its steep flanks. I had a sudden hunch we should leave the plateau till later and cross the divide to explore eastern scarps of the second creek. It was a fortuitous decision.

Several hundred metres around the corner we came on a long, low shelter in the base of the cliff. There were some faded red figures of men and animals, but more prominent was the work of early man. On slabs of sandstone in the right-hand end of the shelter were a number of engraved emu tracks. Some were about fifteen centimetres long and very symmetrical, engraved with great care. They wore the smooth polish of time.

We decided that many large slabs on a forested terrace further north offered good prospects, and split up to explore among them. Three hundred metres further on I saw a huge tilted slab with a large dead ironwood tree leaning against it, and pushed through tall cane grass and bushes to see Dog and Dingo lying in the shade on a dark charcoal floor, waiting for me. They had apparently recognised it as one of those cool places where I would often stay for hours. There was a large panel of paintings on the curved back wall, but I barely noticed them because my eyes were glued to a mass of deep engravings on the southern end of the wall. Excited whoops brought Eddy and Dick crashing through the undergrowth, and we sat on rocks to examine the largest work of early man yet discovered in Cape York peninsula.

The large open shelter was shaped like the inside of a jockey's cap, the curved back wall about twelve metres long and well protected by a high, stepped ceiling, sloping up and out for about twelve metres. It had an ideal westerly aspect and offered excellent shelter in any weather.

The work of early man extended over a panel about five metres long and one to two metres high. It was a connected maze of meandering lines, geometric shapes, circles, emu and scrub turkey tracks. Round pits with diameters of up to four or five centimetres were placed at seeming random throughout the design. A row of four natural, shallow, oval-shaped holes in the centre of the maze had been pecked around or engraved in, to incorporate them as part of the overall design. The lower part of the panel curved outwards to form a ledge, a section of which had broken away and lay partly buried in the floor. Where the sloping panel entered the floor, the engravings continued to an unknown depth below ground level.

The engraved wall was very weathered, with the engravings almost eroded away in some parts; in other areas the engravings were still up to two centimetres in depth. Although water apparently flowed down part of the engraved wall during rain, there was no trace of any silica skin.

The left-hand panel of heavily superimposed paintings had only a few engravings under them. They were the usual motifs of humans, and many species of animals, birds and reptiles. The most unusual

126

figure was a portrayal of the dreaded giant Quinkin, Turramulli, a no-neck monster having only three fingers and toes on each hand and foot.

It seemed that the panel of ancient engravings was the work of early man, and the panel of paintings the work of a much later people, with a long hiatus between the two styles. Our knowledge of early man was limited to his engraved art, which was usually found in the most favoured shelters, offering the best protection from weather, of easy access, and located near permanent water.

The massive work involved in engraving the wall of the shelter hinted at powerful motivations—early man was concerned about something, and emu and scrub turkey tracks incorporated in the design suggested the concern included those birds. Engraved round pits can represent many things when included in a design—a water-hole, a camp site, fruit, yams or eggs; when associated with bird tracks it was logical to assume they represented eggs.

Many of the other early man engravings also contained emu and scrub turkey tracks, and if the pitchfork designs did represent thunderstorms, then early man was concerned about drought and the effect it was having on his birds.

Dick thought the rows of conjoined emu and turkey tracks might represent the short, strutting steps made during a mating display by the male bird. The tracks may not have represented the smaller species of today; the emu could have been the extinct giant, Genyornis and the turkey, or four-toed megapode, may have been the extinct giant megapode, *Progura gallinacea*, about three times larger than the present scrub turkey. Like most engraved early man sites elsewhere, some later artist had also added an engraved pair of kanga-roo tracks to this site, as they were much fresher and unpatinated.

We named the new gallery Early Man, and the unnamed creek it was on, Early Man Creek. It was such an important archaeological prospect that we decided to postpone further exploration of the area, and to concentrate on surveying a Landrover track to get a future arc-haeological expedition as near as possible to the site. We returned to base camp to make preparations for camping on Early Man Creek.

We took a slightly different route back into the new galleries and found a few more small painted sites on the slopes of the plateau which had been the original target area. Less than a kilometre from Early Man and further west of our original track, we came on more big slabs and found another long, tilted gallery containing many bright figures. The most striking was a big white and red emu, about two metres long and one and a half metres high, standing over a clutch of nine eggs. Other smaller figures of men and kangaroos were under and about it. Immediately in front of the emu was a finely drawn scrub turkey and a fish, both bichromes in white and red.

Higher up in the southern end of the shelter was a smaller bichrome emu, also in white and red. It was standing over a clutch of four eggs. The bird was depicted as reaching under its body to turn the eggs over with its beak to control temperature. It was one of the most sensitively animated paintings we had discovered.

The lower northern end of the cave had been the main camping area, and its walls and ceiling were decorated with a snake and some Quinkin figures. On the outer sloping ceiling, a row of stark red foot-tracks of a man stalked after an equally stark red goanna. The goanna was over a metre long and was impaled on a spear near one hind leg. The hunting scene had such impact that one could almost hear the stealthy footsteps of the hunter, the click and rattle of the womera-flung spear, followed by the threshing and hissing of the writhing reptile. Dick sat looking at the goanna and remarked, 'It's a nice fat one—might have plenty eggs inside.'

Lower on the ceiling was an X-ray painting of a tortoise, portrayed as being full of eggs, always an unexpected bonus for the hunter, and perhaps an assurance there would be an abundance of tortoises.

The finding of Goanna Gallery was a bonus for us, and we continued on to Early Man wondering just how long had mankind been caring for emus, scrub turkeys, and all other flora and fauna of the region. Perhaps some answers lay under the floor of Early Man, waiting to be excavated.

By the time we had finished recording the new sites, it was time for me to take up a Churchill Fellowship I had been awarded to do a world tour of prehistoric rock art sites, not only for comparative purposes, but also to study what other nations were doing to protect and preserve their sites.

I had four months' long service leave from aviation, and had allocated the time to spend the first two weeks in Quinkin country, three months on the world tour, and the final two weeks back in the Quinkin bush. I had selected France, Spain, South Africa, Zimbabwe and North America for the overseas study.

The value of the ancient and magnificent Magdalenian and Aurignacian art bodies had long been recognised by France and Spain. Mostly subterranean, the entrances to the caves were protected by steel doors like bank vaults. The paintings and engravings were protected against any damage and flash photography was not permitted. Tourism to the caves was obviously yielding large profits annually, but the aesthetic quality of the art was downgraded in most places by over-exploitation, where huge crowds of people jostled each other to view the art.

It was fascinating to see figures of extinct animals of the Ice Age, painted by our European ancestors, with the similarities and differences from Aboriginal art. The motivations behind the art appeared to be mainly associated with hunting magic, and some sorcery. People were seldom portrayed, and there was little to convey any feeling of what life was like in those times. Unlike the Australian art, it was not explained, supported and enriched by mythology.

The sites visited in America, in Arizona and New Mexico, were well protected and presented, especially old Indian village sites, but the rock art, mainly engravings, was rather impoverished and attracted little interest there. Some of the best paintings were in Utah, and large galleries in Baja California rivalled those in Cape York peninsula, but once again the lack of knowledge of who painted them and why diminished the experience.

South Africa had thousands of sites containing the beautiful art of the largely vanished Bushmen. Like the artists themselves, the figures were mostly very small, and located in small shelters; but the draftsmanship was superb, for beauty of line and proportion no artist anywhere had ever exceeded the Bushmen. They had captured to perfection the flowing grace of the felines and antelopes and the portrayals of people hunting them, or miming them in dance. Unlike the mainly static, symbolised art of the Australians, the Bushmen art was alive and active. The Bushmen, like the Aborigines, were in complete harmony with all the life and landscapes of their environment. Their art conveyed the fullness of being Bushmen.

Vandalism was rife in the Bushmen galleries. Names were scrawled over paintings and engravings. Paintings had been hacked out of rock faces in some places. Worst of all was the practice of sloshing and spraying water over the painted surfaces to provide better photographic conditions. Protection of some sites had been attempted by erecting heavy mesh enclosures to keep people and animals away from the art, but in every such place the mesh had been torn away or the gates sagged on broken hinges.

It seemed the exquisite Bushmen art had little future in South Africa.

Zimbabwe was a different story. In Matabeleland, near Bulawayo, the granite rock shelters of the Matopo Hills held a treasure trove of Bushmen art. The huge, deep shelters offered ample scope for panels of large paintings, with hundreds of figures superimposed in layers, as in Quinkin country.

Across the walls and ceilings the elephants trumpeted, the felines slunk, the antelopes leapt gracefully, and giraffes cantered in rocking motion. Naked, or sometimes cloaked, hunters danced gracefully, hunted animals, fought lions and invading Bantu warriors. There were scenes of Bushmen running off with herds of Bantu cattle, hotly pursued by Bantu warriors. There the Rainbow Serpent was an antelope, its metres-long body having an antelope head each end. Although the figures were all motion when compared to the static

Quinkin art, there was the same feeling of magic, mystery and legend, with overtones of humour. The Bushmen and the Aborigines would have appreciated and understood each other.

During my absence overseas on the Churchill Fellowship, Eddy had been busy. A mining company had been carrying out intensive exploration of the Quinkin sandstones, using helicopters so geologists could collect rock samples from a close-patterned grid over the entire area. They had found some of our sites already recorded on the Deighton River, and others near its headwaters which we had not seen. Eddy had accepted their offer to be flown in and left for a few days to record the sites and explore for more.

Eddy had also continued exploration of Stone Axe Creek and had found a modest gallery of paintings along its southern scarps; among the figures were four small paintings of mounted horsemen. We decided to have a look at them and continue exploration.

The Mounted Horsemen site was about eight kilometres up the creek from the Laura, located among broken slabs of the top scarp. It was a good quality shelter with the usual secular figures associated with love-magic, sorcery etc. A man painted in red ochre had a large red catfish hanging from one finger; presumably he had been stung by a poisonous barb of the catfish. The horsemen had been painted as silhouettes in dark purple red. There were four of them and one was depicted as standing on the back of the horse while holding the reins; the others were in the conventional sitting pose. The horses looked more like kangaroos than horses, the tails were like bottlebrushes, and instead of hooves there were horse-shoe shapes suspended from the bottom of the legs. The artists had probably looked fearfully at the strange animals from a distance, and later gone to look at the tracks and deduced the shape of the feet from them.

We continued along the broken scarp for a couple of hours and eventually reached the head of the creek, finding only three small shelters with a few old faded figures. The northern side of the gorge appeared to have no worthwhile shelters, so we commenced a return along a lower terrace which offered easier walking. We were almost back level with the Mounted Horsemen when we topped a low ridge to see a large slab on the terrace ahead. It had a wide, stepped overhang crammed with paintings. Weariness departed in a flash and we ran forward cheering to inspect the new find.

It was an excellent living shelter. The sandy floor was dark with charcoal and littered with stone tools. It was about twenty metres long and five metres deep. The back part of the ceiling was only about a metre high, but two stepped faces sloped up to about three metres in front.

The author with buried engravings uncovered at the Sandy Creek site.

The author and Dick examining engravings at the Early Man site.

Dillybag Gallery. Eddy Oribin drawing two ancestral beings.

Quinkin Mountain Gallery. An Imjim Quinkin with five replicas inside himself for use as spies.

Giant Wallaroo Gallery. Giant red wallaroo being attacked by a dingo.

Le Chu Gallery. Black Police troopers. The main police trooper wears a cap, pants and boots and has a rifle.

Echidna Dreaming. Eddy Oribin drawing on a scaffold platform at the Echidna site.

Dillybag Gallery. A faded red painting of the extinct giant emu, Genyornis.

St George River. The large bichrome figures of people and animals were superbly drawn.

Eddy Oribin photographing Magnificent Gallery.

Magnificent Gallery. *Above*: Dick admires an owl, *below*: the author
contemplates a tall white guardian-style figure.

Above: Koala site, Mosman River. A koala was a striking figure in a Mosman River site. *Below*: Blue Figure site, Deighton River. An inverted blue sorcery figure with many superimpositions.

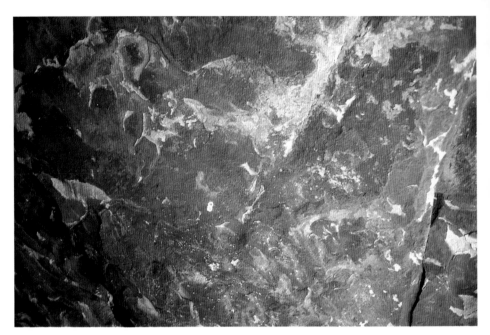

Diprotodon site, Deighton River. *Top*: The ancient painting of a
diprotodon is faded and exfoliating. *Bottom*: A portrayal of diprotodons by
the author, based on the Aboriginal drawing.

Layers of paintings were superimposed on all smooth surfaces. Most of the figures looked comparatively recent, and they were large, colourful and well drawn. There were kangaroos, echidnas, fish, snakes and crocodiles among the usual motifs. Two small Imjim Quinkins, male and female, were side by side on top of other figures. A large figure of a man on the outer ceiling had several spears thrust through his body. Some of the barbs of the spears were later additions in different shades of red, indicating that the same sorcery magic had been reactivated on the figure time and time again.

The strangest figure, partly obscured by later figures, appeared to be an armless woman. Only about a metre of the horizontal figure emerged from under other paintings, it was cream with red outline and decoration. There were red lines which appeared to represent hair, two round eyes, and shoulders which sloped away to become breasts with nipples.

The figure which delighted me most was a large white and red kangaroo, curled up neatly to fit in a round recess, which had been formed when an oval-shaped slab had fallen out of the sloping ceiling. The curved top of the sharp-edged recess had suggested the curved back of a kangaroo to the artist, and he had painted it in there, curving the tail and legs to fit the niche, only the head extended out over the left-hand side of the recess, like a young kangaroo curled up in the pouch, looking out of it.

At Altmira in Spain, ancient Magdalenian artists had seen round protruberances, about a metre in diameter, hanging from the ceiling, and used the surfaces to portray neatly curled up red and black bisons. In a booklet about the paintings the Spanish proudly claimed that nowhere else in the world had prehistoric man employed natural shapes to emphasise outlines of figures. Since then we have found many examples of using natural shapes for design.

There were no ancient engravings in the Armless Woman Gallery, but it appeared to have been a main wet season shelter for a very long time. There were no paintings reflecting the European invasion, like the four horsemen on the steep hill above us. It appeared that the traditional shelter on the terrace was too accessible to mounted Black Police, and during the troubled times the clan had used the high safe site, and had painted the Black Police for sorcery purposes.

In 1973 Dick was busy with the Aboriginal Art Board and was not able to spend as much time in the bush with us. I usually saw him when he passed through Cairns for meetings in Sydney. On one trip he brought me a special message-stick from Warrabudgera, inviting me to attend a Luragal ceremony next year, when they would be putting three young men 'through the smoke'. On one side of the short stick a half-circle was engraved, which Dick interpreted as the sacred ground, the galun; across the circle were three short lines representing the three initiates lying down; there were ten knicks cut in one side of the stick, and nine in the other side, each representing an elder inviting me to attend. On the other side of the stick was a long spear, which symbolised good hunting—there would be plenty of dugong and turtle.

Our next trip was a return to the Normanby River region to look for more incipient X-ray figures like those found on Bull Creek. Access had been improved by a new track bulldozed through the area to link Cooktown to Laura via Battle Camp.

It was poor country, with the low open forest more stunted and scraggy than the Laura forest. The decaying sandstone scarps had weathered into lines of rounded dark grey slabs. We camped on a small running creek and next morning headed south-east to where aerial sightings had revealed large clusters of slabs near the head of the creek.

We finally came on them and were disappointed that none had shelters. Eddy suggested we cross a ridge to get nearer the Normanby, but an inner urge made me persist with the big rounded grey slabs. We were about to give up when we noticed a hole about a metre high under a big slab ahead. We stooped through it and stood up inside a huge igloo shelter—and the wall all around bore a mass of ochre figures.

The slab's exterior height was only four metres and the inside domed ceiling was about three metres high. Eddy maintained later that as I had persisted with the one heading all morning and seemed to know where I was going, I must have been an Aborigine of those parts in an earlier life.

Most of the large figures were white with yellow outlines, or yellow with white outlines. Horrific Quinkins with big ugly heads, distorted bodies and genitalia, were the dominant figures. A large, bright yellow emu and a very symmetrical, long-necked tortoise, also in yellow and white, seemed to be the most recent figures. Faded red figures of emus and kangaroos exhibited internal organs like those further down Bull Creek, so an X-ray technique was a feature of an older Bull Creek style, which for some reason had not become as highly developed as in the Arnhem Land art.

It was a perfect living place and had been used as such for a very long time. It was typical of the places favoured by early man, and a couple of big slabs lying near the wall were ideal places for his engravings; but there was no trace of his work, and we thought it gave ground to our theory that the area had been under dense rainforest in the times of early man.

A thorough search of the rest of the creek yielded no other suitable shelters or paintings.

A few weeks later we set up a base camp on the Laura River, near the junction of Early Man Creek, to continue recording of sites found, and further exploration, expecially to the north of Early Man site, where aerial surveys had revealed large outliers along the fractured scarps of Conglomerate Creek.

We had developed the practice of finding a major site in a new area, then leaving further exploration until we returned to record the site. Then each day we worked making scaled drawings until about 4 p.m., when it was cooler, then we spent a couple of hours each evening systematically exploring in all directions. It added excitement to each day, and kept us fit.

The entire area was rich in art sites. Every day we found more, ranging from small sites with a few hand stencils, paintings or engravings, to large shelters with scores of superimposed figures. The first big find was less than two kilometres north of Early Man.

It was a very large and excellent shelter of the igloo type, under a huge slab of sandstone forming part of the disintegrating scarp of the plateau. It could easily have sheltered a hundred people. Dingoes, kangaroos, crocodiles and human beings were among the life-size figures. A cream snake, a third of a metre wide, meandered all over the ceiling for about twenty metres. A painting of a possum was an exciting find, being the first of the species we had identified. It was old and faded, in creamy brown with a red outline, very well-drawn with typically rounded head and ears, and a curled tail. Possums were rare in Quinkin country and we had sighted only a few in all our years of exploring. Later, we found three more very faded red paintings of possums in a small shelter further east along the scarp.

We named it Possum Gallery, and then found six smaller sites in the immediate vicinity. One contained the silica-glazed work of early man, and another featured a small snake painted in tight coils. A few metres away was a large beehive with a swarm of bees departing. The rate of discovery was far out-stripping our rate of recording.

'The most interesting figure was a faded, but very distinct, red silhouette emu . . . Near the rear of the emu was . . . a human figure holding a stick like a shepherd's crook . . .'

13

An ancient emu

The monsoon came early in 1974. The towering, black mass of the inter-tropic front, trailing its silver curtain of torrential rain, engulfed Quinkin country in mid-December. After weeks of heavy rain every watercourse rose to raging flood. We knew all about Quinkin country in the dry season, but often wondered what it was like to live in a cave in the hills during a heavy wet season. It was a good year to find out.

The monsoon was usually at its height about the end of February, so we chose that time to mount a small expedition. It was easy to organise as we had bought the Laura pub the previous December, as part of my preparation to quit airline flying, and establish a base in Quinkin country. I had also purchased a Cessna 206, VH-SIR, and took out an air-charter licence, so the plane would earn its keep, and be available for essential surveys after art sites.

Dick, Eddy and myself were joined by Jimmy Archer, the ranger for the Aboriginal Trust. One afternoon the Laura River dropped low enough to expose most of the log bridge, and we surged across in the Landrover and drove to where Hell's Gate Creek crossed the road, and prepared to backpack south up the creek into the gorges.

Our destination was a big painted shelter high in the western scarps, where we would record the art, and investigate the quantity and quality of natural food resources available in the area during the wet season.

All the country was incredibly lush and there was every possible shade of green. Water rushed down the creek, the ground squelched underfoot, brilliant green vines embraced most of the trees, and wildflowers of every colour starred the open forest. The heavy air throbbed with the cadence of cicadas, and flocks of red-winged parrots flashed crimson as they flapped ahead of squawking pale green fledglings.

A few kilometres up the creek we commenced climbing a long ridge leading up to the western cliffs. It was like walking in a sauna, the air so hot and humid that all our clothes were drenched with perspiration, so it mattered little when the usual afternoon storms rolled thunder through the hills and literally bucketed us with rain. Dog and Dingo scouted eagerly ahead through the ironbarks, overjoyed with the wet season adventure.

The sandy floor of the veranda-like shelter was dry and had ample room for the four of us to roll out swags along the back wall. There was even dry wood, left over from the last fire of Aboriginal occupants of long ago. We put our billies under streams of water falling from the dripline and prepared for an enjoyable and interesting week. There were no sandflies or mosquitoes, mammatus clouds from dissipating storms provided a fiery, glowing sunset, and a cooling breeze tossed the bloodwoods. It was the ideal place to spend the wet season.

Each morning we spent several hours exploring, and found several more small galleries, but the questing noses of the dogs seldom found anything to excite them. Twice they briefly pursued big, dark grey wallaroos, and three or four times roused agile rock wallabies. We found no trace of bandicoots, possums, echidnas, emus or other animals, all common motifs in the galleries, and present in reasonable numbers eastward nearer the coast. Most of the large reptiles, goannas, snakes and frilled lizards, had disappeared soon after the advent of the poisonous cane toad.

We thought that overuse of fire by graziers, who burnt most of Cape York peninsula each year, was probably responsible for the dwindling numbers of marsupials. The master managers of clan estates, the Aborigines, burnt the country very carefully, using a mosaic of burnt and unburnt country, to provide green shoots of grass adjacent to long dry grass where smaller animals could hide from predators.

Burning commenced as soon as possible after the wet season, firing areas which had not been burnt for three or four years. Heavy dews extinguished the fires each evening, and the mosaic burning continued until early August, when the dews were becoming too light to stop the fires. The mosaic pattern prevented massive wild fires from sweeping the country bare during hot windy weather of early summer.

After the wet season a team of archaeologists from the Australian National University arrived to excavate Early Man shelter. They were led by Dr Andrée Rosenfeld, whom I had met in Spain, where she was excavating and studying prehistoric art in caves in the Spanish hills. I had enthused to Andrée about the archaeological potential of Early Man, and as she was about to take up an appointment with ANU, she had expressed interest in an excavation.

We had hacked out a precarious four-wheel drive track up Early Man Creek so the team could set up a base camp on a spring just below the site. During the course of the excavation Eddy and I continued recording sites, and explored areas to the north-west.

We found several small galleries further west along the scarps of Early Man Creek, but our best discovery was about two kilometres north-west across the plateau, among big blocks of sandstone on the Conglomerate Creek fall.

One outlier on a terrace above the creek had a wide, upward-tilted overhang on the west side, and a large igloo-shaped shelter under the east side. All smooth sections of the walls and ceilings bore layers of superimposed paintings. As a motif the emu easily outnumbered all others, not surprising in view of the many nonda and lady-apple fruit trees in the area, but there were kangaroos, a dingo, crocodiles, Quinkins and many human figures.

The most interesting figure was a faded, but very distinct, red silhouette emu; its heavy beak was curved like that of a flamingo. It was very carefully drawn and looked very old. Most of the original red ochre paint was gone, leaving a clear permeated stain of light red on the sloping ceiling. Although all other areas surrounding the mysterious bird were heavily superimposed with many figures, no other painting had ever been superimposed on it. Near the rear of the emu and merging into it was the upper part of a human figure holding a stick like a shepherd's crook. It appeared to be associated, and contemporary with, the emu, both being in the same faded red.

We speculated that it was a portrayal of the extinct giant emu, Genyornis, described by palaeontologists as being over two metres tall, with comparatively small feet for its size, and having a thick strong neck. The shape of the beak was unknown, but the strong neck suggested a heavy one. It seemed that when later generations of people realised the portrayed bird had vanished forever from the landscape, they had elected never to obscure it with other paintings.

The man with the crooked stick may have represented some way of catching the emu. Present-day emus are so curious and stupid, that they can be attracted to almost within touching distance by anybody lying on the ground and waving their legs in the air. A crook made from the forked branch of a tree to hook a leg, and a club, were all that was needed to capture emus. The portrayal might also mean that the ancient birds were domesticated in remote times.

There were three other small galleries near the main site. One contained a few small Quinkins with distorted genitalia, another had human ancestral figures, and the third faded red stencils of human hands and feet, and boomerangs, some of the latter being shaped like the head and neck of an emu.

It was almost dusk when we came to another small shelter about two hundred metres north down the slope from the main site. I bobbed down to enter the shelter and saw what appeared to be a striped snake coiled on a ledge near my nose. I blundered into Eddy as I hastily withdrew; but cautious investigation revealed the 'snake' to be a brown and fawn striped dillybag. Beside it was a steel tomahawk, and scattered about the floor of the shelter were several spears and a stout digging stick. The grass-fibre dillybag was in good condition and found to contain a ball of fibre string and the beginning of a new dillybag, with a small curved stick for its weaving, a ball of black bees-wax, a small, fringed, women's pubic apron, made from old-style trade beads, a small silver Chinese spoon, and a steel fishhook.

We wondered what drama had caused the abandonment of those personal treasures by a man and a woman. Had they been surprised by the sudden advent of a party of mounted Black Police, and fled, or had they been shot or captured?

We named the new group the Dillybag Galleries.

Meanwhile the excavation at Early Man was proceeding smoothly, yielding stone implements, faunal material and charcoal, as clues to the lifestyle of its human inhabitants from recent to remote times. The diggers found that the engravings continued underground along the back wall, until they curved down on to the floor, over a metre below the surface.

Carbon dates for two styles of engravings were obtained. The oldest engravings were found to have a minimum age of a little over 13 000 B.P. The later style proved to be about 4000 to 5000 B.P. The dates gave no indication of duration of the styles in question.

We thought that the date of 13 000 years probably related mainly to the painted panel, its first figures being executed by the first occupants after the droughts. But the date was the oldest and most important for the minimum age of ancient engravings, and the later reworking of parts of them could have accounted for the lesser date of 4000 to 5000 years.

Eddy Oribin, the author and Dick Roughsey recording the panels of paintings and engravings at Early Man site.

'. . . a two metre long white and red wallaroo . . . dominated that section of the gallery . . .'

14
Jowalbinna

Back in the early 1960s Dick and I had explored parts of the lower gorge of Shepherd Creek, south-west from Laura. We had found only a few small sites, but the most notable thing was Shepherd Creek itself. Despite several years of semi-drought it was still flowing strongly near the end of the dry season, with eels, catfish and freshwater shrimps swimming about, and there were tracks of small freshwater crocodiles.

Where we came down on it the creek ran through a broad gorge, walled by red and grey sandstone cliffs. It was cool and shady, overhung with huge paperbarks and fig trees, and fringed with red-flowering callistemons and other shrubs, the sweet, crystal-clear water flowing over a wide sandy bed. After the dry hills it seemed like paradise, and I thought it the most beautiful part of Cape York peninsula I had seen.

I found out later that most of Shepherd Creek was contained within the leasehold of Staunton, a forty-square-kilometre cattle run. It was put up for auction in June 1975, and prior to it I took Wally O'Grady out for an inspection. It was a beautiful expanse of wilderness, and adjoined the Quinkin Reserves, covering much of the red gorge country of Shepherd and Brady creeks, which ran clear water even during droughts. There were two large fenced paddocks, and a huge, concrete-floored shed was the beginnings of a homestead. We decided to attend the auction and bid for it. On the day of the sale I was stuck in Cairns waiting on an oil seal for SIR (the Cessna plane I had purchased), and was highly delighted when Wally rang to say our bid had been successful. We decided to call it Jowalbinna, the Aboriginal name for the towering red bluff that marked its north-eastern corner.

We bought some horses and saddle gear, and a few weeks later I went with Beverley and Wally to continue exploration of Jowalbinna. While inspecting fence lines Wally had seen ancient engravings on a huge weathered block of sandstone on top of the northern escarpment.

It was an impressive place. Two big, rectangular blocks of red sandstone brooded among gnarled bloodwoods on a point of the scarp. The eastern block had a large shallow recess in its southern side, and early man had engraved emu tracks, geometric, meandering line and star-shaped designs there. The reason it had been chosen for emu Dreaming was readily evident—part of the rock face had weathered to produce the natural shape of a very large emu in side profile, only the head and lower legs were missing. It was as tall as the extinct emu, *Genyornis*.

Three round pits, over ten centimetres in diameter and about four deep, had been engraved in the rear of the emu, representing eggs, as they sometimes do in painted portrayals of emus. There were also several rows of smaller round pits, similar to those at Early Man. Some of the weathered engravings had been more recently battered out again, and repatination had not yet occurred. A large, very faded red man, with outstretched arms, and hands having only three fingers, like an emu track, was painted near the emu. It was obviously a sacred Dreaming site and had held that role for many thousands of years—until that fateful day when the first Snider rifle shots echoed and re-echoed across the red gorges.

On the western block there were two small paintings of men, very faded and old. Near them was a small shelter which had been much used for camping. Stone tools lay on the floor, along with the rusty head of a steel tomahawk. The shelter would have been used by the custodians of emu Dreaming when they came on the annual pilgrimage to 'wake up' old Ichamba, their emu ancestor, doomed now to sleep forever.

Red cliffs on the south side of the gorge beckoned, and we crossed to examine them. There were no shelters in the cliff base so we climbed up and crossed the plateau to the eastern side, which did have shelters. Every small shelter suitable for camping had been used and all contained a few paintings of a secular nature; we counted over a hundred figures in all. Near one shelter we found an old, rusty, handmade shovel. Its handle had been burnt by bushfires, and one side of the blade had been cut off to make steel spearheads for the deadly shovel-nosed spears, so effective in killing cattle.

Next morning we saddled horses and rode up the creek, heading for the western scarps of its main tributary, Brady Creek, which we had inspected from the air. It was a pleasant ride in the cool morning air, our passage heralded by screeching white cockatoo clans. The creek was home to many species of birds, quail exploded into whirring flight from under the horses, pale-headed rosellas chattered to each other, flocks of rainbow lorikeets shrieked past, pardalotes called from high white branches of Morton Bay ash, banana birds heckled the dogs, and high on the ridges flocks of black cockatoos uttered harsh, eerie Quinkin calls as they fed on bloodwood nuts.

The entrance to Brady Creek gorge was dominated by a towering peak which marked the beginning of its eastern scarp. Perched on top of the peak were big blocks of weathered sandstone, two of which looked like the heads of dogs, one looking south-east, the other south-west. I felt sure they would have loomed large in the local mythology so we called them Dingo Rocks.

We tethered the horses at the junction of the two creeks, under a huge shady, fruiting fig tree, where they could eat the fallen red and yellow fruit, and reach the water. We walked west across a grassy, grey-box terrace and climbed up through ironbarks on the steep scree slope to the base of the red cliff.

We turned south and almost immediately found two paintings under a shallow overhang, a long-necked tortoise and a fish, both stark white silhouettes. There were no more shelters for several hundred metres, then we found a good one under an outlier just below the cliff. It was full of bright figures in red and white, 34 in all. It was a good dry living place, and apart from the human figures, the motifs portrayed the aquatic life found in the creek below, garfish, crocodiles, perch, catfish, eels and tortoises. We called it Garfish Gallery.

The cliff ran east above Garfish and about a hundred metres further on turned abruptly south again. There was a rock terrace on the point which would afford a vast panoramic view over the trees, so we climbed up to it, and found people already staring out over the splendid view. The main figure was a life-size, dark red lady, with arms wide-flung. There were other human figures, all in red, a very large dark red wallaroo and a dingo. The towering red cliff leaned outward to give some protection from the rain. All the red figures appeared to be very old, a man and woman standing side by side were almost obliterated by a milky silica flow. There were no recent figures and it was not a suitable living site, so we concluded it was an ancient sacred site, many thousands of years old. We left the red lady to her vigil, and pressed on after more treasures.

About three hundred metres south of the corner there were two more shallow shelters with small paintings, one had four figures and the other ten, mainly aquatic animals. Just ahead was a small steep gully with a swamp choked with ferns, vines and razor grass. We scrambled down the slope to pass below the swamp, and noticed a shelter under a big outlier about sixty metres from the cliff.

A large, faded red echidna was under an overhang outside the shelter, and we entered to see figures scattered all over walls, ceiling and fallen slabs. Long ago a wide thick slab had fallen from the ceiling, snapped in half, and had come to rest leaning one against the other to form a tent-shaped shelter within the main shelter. Its inner walls bore paintings of large humans, a dingo and three scrub turkeys.

The most striking figure was an ancestral guardian-type man about three metres high. Painted in red and decorated with white, it was skilfully drawn, and the magic charm of a pearl-shell pendant hung from his neck. An aura of virtue and protection emanated from the powerful figure, which was painted over an old white crocodile.

Rows of red stick men were painted on one outer side of the tent, and on the wall above were three quaint little Quinkins. Near them was a very small painting of a white cockatoo with a raised crest, the first portrayal of that bird we had found. There were large red crocodiles, an eel, tortoise and another echidna. Among stone implements on the floor was a rusty steel spear blade, about the size of the piece missing from the shovel we found the day before. We called it Tent Gallery.

Beverley and Wally decided to go down and explore along Brady Creek for aquatic life, while I continued along the cliff face. About a kilometre further on the scarp turned abruptly west into a small branch of Brady Creek, so I turned back to look among big blocks at the foot of the steep slope.

There were no good shelters in any of the large slabs but I found two large red figures painted on an exposed wall of one of them. The silhouette kangaroo and crocodile were exposed to every shower of rain, and the sun every afternoon. They were faded but distinct, and it was obvious the fine red haematite particles had permeated into the sandstone and stained it, probably several millimetres deep, and so the figures will still be there some thousands of years in the future.

There was a house-high block of sandstone on the creek terrace just above a deep waterhole. The block leaned east to provide some shelter, and a large ironwood provided solid shade. It had been used as a camp site and the leaning wall was covered with old faded paintings, mainly of women. A white and red female Imjim Quinkin was the clearest figure.

Beverley and Wally returned and said they had found large, deep waterholes and Livistona palms. Wally had seen a three-metre freshwater crocodile launch itself into a waterhole, and they had seen a large mottled eel and some tortoises.

Riding back down the creek we planned a systematic exploration of Jowalbinna, and the vast area of wild and rugged country surrounding it. We would need more horses, especially packhorses and packsaddles. Hank Morris, who ran the Laura pub for us, was a former cattleman, so we decided to fly him down to the next Mareeba horse sale.

A couple of weeks later I returned with Dick and Eddy. They went to explore the northern scarps of Shepherd Creek, while I went up to record Emu Dreaming. Early morning sun was still on the engraved section, making it too hot to work there, so I decided to go exploring for an hour until the sun shifted.

Walking west along the plateau I came on huge sheets of exposed grey sandstone, and went to look in a shallow gully eroded into the edge of it. There was a split in the rock which extended into a three-metre-high tunnel running deep into the sandstone. Near the entrance, in a shallow recess, were a number of children's hand stencils in dark red. I walked into the tunnel looking for paintings, followed by Dog and Dingo, but as the tunnel got darker, Dingo stopped and commenced a nervous squeaking. The air had a musty smell of bats and/or big snakes and I presumed she was worried about them. I struck matches and searched the walls but there were no paintings or engravings. The tunnel narrowed and continued on into total darkness. Dog followed me into the darkness, but Dingo stayed back in the light squeaking her concern for us. When I turned and came back she bolted for the entrance and could never be enticed in there again.

The boy's hand stencils at the entrance were like those found at many initiation sites, and I thought the dark mysterious tunnel would have been the reputed home of some mythical monster, the boys being brought to the entrance and adequately terrified by the accompanying myth, as part of their initiation ceremony.

About a hundred metres on, at the head of the gully, there was a small but good living shelter, being hastily vacated by a large brown snake as I walked up to it. There were about twenty-five paintings on the ceiling and walls; some ceiling figures were partly obscured by lichen, but visible was most of a big, red and white crocodile, the torso of a well-endowed woman, and two long snakes, one white and one red. Stone implements on the floor included a dished seed-grinding slab with the top grinding stone still in place. I named it Snake Place.

Another two hundred metres west, near the edge of the cliff overlooking Shepherd Creek, there were ten large figures of humans and animals painted on rock surfaces exposed to weather. Like those on the terrace of Brady Creek they were stains which had permeated into the sandstone. It seemed that the permanent creek waters below would ensure that every habitable shelter in the region would contain paintings. It had probably been a refuge area when prolonged droughts ravished Australia about 17 000 years ago.

Dick and Eddy arrived back in the afternoon to report some panels of curious, simplified portrayals of human beings, located under a huge bridge of sandstone arching over a gully. They likened the figures to those at the entrance to the mortuary site in the Quinkin group. Dick thought the archway might symbolise the entrance to Woolunda.

During the ensuing wet season, charter flights out of Laura presented opportunities for further aerial surveys, especially parts of the Chillagoe Formation, ancient coral reefs outcropping in high jagged masses from Chillagoe north to the Palmer River. Just south of the Palmer I located a big shelter in the west face of a hundred-metre-high mass of limestone.

When the country dried out I set out with Dick and Jimmy to explore the limestones. It was a day's drive over rough tracks and through the bush to make camp among the gloomy grey spires.

Next morning I used a high-peaked hill as a landmark and located it about ten metres up the cliff face. It was easy to climb up but great care was necessary as the hard limestone had weathered into knife-edge serrations, and a fall would have resulted in severe injuries.

It was not a camping place, the rough stony floor bore no charcoal, but there were panels of small figures of men painted in monochromes, about sixty in dark red, six in orange and five in black. They were executed in the simple style of mortuary figures, representing spirits of the dead. Dick and Jimmy were convinced it was a secondary burial place, pointing out holes going away down into the limestones, where bark mortuary caskets could be dropped. A stone dropped into a hole rattled for a few seconds then fell into an abyss, and one could imagine the bones being pushed in, to rattle away into darkness, going on an equally mysterious journey as that already undertaken by the spirit.

The limestone boomed when struck and was obviously hollow. Proof of that came later when further north on the outcrop we saw hundreds of small grey swiftlets circling above a spire, then diving into the top of it at tremendous speed, obviously entering a big cavern inside. The rows of limestone outcrops just south of the Palmer River are the largest of the Chillagoe Formation and may be connected by a vast system of subterranean caves.

We found no suitable camping sites among the limestones and decided to shift camp ten kilometres north of the Palmer and make a survey of the southern end of the sandstone plateau, which lay west of the telegraph line. Next morning we followed a creek to the base of the plateau and climbed up the south-east corner. There was a small shelter which contained red and white figures of five people, including a plump-breasted woman. They were well drawn and decorated, and raised our hopes of finding a large gallery.

By mid-afternoon we had found five more painted sites in the heads of shallow gorges running west across the plateau. Although we spent little time examining them they appeared to be Dreaming sites of various creatures, probably belonging to a tribe whose main clan country lay along rivers further west. An interesting site was a small shelter with paintings of three women and three dingoes. The women were less than a metre tall and all figures were silhouettes in stark white, with red outlines and decoration. One woman was apparently suckling a dingo, a common occurrence in tribal life. All figures looked as fresh as though they were painted the day before—all execpt the hind leg of one dingo, which was a very faded white with a faint red outline. The process of repainting the old figures was not quite completed, perhaps interrupted over a hundred years ago by the Palmer gold rush. It was also mute evidence that repainting of sacred figures was done very carefully and perhaps over a long period of time.

On the way back we walked along the edge of the sheer eastern cliff looking for a way down. Crossing a shallow gorge we found a faded painting of an eel, and opposite it was a big shelter with no paintings, but a bark bone casket was on a ledge about three metres above the floor. Some of the bark had rotted away and the skull stared solemnly down at us. A couple of long bones had fallen to the floor, so I climbed on a low ledge and Dick passed them up for replacement with the rest. Most caskets were usually eaten by termites, bones and all, the termites building long tunnels up rock faces to reach them. The surface sandstone in that shelter was loose and friable and the termites could not build on it, so it had survived.

Aerial surveys of Jowalbinna had revealed many areas with a high potential for rock shelters, and when there was a lull in charter flying I drove out with Dick and pushed a track north-west across the plateau and drove down to camp on Pine Tree Creek by a small waterfall.

Next morning we crossed to the western scarps of the creek, and after finding only hand stencils, climbed a peak of the scarp to scan the rugged area with binoculars. A few kilometres away to the south was a high round plateau with sheer red and grey cliffs, and about a kilometre in diameter. It had a scar on the north face caused by an ancient rock fall, and we made it our first objective. Two kilometres beyond the east side of the plateau were rows of grey sandstone domes, which I had noted from the air as a good prospect. On the eastern scarps of the creek were a series of weathered sandstone domes, shaped like huge gunyahs. We set off to explore the three places.

An hour later I scrambled up among the rock fall to the base of the cliff, and saw a large white Imjim Quinkin glaring at me from the wall of a shallow cave. It was a splendid portrayal of his kind, and unusual in that four small replicas of himself were painted within the gridded decoration of his torso, and a fifth was upside down just below his neck. Dick interpreted it as small versions of Imjim which he could spit out and send to the four winds as spies and then swallow them back down again. There were many other paintings, including inverted humans, a fine, large barramundi, and several large white and red kangaroos.

Just west of the first shelter was a steep gully where a spring ran from under the cliff. It had been dammed at the lower end in ancient times, to form a deep permanent waterhole. Tree roots had laced all over the earth dam to consolidate it, and it was fringed with a prolific growth of ferns, mauve-flowering lasiandra shrubs and trees. The pool had probably been part of a fish-farming operation, where fingerlings could be brought in coolamons, to grow in safety until wet season floods returned them to the main creek, which was also noted for its large mottled eels.

On the other side of the waterhole another shelter contained more white and red kangaroos, and lots of curious, tiny Quinkins with misshapen heads and limbs. It was a delightful find and Dick thought the fitting name would be Quinkin Mountain.

The first shelter among the grey domes contained a few hand stencils and impoverished paintings, but around on the eastern side there were lots of lady-apple trees, and pushing through undergrowth we glimpsed large dark red figures at the base of an outward-leaning cliff. It was another major art site.

An ancient rock-fall had created a stairway up the side of the sheltered cliff face, and it had been used to paint a stepped series of large red wallaroos on the cliff. There were ten of them, all in dark red with faded white outlines, powerfully drawn and from two metres to over three metres long. Most of the wallaroos had a dingo painted under their tails, as though attacking the flank of the large animal. A more recent dingo, in white with red outline, had been placed near the faded dingo behind the largest wallaroo. There were several echidnas, large eels in both red and white, tortoises, red yams, possums and other small marsupials. Early man had been there to batter out a long row of round pits. They were not patinated and had apparently been re-worked in more recent times.

On the ceiling of a low recess under the largest wallaroo there was a series of superimposed figures. A red woman was being bitten on the foot by a metre-long red snake, there was a white and red dingo, and a small white circle with red lines across it, suggesting a ball bound with string. The rock fall had created another tent shelter, and its inner and outer walls were covered with faded paintings, including a large kangaroo and a big beehive.

Further north along the cliff face there was a large yellow Quinkin, looking like a real no-neck monster, with a big domed head and three clawed fingers on each hand, which we found out was the dreaded monster Turramulli, who ate people. Beyond him was a thin, attenuated Timara Quinkin. Thirty metres north along the cliff a low cave had a small group of figures, two red women, and a red dingo with a pup. On an outer wall of the cave was a white and red eel, a faded red dingo sniffed the tail of another dingo, and a stark white dingo was just around the corner from them. The last painting was high on the outer wall and depicted a large jabiru about to swallow a small eel-tailed catfish, its favourite food.

Southward into the head of the small gorge we found another immense shelter, about fifty metres long and up to ten metres deep. On the wall of the northern end was the largest wallaroo of all, over four metres long. It was painted in faded white, with a thick, dark red outline and red dot decoration. The slitted eye was a natural hole in the rock, which had probably prompted the creation of the figure there, as the place where the ancestral wallaroo had located himself in the rock. The bottom part of the hind legs had been repainted as far up as could be reached. There had been a ledge from which the original figure was created, but it was long gone.

There were three panels of red stick figures near the wallaroo, one panel had an inverted sorcery man, and they were probably all mortuary figures.

At the southern end of the great cavern, an ironwood pole leaned against the floor of an upper cave, giving access to an excellent resting place for bark caskets, but crumbling sandstone made further investigation too risky. Two large, stark red eels, and a smaller wallaroo, were also in the southern end.

Unlike the first wallaroo site, there was no charcoal or camping debris, and it was obviously a wallaroo Dreaming, and mortuary site, and we decided to call these the Giant Wallaroo sites.

We crossed to the eastern scarps and explored among huge blocks along its base, as we headed toward Gunyah Rocks. There were no shelters, but Dog and Dingo had a fun chase after a pair of big dark grey wallaroos.

We found the Gunyahs to be weathered turrets of exposed sheets of bedrock sandstone. There was a long low shelter under the side of one sheet and it contained about thirty small figures of animals and people, including some fine paintings of women on the ceiling, apparently associated with love-magic. It had been used as a living site for a long time as the silica-glazed engraving of early man's pitchfork design was also there.

Further aerial surveys revealed more good prospects west of Giant Wallaroo, and further west on the headwaters of the St George River, where I had seen a narrow bluff running westward out from the main scarp. There was a long shelter under the north side, and flying very low along the south side I had glimpsed large red paintings through the screening trees along the base. It was about twenty kilometres across the ranges from Jowalbinna, so we decided to make it a pack-horse trip, exploring the country across to it, and recording Giant Wallaroo on the way back.

Eddy, Dick, Jimmy and myself spent a day shoeing horses, preparing pack-saddles, hobbles and other essential gear, while Stephen, with two Laura Aborigines, Fred Coleman and Teddy George, brought extra horses out from Laura.

We decided to establish a base camp as near as possible to Giant Wallaroo and next day loaded pack-saddles and all other gear into two Landrovers, and Eddy and I set off to make a track down into Pine Tree Creek Gorge, with the others to bring all the horses over when they arrived from Laura.

There was a break in the cliff near the Gunyahs and we bumped down into the gorge and pushed through high grass and dense undergrowth to a good camp site by the creek, only a few minutes walk from Giant Wallaroo. We set up camp and built a small single-rail yard with saplings to hold the horses. Fortunately it was near full moon, as Steve and party did not arrive till well after dark, having had trouble with some of the horses.

Next morning we loaded three packhorses and rode across the creek to follow a small tributary of it westward past Quinkin Mountain, to get on a long, stony, bloodwood ridge running up to the watershed. It was a very hot day and the steep ridge was hard on the horses, so we led them up the steep pinches. The watershed was a broad sandy plateau with outcrops of red sandstone among a tall open forest of stringy-barks. We were fortunate in finding a spring at the base of a low cliff, and stopped there to spell the horses and have lunch. There was a good shelter under the cliff and it contained about thirty paintings, mostly small human figures.

By mid-afternoon we reached the far side of the watershed and from the top of a high cliff had a grand panoramic view of the rugged St George waters. Only a kilometre away was the grey bluff which was our destination. One of the packhorses was exhausted, so we stopped in shade to spell it while Eddy rode south and Jimmy north to find a way down off the cliff.

In an hour they were both back—there was no way down for horses. I should have surveyed the route by air beforehand. We were almost out of water so an immediate return to the spring was essential. Eddy said he had found a big shelter which looked out over the St George, and estimated it contained about a hundred figures. Steve's saddlehorse had experience carrying packs so we loaded packs off the distressed horse on to him, and Steve trotted along behind the pack-horses. All of us, men, horses and dogs, were pleased to reach the spring under the light of a full moon.

Next day Eddy and I made scaled drawings of the paintings in the nearby shelter, while the rest of the party rode out in all directions to scour the country for more art sites. They found none, so in the afternoon we all returned to the base camp on Pine Tree Creek, where Eddy and I stayed for a few days recording Giant Wallaroo, and the rest returned the horses to Jowalbinna.

A few weeks later we heard that a mining company was prospecting along the Palmer with a helicopter, so Eddy and I drove over to see if the prospectors would airlift us into the St George cliff site, about fifty kilometres north of their camp. They were delighted to help, and the experienced helicopter pilot dropped us and our gear in a tiny clearing by a waterhole only a few hundred metres from the cliff. We took recording gear and walked across to it.

It was a site of huge proportions. The fifty-metre-high cliff leaned out to provide shelter for over a hundred metres at its base. Most of the larger-than-life figures were painted in dark red or purple-red ochres, with white outlines and decoration. We were astonished at the quality of draftsmanship because the entire lower cliff face was composed of extremely rough pudding-stone conglomerate, yet every sweeping line of the figures was perfect and symmetrical. Close examination revealed the outer edges of the figures had been drawn carefully over protruding stones and down into crevices, and every bit of the figure blocked in until it was all solid colour.

We thought that the clan of that region, after visiting neighbours who owned fine paintings on smooth sandstone, had resolved to create their own fine figures no matter what the effort required. The figures appeared to represent ancestral beings and Dreaming animals, and were probably repainted several times.

A large purple-red emu was a particularly fine figure. A smaller bird, shaped like an emu, but with an upright stance, had six toes on each foot, as though to emphasise it had more than the emu's three toes. We thought it was another portrayal of the extinct giant megapode, *Progura gallinacea*. Down the eastern end of the shelter was a two-metre-long red wallaroo, and a long thin snake. A ground-edge stone axe was among other implements on the floor.

The shelter on the north side was even larger, being a vast high cavern nearly a hundred metres long. Most of its back wall ceiling was conglomerate, but there were areas of smooth, rather friable sandstone. The living area was at the western end, and had a few small paintings of a secular nature. High on the wall of the eastern end, above a ledge, were three life-size sorcery figures, two men and a woman. One of the men was inverted.

The chopper returned three days later. The pilot had asked us to find a large clearing for take-off, and we located one from the top of a hill. We carried our gear there and lit a smoke fire as beacon. While we were waiting we suddenly realised we were on an old corroboree ground. It was a circular clearing about forty metres in diameter, with a sandy centre, now used as a cattle camp. Under surrounding shady trees we found the large flat stones used as working platforms. It was a very fitting launch pad to depart that part of Quinkin country.

Dick and I had an exhibition coming up so we went to Jowalbinna to paint. He had worked as a stockman on the Gulf cattle stations when young, and was always glad to see the horses, so we took the occasional day off from painting to explore the eastern scarps of Garden Creek, a part of the Quinkin reserves. We rode up a convenient ridge and tethered the horses while we explored the cliff base on foot. There was little art in that part of the creek, and in three days of exploring we found only one site containing ten figures, including four little black emus, an engraved boomerang, dotted beehives and stencilled boomerangs.

The next packhorse trip was organised to explore the headwaters of Shepherd Creek. Wally, Matt and Steve were keen to see the country, and joined Dick and myself. Some of the horses were fresh and frisky, and mine threw me twice before he tired of it, but they all quietened down once we left the home paddocks and they sensed a new adventure.

About sixty head of wild cattle went lowing and bawling up the creek ahead of us. We saw large mottled eels in the clear creek water and the tracks of small crocodiles where they had been sunning on sandbars. By late afternoon we were looking for a good camp site to hobble out the horses, when we came on a deep gorge coming in from the north-west. It was walled by red cliffs high up and I had a sudden urge to explore it. A grassy box flat lay just ahead, so we decided to camp there and explore the gorge next day.

Early next morning Dick and I set off to explore the gorge on foot, while Matt, Steve and Wally went to look for shelters I had located from the air, situated on a high terrace several kilometres upstream on the left side. The scree-covered sides of the gorge were extremely steep and scrubby and we were glad to reach the base of the cliff, with easier walking along the wallaroo track. Almost immediately we began finding isolated and mostly faded figures of people and animals, in small shelters and on open rock faces. About a kilometre up the gorge on the east side we found a gallery of old faded figures, and just around the corner a group of large, stark white figures, most of them outlined and decorated with red.

The white clay figures were in a high corner of an open, rocky shelter, protected by a very high overhang, but the lower parts of a couple of paintings had been exposed to windblown rain and had run down the rock. There were six men, a horse, a crocodile and a stone axe. The largest man was less than two metres tall, wore trousers and boots, had a long rifle under one arm, and had a red line drawn across his brow to indicate the peaked cap of a Black Police trooper. The large white stone axe was poised above his head as though about to smash his skull. Another large man also appeared to be wearing trousers, but had no rifle or peaked cap. The other four smaller men appeared to be sorcery figures but were not identified as Black Police. The white horse looked more like a kangaroo, but inverted horseshoe shapes were painted on the bottom of each leg. All the figures were fresh and may have been painted early this century.

The site was spectacularly located at the base of the high red cliff, and offered a panoramic view of the rugged gorge country. Far below on Shepherd Creek we could see our horses grazing on the grassy flat. I remembered Caesar Le Chu's stories of his childhood, and how the black troopers had pursued his family through these wild gorges, but they had always eluded them by climbing steep slopes where horses could not follow, then they went up through a dark tunnel and came out on top of the cliff, from where they could abuse the police with impunity. Caesar said he had seen paintings but couldn't remember where, as he was only five or six at the time. I wondered if the main black trooper portrayed there was Harry Mole, who had been stationed at Laura from late last century till the late 1950s.

We continued up the gorge, which turned back to the east and narrowed. Progress through it was difficult, but melodious, as the gorge was alive with scores of currawongs, filling the vivid morning air with bell-like music. There were no more shelters and there appeared to be no way out of the gorge—until we descended into the creek bed and followed it into a gloomy tunnel under massive black rocks, which brought us out on top of the plateau; the Le Chu escape tunnel.

The hated Black Police had never taken any of Caesar's clan, the Oco Carnigal. They had lived free until Caesar was about fifteen, when his parents decided to 'come in', and they all went to work for Maitland cattle station, south across the ranges.

We decided to call it the Le Chu Gallery, on Currawong Creek. We turned west and struck the head of another gorge, which contained a beautiful, fern-fringed pool of crystal-clear water. The shelter above it was unsuited for camping, but contained one painting, a love-magic figure of a woman in red and white. I suggested it might be a favourite trysting place for lovers, but Dick thought it to be a nice cool place where love-struck men sat to sing the magic love songs of the moon.

The next gorge contained no shelters, but near the point of the upper scarp on the western side, we came on a good gallery containing large, strong, dark red and white figures of four dingoes and a woman. The largest dingo was more than a metre long. They were in a shallow recess in the wall a few metres above ground level. It was obviously another site of dingo Dreaming.

153

In late afternoon we descended a steep, knife-edged ridge toward our camp, and saw Matt and the others returning along the creek. They had found about two hundred excellent figures in several spectacular shelters in the high terraces. They reported more dingoes, big yams, a long red snake, groups of flying foxes, large humans, kangaroos and other animals. It had been another successful day.

One of my best aerial prospects was in the grand red gorges of the upper Mosman River region. In a side gorge west of the main Mosman, I had noted a long grey cliff, and a big fall-out had occurred in its base, leaving what appeared to be a long deep shelter. An earlier attempt with Eddy had failed to find it, and the special feeling I had for the place strengthened every time I flew over the wild area. Dick and I decided to make another search for it.

We drove up onto the Great Divide along the old, rough and hair-raising Cobb and Co. coach track. At an appropriate place we left the track and drove east through the bush, sometimes crashing our way through dense stands of stunted ti-tree until we reached the rim of Mosman Gorge.

The gorge was a side branch and we walked along its northern cliff until we came out on a point shaded by tall bloodwoods. It offered splendid views of the red-walled gorges of the upper Mosman. It was all contained within the boundaries of the Quinkin Reserves, and was such a beautiful place we thought it should have a name. Dick suggested Percy's Point, and I thought it a jolly good idea.

It was obvious that we were too far south for the long grey cliff, but the area looked interesting so we spent most of the day down in the gorges and found five sites, the largest containing about seventy figures. We then drove north until we came to the head of another side gorge, which ran north for about a kilometre before turning east into the main gorge.

We walked down on to the lower terrace above the gorge and found shelters on the west side of it. The largest had about two hundred little stick figures of men, or boys, painted in panels on several parts of the back wall. It was a good wet season camp site, and exhibited many signs of having been a 'boy seclusion' place. Such places usually had many small hand stencils, but Dick thought that there they had used a small stick figure to represent each initiate passing through it.

Coming out of the last shelter I looked north and saw the long grey cliff we had been seeking, and could see there was a huge, long shelter under its base. From where we stood there appeared to be no way down into the sheer-walled, deep gorge. It was near sundown so we decided the grey cliff would have to retain its secrets until we could make a return trip.

154

Dick had family problems on his return home, and had to go to Mt Isa. He was not able to accompany Eddy and I when we left Jowalbinna in November to investigate the long grey cliff. Up on the Divide we were able to follow our previous wheel tracks through the Mitchell grass, which was dry then and of a pale, red ochre colour. In one clearing three stately plains turkeys stalked through the grass.

After about two kilometres the country began to fall away into the gorge ahead, and when it became steep and stony we left the vehicle and walked down a rocky, forested ridge on to the rim of the deep gorge. It offered a splendid panoramic view of rugged wilderness; orange-red cliffs opposite were partly screened by lush, golden green foliage of large bloodwoods. Further north-east the gorge widened rapidly and turned east, its far northern scarps softened by blue smoke haze from distant bushfires. The wind carried the sound of tinkling water from below, and immediately in front of us a natural stone stairway angled through a narrow crevasse down to the bottom of the cliff. It had the appearance of an old access track, still used by animals. We scrambled down it with mounting excitement.

A narrow rock ledge above fallen slabs led north around a corner, and a few metres past it we looked ahead to see a very long, deep, high shelter, its back wall covered with a mosaic of ochre figures. Whooping with excitement we jumped down over broken slabs and entered the southern end. There was a life-size, white and red emu, a large cream slurry fish, red dillybags, a dark red echidna, and several big portrayals of human beings, one of them horizontal. A small white scrub turkey and a red owl were nearer the charcoal-dark floor, on which there was a dished slab of sandstone with a large piece of orange ochre resting on it—art material left by the last artist, and conveying to us a feeling of intrusion.

A few metres further along, a two-metre-long white and red wallaroo, high on the wall, dominated that section of the gallery. The wallaroo's tail was superimposed on a large, plump-breasted white and red woman, who wore the crossed-bandolier strings indicating widowhood; she was in turn painted over a very large red barramundi, and she had a large red and white eel over one foot. The front paws of the wallaroo were placed squarely over a big red and white dingo. Below them, near the floor, stood a metre-high red and white bird of upright stance, with six toes on each foot, almost identical to the portrayal of the extinct megapode we had seen in the St George River site, and on the Deighton River.

The mosaic of superimposed figures extended over nearly forty metres, and contained virtually every motif common to the Quinkin art body. There were many yams, flying foxes, tortoises, echidnas, snakes, crocodiles, goannas, a jabiru, emus, scrub turkeys, large and small kangaroos, possums and many human beings. We counted about four hundred figures.

A special figure was a female Timara Quinkin, painted in dark red and having glaring, white eyes. She stood about three metres tall, with extremely long thin arms, and legs with stone axe bumps on elbows and knees. Her outspread arms were about five metres from fingertip to fingertip and were superimposed on many other figures.

Near the northern end of the gallery, a male ancestral guardian figure stood about three metres tall. Painted in white with red outline and interior decoration, he had wide-flung arms, with a left hand across the face of a male Timara Quinkin, as though giving him a back-hander across the mouth. Nearby a life-size emu, in white and red, stood over a clutch of white eggs.

There was a string of small figures along the wall just above the floor, including humans, birds, a delightful little dingo with ears pricked forward, and other animals, which we thought had been drawn by children, perhaps when Dad went away, leaving inviting ochre on a dished slab.

The shelter itself was immense, over fifty metres long and up to eight metres deep, with a flat ceiling about nine metres high. Some of the fall-out slabs remained in front of the shelter, providing additional protection against weather. Some of the slabs bore the engraved pits and emu tracks of early man. It was a magnificent shelter which had been home to hundreds of generations of first Australians.

The flat rock floor was exposed at the northern end, but had almost a metre of sand, charcoal and other occupational debris in the middle and southern sections. A circle of cooking stones marked the position of the last hearth, and near it was the butt of a grasstree, from which resin would have been extracted and mixed with beeswax, to seal string bindings. A broken spearhead had some of the mixture adhering to it.

There were no paintings reflecting the European invasion, or other contact, and we assumed that as the site was so close to one of the routes to the Palmer gold rush that it had been abandoned abruptly as the owners fled to the safety of the coastal rainforests.

The view from the shelter was magnificent. The red-walled gorge was about three hundred metres wide, and clothed with an open forest of bloodwood, stringy-bark, ironwood acacias and shrubs. Some lady-apple and nonda fruit trees were scattered down the steep scree slope, and pandanus palms along the creek indicated permanent water. We decided to call it Magnificent Gallery, realising how proud the inheriting generations of families must have been of their colourful wet season home, decorated with the symbols of everything that gave meaning, direction and purpose to their lives.

'. . . a male ancestral guardian figure stood about three metres tall . . .'

'Our first task was to record Echidna Dreaming . . . We decided to build
a scaffold platform to get alongside the figures.'

15
Garden Creek and Green Ant Mountain

The main headwaters of Garden Creek lay just west of Magnificent Gallery. In 1978 we established a camp on its eastern scarps and commenced exploration.

The first thing we found was the old wagon road, and a cutting blasted out of the top scarp, used to get the heavy, ore-crushing stamper batteries to the top of the plateau, on their way to the Maytown goldfields. The Cobb and Co. coach road had been too steep for the wagons, and they had used a more gentle ridge east of the coach road. At the top of the cutting they had cut a half-metre square hole in the bedrock to hold a winch-block to winch the wagons up the last steep pinch.

Just along the low cliff from the cutting we found a small shelter which featured three panels of colourful stick figures, scores of them in red, white and yellow. They were all male and appeared to be associated with rituals. We found six more galleries further south around the rim of Garden Creek, all of them living sites with secular paintings.

One of the shelters was on a terrace near the main stream of the creek, which poured a silver curtain of water off the sheer cliff to a tropical garden thirty metres below. Beautiful tree ferns and other broad-leafed shrubs and trees sparkled with water droplets, survivors in that small oasis from giant rainforests of ages past.

We were looking at paintings of eels and kangaroos when Eddy said, 'What's that squeaking?' I replied that it was probably tree branches rubbing together in the wind. Then louder squeaking was heard coming from a low tunnel in the back wall. We knelt down and looked in to see five tiny dingo pups taking a lively interest in our presence. They were only three or four weeks old and still unsteady on their feet.

Poor Dog had been killed in a vehicle accident the year before and I realised it was a splendid opportunity to replace him with a dingo. The pups were out of reach so I went out of the shelter to get a stick on which to rig a noose, and almost collided with the dingo mother. She was carrying a young echidna, and, giving me a startled look, dropped it and fled.

I wasn't surprised to see the dead echidna, having observed the techniques old Dingo employed to overcome the prickly problem. At first sight, sound or scent of danger the echidna moves to any place where it can start digging in, which means anywhere except solid rock, and without exposing even a toe, is half-buried in seconds, with only its unassailable spiny back exposed. A hungry dingo will lie quietly behind the buried echidna, waiting patiently for as long as it takes for the echidna to feel sure it is safe to venture on. Echidnas have a long special grooming claw on each back foot, and the dingo waits for a claw to show, seizes it, flips the echidna on its back, and slashes into the soft underbelly before the echidna can roll up into a ball. Dog usually spoiled Dingo's act by yapping in frustration at the stalemate, until Dingo gave up in disgust.

The most curious and adventurous of the tiny pups was female, so I lassoed her and pulled her out. The fur was dark grey with just a tinge of the warm golden orange which would be her mature colour, and the tip of the tail and the four feet were pale cream. She looked more like a lion cub than a dingo pup. I named her Lasca, and following Aboriginal custom, put her nose into my sweaty armpit to bond her to me.

Dingo came rushing out to greet us when we returned to the pub, but when I produced the pup out of my shirt she snarled, gave both of us a baleful glare and stalked off, to ignore me for days, until I put Lasca back in my shirt and flew down to Cairns to place her in the care of our delighted five-year-old Aboriginal foster-daughter, Patty. Aboriginal children and dingo pups were made for each other.

The Koolburra plateau was the westernmost portion of the Quinkin country sandstone. It lay about fifty kilometres west of Laura, rearing out of grey-green eucalypt forest, and looked very interesting from the air. Eddy and I decided to drive out and commence exploration of its north-western parts.

We found it was possible to drive in among huge blocks of sandstone scattered through the forest at the base of the low plateau, and saw red hand stencils before we got out of the vehicle. We found seven art sites on the north-east point, which was called Green Ant Mountain.

The largest site was a very good living shelter and its back wall was covered with a mass of superimposed engravings and paintings. The ancient engravings of meandering lines, enclosed geometric shapes and pits were fully patinated, and in many places disappeared underground. A much more recent style of engravings had been superimposed on parts of the old engravings. There were many pounded lines, both straight and meandering, kangaroo rear foot-tracks, a fully battered out flying fox, and what looked like a human foot-track, and an engraved, large, wide, human hand print. The latter two may not be human prints, but could represent footprints of one of the extinct megafauna, a large wombat or a diprotodon. A few bichrome paintings of humans, and a crocodile, had been superimposed on the engravings.

Further round to the south-west we found seven more sites, some under outliers near the foot of the scarp, and others in shelters on the tessellated top cliff. It was obvious that Koolburra plateau contained a very large body of art which might differ significantly from the Laura art. We estimated it would take about two years to explore and record the entire plateau.

There were still many unexplored pockets of country in the rugged gorges and plateaux of Jowalbinna, and whenever one of us had a spare day we would look at another section; if there was a useable shelter there was always something, from a few faded red hand stencils to a solitary ancient engraving.

Steve inspected a section of Shepherd Creek scarps we had always ridden past, because from below there appeared to be no adequate shelters. He climbed up and soon found a small shelter which was not useable because of a steeply sloping rock floor, but it contained a few dark red figures of humans in an old linear style. A little further west around the cliff base he saw a short, almost vertical tunnel among big slabs still jammed against the cliff face. With a little climbing and wriggling he got up through it and found Yam Dreaming.

It was instantly recognisable as a ceremonial site, but a very ancient one, and it was concerned with yams and flying foxes. A yam man presided. The shelter was on a broad rock ledge, with large tumbled slabs on its outer edge forming the entrance tunnel, and the cliff face leaned out over to protect it. There was a splendid panoramic view across the tops of bloodwoods to the northern cliffs of the gorge, and away east to the red bluffs of Jowalbinna.

Yam man was about half-a-metre tall, and finger drawn in dark red. He was the epitome of a man in the process of turning into a clump of yams; his ears were becoming yams, and yams were sprouting from his elbows and knees. His penis and testicles were already yams. A thin skin of silica sealed him into the rock. He was very reminiscent of the finger-drawn, first version of the ancestral beings at Split Rock.

There were several large drawings of yams in dark red, portraying two different species. They were over a metre high and two of them were clumps of tubers emanating from a central point; some tubers were phallic shaped. The top branched into several vines, some of which meandered for metres across the rock face, and mingled with groups of hanging flying foxes. The yam drawings were probably portrayals of the native grapevine with its tubers.

The flying foxes were painted as life-size, dark red silhouettes, hanging upside down in groups, with their leathery wings wrapped around themselves. Some of them were almost obliterated by milky silica skins, and parts were missing where exfoliation had occurred. There were no paintings on top of the silica skin, and those under it probably had their origin in some remote time before the great droughts of many thousands of years ago.

Down in the dark crawl tunnel, gleaming with polished silica, one could almost see the shining faces of the children of early man, crawling up toward their initiation ceremony, and their ensuing rights to join in the feasts of roasted flying foxes and yams.

A week later Matthew climbed up the steep ridge to view Yam Dreaming. On the east side of the ridge was a broad gully, full of tangled vine scrub, huge blocks of sandstone, and many large nonda and lady-apple trees. It was a scrub turkey habitat, and on the way back he entered among the tumbled rocks and found Yam Camp.

Yam Camp was one of the best living sites on Jowalbinna and the charcoal-dark floor attested to its constant wet season occupations. It was a large overhang with leaning slabs creating tunnels for extra living space, and every smooth area of the walls and ceiling contained layers of paintings of all shades of ochres, portraying people and animals. The largest figure was a huge, irregularly shaped catfish, over three metres long. It was in silhouette and was dark red with white outline and decorating dots. On top of it were several crudely executed small white human figures, one of them a plump-breasted woman with thin stick arms wide-flung.

Underneath all the paint on the back wall was a large panel of geometric engravings of early man, so old and timeworn, covered first with silica, then layers of ochre, that no meaningful interpretation could ever be made of them. The lower part of the engraved panel had broken away a long time ago and was probably buried deep in the floor. It was a choice archaeological prospect.

There were two small tunnels in the back wall, about two metres above floor level. A white Quinkin had been painted on the ceiling of one, and it appeared to be hovering in midair as it flew out of the tunnel. The other tunnel contained fragments of bark, and a few human bones, including a skullcap, all that remained of poor old grandma or grandpa. Stone tools, including a small stone axe, lay about the floor.

Lasca had grown into a fine dingo and we took her along on our next exploration trip into the lower parts of the massive Mosman Gorge. It had taken many months for old Dingo to accept Lasca as part of our team, and to cooperate as a hunting pair. We camped on a shady waterhole at the mouth of the gorge, and as it was hot November, left at dawn next morning to explore along scarps to the west of the main gorge. Dick had not done much walking for some time and decided to explore a small gorge and return to camp before the midday heat. Eddy and I headed west to commence at the point where Dick would finish.

There were very few shelters along the cliffs and by noon we had found only two. The first, on a point running out to the north, had about thirty figures, most of them being of humans, but including a very large red snake. Several kilometres further west we found the cliffs were much lower, but in a long, low shelter we found another twenty human figures, most of these damaged by water seepage.

It was a hard slog in fierce heat back to camp. We were following a cattle pad along a dry creek when suddenly two scrub bulls burst out of low bushes to confront us. They were big, grey and black beasts, with huge gleaming horns, and began pawing up the dust and bellowing. I realised they were probably bulls which had beaten bulldoggers during the last muster and were no longer afraid of men on foot. It was also the beginning of the breeding season when all bulls were stroppy. They were less than thirty metres away and I had forgotten to strap on my revolver. I warned Eddy to stand our ground and to give a mighty yell if they charged, when Lasca suddenly leapt up out of the creek bed and confronted the bulls, to be joined a second later by Dingo. The bulls turned and bolted, hotly pursued by the dogs.

We collapsed in shade for a rest and to let the adrenalin burn off. It was clear that Lasca had recognised the confrontation and taken appropriate action, as she had been in a cattle muster and knew about charging bulls.

Dick had found three sites in the small gorge, one had six figures, another he estimated at about eighty figures, and one with a solitary sorcery figure.

We entered the main gorge next morning and within two kilometres found a small site with fifteen figures, including a linear Imjim Quinkin. Then Eddy called us down to see an excellent shelter under an outlier on the terrace. It had over a hundred figures, including a red horizontal man two metres long, and a red and white eel well over two metres long.

Dick's best find was a rain-making site and he took us up a terraced hill to see it. It was a large outlying slab just below the top terrace on the south-west corner. The upper parts and top of the sandstone block were covered with dark grey lichen, and a shallow overhang provided shelter for some paintings on a pale pink and yellow back wall. Viewed from a distance the ten-metre-high rock could be perceived to symbolise a black-topped thunderstorm with pale curtains of rain falling from it.

The ochre paintings in the shelter were all faded. On the left side there were three human figures in red monochrome, all portrayed with arms wide-flung. The first was a man about a metre tall, his lower parts completely faded; about two metres further right there was a large woman almost two metres tall, and another three metres to a smaller man. Above the human figures there were six red figures which appeared to represent lightning bolts, each having five or six wavelike lines emanating from a round ball, spraying down like forked lightning. Each figure was being struck on the head by a lightning bolt.

Below the lightning bolts a series of red vertical stripes each about two centimetres wide and ten centimetres long, represented falling rain. Further right there was a separate panel of similar stripes about 1.5 metres square. It was less faded than all the other figures and was either more recent, or had been repainted.

It was a very explicit rain-making site, but the human figures being struck by lightning suggested it had a dual role, and that signs of sorcery were present here, as well as rain-making symbols employed to conjure up the first October storms.

Walking back down the ridge we saw a stand of four small ironwood trees, each with an oval scar about the size of a bullroarer, and we wondered whether bullroarers had been used in the rain-making ceremony.

We had taken Dr Josephine Flood, archaeologist from the Australian Heritage Commission, to see the main engraved site at Green Ant, and she was determined to raise an expedition to excavate it, while we continued exploration and recording of rock art. A recession in Australia had dried up all funding for scientific field work, and we were pleased to accept funding from American Earthwatch of Boston, which funded scientific field expeditions in many disciplines around the world by recruiting volunteers who worked on the expeditions and paid a share of the costs.

Most of the volunteers were Americans, a cheerful lot who were keen for adventures in the outback, though some were astonished at how far outback Green Ant really was. The logistics of transporting, camping and catering for about twenty people in a remote region were formidable, but Dick and Beverley gave a hand and in one day we transported them from Cairns to Green Ant tented camp, where Jo Flood was soon showing them the site to be excavated.

Dick and I headed the small exploration team and commenced systematic investigation of the plateau. We soon found that the north western parts of it were largely associated with old red hand stencils. There was one very interesting composite stencilled white figure which appeared to represent a centipede. The composer had used his bent little finger to form all the legs of the centipede.

In another small shelter nearby we found an old returning boomerang under a low ledge. Small softwood parts of it had been chewed off by termites. The gorge below was probably a fly-way for flying foxes streaming out of their camp in late evening in search of blossom. One could visualise the hunters, silhouetted against the last glare of the sun, standing on the edge of the cliff hurling boomerangs out into the stream of bats; if one failed to strike a flying fox it returned to the thrower, and when it did strike a bat they both fell together and were easily retrieved. We named it Boomerang Creek.

Our best find was further east on Lakes Creek. During an aerial survey I had seen a large shelter at the base of the cliff on the east side, and sent Graham, an Australian, up to look at it while the rest of us continued along the creek. About a kilometre into the gorge we came on a huge outlier with an excellent shelter under its west side. There were a few paintings on the wall and ceiling, including a fat, red, fork-tailed catfish, but the most important feature was the mass of ancient engravings all over the walls. Like those at Yam Camp they were so worn and smooth with time that, except for round pits and emu tracks, there was no identifiable design. The floor was dark grey with charcoal and we estimated it could contain up to three metres of deposit, and was an excellent excavation site.

On the way back we saw Graham coming down a steep ridge from the top scarp. He was grinning like a Cheshire cat and was very willing to go back up and show us his remarkable discovery.

There was a very long shelter under the cliff, much of it littered with rock-falls, and there were groups of paintings scattered along the back wall. The main group of large figures were at the eastern end. The rock floor below them had fallen out and disappeared long ages ago, leaving the paintings stranded three to four metres above the present ground level.

Most of the figures were strange anthropomorphs in silhouette white, with dark red outlines, having both animal and human traits. By close examination we ascertained that the figures portrayed people, both men and women, changing into echidnas. The men had headdresses looking like rayed spines of an echidna, all with short legs, arms and penises. The women were generally more slender, with breasts displayed laterally. Their headdresses were composed of two vertical projections, looking like the lateral view of a partially open echidna snout. The women wore short, fringed pubic aprons. In many of the figures only the red outline remained, others retained traces of the original solid white infill.

It was a ceremonial site of considerable antiquity and we named it Echidna Dreaming. The main living site of recent times was under the outlier down by the creek.

The following year we returned with another Earthwatch team to continue work on the Koolburra plateau, camping at the entrance to the gorge on Lakes Creek, where Jo Flood and Nicky Horsfall were going to excavate the site under the outlier. Our first task was to record Echidna Dreaming.

Getting drawing grids over the large figures high on the wall was a problem. We decided to build a scaffold platform about three metres high to get alongside the figures, and cut long poles from the bush on top of the plateau and lowered them down the cliff. It took Dick, Eddy and myself two days of hard work to cut and lash the poles in place.

We recorded about twenty sites along Echidna Creek, then went further east to explore Black Dog Creek.

There were a lot more paintings of echidna people on Black Dog Creek, with many variations on the theme. There was one composition where a faded pair of echidna people, a man and a woman, were enclosed by a painted double arch; the male figure had an exceptionally long toe on each foot, to symbolise the long grooming claw of an echidna. We found several pairs of humans under arches and came to the conclusion the compositions represented people living in domed structures, probably huts.

Many of the figures were high out of reach on the back walls and ceilings of the shelters, because the original floor from which they had been painted had eroded out and disappeared. We found forty sites on the creek, with most of the figures extremely old and faded, and very little recent work.

Aerial surveys had revealed some excellent prospects in the south-east side of the plateau, which overlooked the Kennedy River. We took a small party around there and soon found more sites containing the old echidna figures. After lunch in one of the shelters we decided to take a short cut across the plateau to where a short gorge held one of the best prospective sites.

We were walking south along the scree slope of the plateau when Lasca suddenly lunged in under a rock slab in pursuit of something, then hastily backed out and gave me a meaningful look which clearly said 'You have a go'. I looked under and saw a large echidna desperately trying to dig down in the stony ground.

Echidnas were rare animals so we captured it and put it in a backpack to take it back to camp for photographs before releasing it again. It gave me time to look about and consult my map and I realised we were heading in the wrong direction; the gorge we sought was back to the north-west. I felt as though the echidna people had sent a messenger to turn us the right way.

Some of us crossed to explore the left side of the gorge, while Eddy and others continued along the right side. We found nothing but as we approached the scrub-filled head of the gorge we heard excited chattering and went on to see Dick and Eddy explaining figures to Americans Jack and Jane Scott.

It was an excellent large shelter and housed scores of painted figures, most of them faded echidna people arranged in rows. Dick pointed out a large faded dark red snake shape under the echidna figures, which he thought was a portrayal of a rainbow serpent. It was our most important discovery since Magnificent Gallery. There were no figures which could be said to be of recent origin, and we thought it to be an ancient ceremonial site. We named it Ancient Dreaming.

Jo Flood obtained radiocarbon dates of about 8500 B.P. for Green Ant's lowest occupation levels, and about 7000 B.P. for the base of Echidna shelter, and concluded that occupation of the Koolburra plateau had commenced about 8500 years ago, and all of the art, including the ancient silica-skinned engravings, were younger than that date.

The early man site excavated by Andrée Rosenfeld had yielded a carbon date of 13 200 years B.P. as a minimum age for the engravings there, which had no silica skin, and in many ways were reminiscent of the younger figurative engravings at Green Ant. The geomorphologists thought that the silica skins had evolved in a humid phase of more than 18 000 years ago, and I thought it probable that the layer of sand-stone which had composed the original floors of the shelters in the Koolburra plateau, had eroded out during that wetter phase, leaving the old echidna figures stranded high on the walls.

In the Sandy Creek excavation we had found a layer of cemented gravelly material almost a metre thick, which had represented a hiatus of an unknown length of time, between the recent occupation and a very ancient occupation. The hiatus probably represented many thousands of years of drought, and the two Koolburra excavations had not penetrated the hiatus layer. The dates obtained represented only the last modern occupation.

My conclusions were that though some reworking and additions may have been made to the younger engravings at Green Ant in more recent times, all the engravings at Green Ant and Echidna sites, and the Ancient Dreaming paintings, belonged to the remote side of the hiatus. Only further, deeper excavations can solve the mystery.

We wondered about the extent of the clan country of the ancient echidna people; it may have been the entire Kennedy River drainage system, but the remaining visible evidence would only be found in the regions containing sandstone shelters. We decided to explore the distant headwaters of the river, where it split into two main tributaries, the St George and Little Kennedy rivers. The Little Kennedy drained some of the south-westernmost sandstone plateaux so Eddy, Steve and myself went out there to commence preliminary exploration.

We camped on the Little Kennedy and next morning climbed up to a terrace on the west side, and immediately found ancient art in a small shelter. It consisted of a panel of rows of round shallow pits, each about three centimetres across. The panel was about two metres long by over half a metre high, and most of it was coated with gleaming brown silica. Pits in the middle section of the panel had been battered out again in quite recent times and had not yet weathered much, indicating that the ancient site had retained significance for much later people.

Steve turned south along the terrace and Eddy and I went north to look at outlier blocks, before going up to the main cliff face. We found the usual small sites with faded red figures, and eventually came on a low cliff which contained a long, low shelter with a metre-long white and red eel, and some white tortoises.

There was a low shallow recess in the southern end, and I knelt down and looked in to see a massive white and red figure on the flat ceiling. It was a catfish, in white silhouette with dark red outline, interior red lines and dots. It was three metres long and over half a metre wide, and was surrounded by other aquatic creatures, including five shrimps, tortoises, catfish and eels, all looking like court attendants surrounding a monarch.

It was a ceremonial site of recent times, with the large hidden catfish symbolising the way a big catfish hides under an overhanging bank, surrounded by lesser fry. The large catfish had been repainted in recent times, as old red dots covered with a new coat of white showed dimly through. We called it Catfish Dreaming.

Steve found the main, modern living site on the terrace to the south, and said it contained large, long figures that he thought might represent beehives. We had not found any echidna figures but decided to return to base camp and bring an Earthwatch team back to do recording and continue exploration.

When we returned I went up to record Steve's main camp site, while Eddy went to do Catfish Dreaming with the Scotts from Florida, who were to continue exploration. I found Steve's beehives to be actually large carpet snakes, a male and a female, their dotted decoration had misled him to see them as beehives full of bees. They were surrounded by groups of dark red flying foxes, the main seasonal food of the big snakes.

The flying foxes usually turn up in August in time for the main flowering of the melaleucas growing along the creeks and rivers. The huge colonies of several hundred thousand animals camp in the same patch of vine scrub each year, and stay until the October storms, streaming out each evening to feed on blossom, and returning at dawn. The big snakes live around the flying fox camp all year, having about three months of feasting to fatten them for nine months of fasting.

Eddy's party returned late evening with news of a spectacular find of ancient paintings, so we were all out early next morning to go up and see them.

It was an impressive huge shelter in the base of a high cliff overlooking a deep gorge. There was a large inner cave which contained very old and faded, but beautifully drawn, echidna people; they were faded white silhouettes with very fine red outlines and internal decoration. The figures were so splendidly proportioned and symmetrical, that even with a grid to assist in copying them, I found it difficult to adequately reproduce the beautiful figures.

The echidna people had obviously lived in an era of plenty, able to devote much time to their art and religion. They had lived all along the Kennedy River in a remote time the other side of the great droughts. The people who came to reoccupy the Koolburra plateau about 8500 years ago were apparently like the people who had reoccupied the nearby Hann River region; times were harder and life more difficult, and the pragmatic people had little spare time to contribute much to the stylistic sequence.

I had a growing conviction that everything about the Aboriginal people, their culture and art, were four or five times older than the 10 000 years of the Holocene, in which many investigators were trying to bracket them. If European people were able to evolve art upwards of 30 000 years ago, why should the Australians be any different? It seems the concept of *terra nullius* haunts us still.

The following year we based Earthwatch operations on Jowalbinna. Frank Woolston came up to be quartermaster, and he and Dick ran the base camp while Eddy and I led teams on field expeditions. Each team of volunteers spent the first few days recording sites on Jowalbinna, as an introduction to the work, then made a couple of field trips of five or six days, then the last few days at Jowalbinna transferring field drawings on to canvas for permanent colour copies of each rock art site for the Australian Institute of Aboriginal Studies (AIAS).

Eddy and Matt took a team to the Mosman River and set up camp on a river terrace under the towering bluffs of the gorge, to commence recording and continue exploration. We needed more trained recorders to oversee the teams, and two Cairns women, Noelene Cole and Mary Haginikitas had volunteered. I took them, with others, to camp near Giant Horse and make an intensive recording of all sites in the area.

We had decided to employ helicopters to penetrate more remote areas of the Quinkin wilderness. There were several small cattle-mustering helicopters working local cattle stations and I had booked one to pick up Eddy, Matt and party from their Mosman camp, and deposit them on the extremely rugged headwaters of Yamba Creek, a tributary of the Mosman, and they would spend three or four days exploring their way back to camp. It seemed a good idea.

When we finished at Giant Horse we went out to join the Mosman party. It was perhaps fortunate for me that by then they had had two days of rest to get over the Yamba Creek trip. Things had not gone well.

There had been great excitement when the helicopter arrived at the camp early one morning. The small mustering chopper could uplift only one passenger with backpack at a time, so Eddy went first to select and be dropped off at the most promising place on Yamba Creek, then waited while Matt and the others were shuttled in. Jack and Jane Scott said they had a powerful feeling of isolation when the departing chopper left them standing among rocks in that remote place.

They found a few faded paintings almost immediately and set off down the creek in high hopes. Then Eddy stepped on a three-metre carpet snake, which objected very strenuously; they soon ran out of water and found the only supply to be in the creek hundreds of metres below. It was very hot and their water-carrying capacity so small, that by the time they had climbed back to the top of the scarp they had again finished their water.

During four days of hard walking they found no more art sites until only about three kilometres from camp, and were then rewarded with at least ten good art sites on Terraced Hill. They reeled into camp well after dark on the last day, looking and feeling like the Retreat from Moscow.

After listening to their harrowing story I immediately revised plans for the next helicopter expedition which I was to conduct a couple of weeks later. The chopper would return and lift us out again after three days of exploration.

We found scores of art sites along the lower Mosman, and they conformed to the general pattern of the Laura art, with many old faded figures in poor living shelters, reflecting the heavy populations of long ago, in wetter times. There were old ceremonial sites with sacred figures, obviously still significant in recent times, and the best living sites with their recent bright paintings.

High on the eastern cliff of the gorge, Matt found an excellent painting of a koala. It was a dark red silhouette with a white outline, much brighter than the first faded koala on the exposed rock face on Kennedy Creek. It was clear that koalas had been a part of the local fauna, and that something had caused their disappearance—perhaps a change in climate or disease.

When we returned to Jowalbinna to commence chart work we found that Dick had suffered a sudden illness and had been driven to Laura to meet the Flying Doctor for transport to Cairns. He returned a week later with grim tidings. He had stomach cancer.

On return to Cairns I went with Dick to see the doctor, who confirmed the diagnosis. Dick was philosophical, declined any operation, which the doctor said would be of little help, and said he would try and 'sing' himself better. We spent a couple of weeks together painting for an exhibition, and working on another children's picture book, before Dick returned to Mornington Island for the wet season.

We had found that the quality of scaled drawings of the rock art turned in by Earthwatch volunteers was often of a poor standard, so we recruited Noelene and Mary, who were very competent at drawing, to take over the major recording work, and kept the volunteers on exploring, and transferring the field drawings of the experts on to the canvas colour charts.

The next Earthwatch expedition was to explore more of the lower reaches of the Deighton River system. Access up along the river was too difficult so we decided to blaze a vehicle track along the top of the plateau which formed the watershed between the Deighton and Laura rivers.

We had 3 four-wheel drive vehicles to carry our gear and party of ten. I led with the Toyota truck to push through the scrub, followed by Jim Royle in the main passenger station-wagon, with Mary bringing up the rear in her smaller vehicle. The first day was fairly easy as we followed tracks we had pushed through in earlier years. The second day found us in very rough country, so I had an Australian farmer, Nev Ellis, driving the truck while I walked ahead choosing a track.

Water was a problem as we could carry only a limited quantity and there was none on the top of the ridge we followed. About midday we were passing the rock rim of a deep scrubby gorge when I heard the clamour of currawongs and realised the birds would be on a permanent spring, so we were able to refill our containers, and nearby found two good rock shelters containing old paintings, one of which portrayed a kangaroo with its joey's head poking out of the pouch.

During the morning of the fourth day we reached our destination, a string of beautiful waterholes in a spring-fed creek just below the top of the main scarp of a Deighton gorge and we camped just above them. Every night we were visited by possums after apples, quolls after meat scraps, and occasionally by dingoes looking for a handout. We found quoll tracks in the sandy floors of many of the rock shelters; in one place, a mother quoll had walked in and five or six young had dismounted from her back to scamper about after food scraps from our lunch of the previous day.

The paintings of very long fruiting vines were in almost every painted shelter we found. The fruit were portrayed as hanging on short stems about every twenty centimetres, and were shaped like elongated ovals. The dark red vines usually had other figures of humans and animals superimposed on them and appeared to be very old. Dick suggested they could represent native cucumbers, which were common to northern Australia and fruited during the wet season. We had not seen them growing, probably because we were usually not out in the bush during the wet season, and if they were so succulent then they were all eaten during the brief fruiting season, and wild pigs may have severely reduced the number of vines.

We returned to the Deighton at the end of the following wet season and found a vine of bush cucumbers suspended among bushes out of reach of pigs. The oval, red and cream striped fruit looked like miniature footballs, about three centimetres long. They were not very pleasant to eat raw, and later on we found a long vine of bush bananas, of which there were several species, and more likely to inspire people to make paintings of them, when they were more prolific during a wetter climate. Their botanical name is *Marsdenia viridiflora*.

That expedition proved to be the last for Dick. We returned to Cairns to open a joint art exhibition in July, and afterwards he decided to return home. He had felt the hand of the 'grim reaper' on his shoulder, and like all Aboriginal people, wanted to die in his own country. He had a wistful shopping spree to take presents home for all his family and flew to Mornington Island.

In late August I went over to spend a few days with Dick and found him to be very ill but cheerful. There seemed to be a telepathic link between us and in the past I had been astonished at the way he would chip into my thought stream as though I had been speaking aloud, sometimes about matters we had not discussed for months. So on a Sunday in late October 1985 as I was packing paintings to send to Sydney I was suddenly overwhelmed by a sense of sorrow, and I knew that Dick was heading for the new horizon of Yili-jilit-nyea. It was confirmed by phone.

The life of Dick Roughsey was the complete Australian Aboriginal rebuttal to the British declaration of a *terra nullius* Australia. Born into the undisturbed, ancient Aboriginal tribal traditions, his early years were spent enjoying and understanding that lifestyle. When aged about eight, Scottish missionaries arrived and gathered up the shy bush children and put them in dormitories for schooling in the ways of the white man.

During his four years in the dormitory Dick learned English, and to write it in a copperplate hand. From the Scots he learned and remembered every Scottish song and ballad, and years later astonished audiences around Australia by appropriately quoting Robert Burns, Shakespeare, Longfellow and a host of other classic poets, and like most highly intelligent people he had a sparkling wit.

After the brief schooling Dick and his mates were returned to their clan countries to resume traditional life with the old people, and he was a hunter and fisher for years until World War II intervened in his life and all the young Lardil men were recruited as stockmen for cattle stations around the Gulf. There Dick learned the finer points of cattle-duffing from his crafty employers.

When he tired of cattle work Dick got a job as deckhand on coastal boats trading around the Gulf and welcomed the opportunity to make friends among other tribes all around the Gulf, and from Thursday Island down to Cairns. He married a 'northwind' Lardil girl, Elsie Wilson, and they raised a family of six children.

After we met at Karumba Dick commenced his career as an artist, and went on to become the leading Aboriginal artist in Australia. Art fascinated him and he worked at it fourteen hours a day, seven days a week, having exhibitions in all major cities. He published an autobiography, *Moon and Rainbow*, became inaugural chairman of the Aboriginal Arts Board, and served in that capacity with great distinction for three years, travelling widely in Australia and overseas. In 1977 he was awarded an O.B.E. for outstanding contribution to art and Australian literature. Dick Roughsey was a most successful role model for all Aboriginal people, and was admired and loved by all.

One of my fondest memories of Dick is of him standing with his back to the camp fire, looking at the stars and reciting from Longfellow's 'A Psalm of Life':

Lives of great men all remind us
We can make our lives sublime,
And, departing leave behind us
Footprints on the sands of time.

Footprints, that perhaps another,
Sailing o'er life's solemn main,
A forlorn and a shipwrecked brother,
Seeing, shall take heart again.

'Blue Figures Gallery was the most densely superimposed mass of figures I had ever seen . . .'

16

The kadimakara

The opportunity to carry out further exploration of the Deighton River system occurred in 1986, when we were offered three teams of Venturers from Operation Raleigh, being conducted in Northern Australia under the aegis of Prince Phillip. Operation Raleigh was a British scheme to provide young people with adventure and opportunities to acquire leadership skills like those available in wartime, but under peacetime conditions. Not surprisingly wildernesses, like Cape York peninsula, were thought to be very suitable for these purposes. The Venturers were men and women aged from seventeen to twenty-four, and each team consisted of sixteen members, and was to stay for three weeks. This, as it turned out, meant that we had a solid nine weeks of exploration ahead of us.

We had some logistical assistance from the Australian Army to set up a base camp on our Deighton block of country by a large tree-shaded waterhole on the river. We split the teams in half, each taking turns at exploration or clearing tracks for the vehicles.

We commenced exploration from where Earthwatch teams had left off. The westernmost tributary we had first camped on had been named Echidna Creek, and we found many more sites on it, but none of special significance.

The next big tributary to the east had been named Quoll Creek, but not yet explored. We sent teams out in groups of four on five day backpacking hikes to explore the entire creek. The Venturers were keen as they had paid a lot to join the expedition, and soon began to turn in astonishing results. During the nine weeks they found 204 art sites, and relying on their drawings and written descriptions we were able to visit the most interesting sites.

The first to draw our attention was the description of life-size paintings of men and women in light blue, a colour we had not seen in the art body. They were in a long shallow shelter in the base of the top cliff, with a wide grassy terrace in front, and a view over the Deighton River from the east side.

Blue Figures Gallery was the most densely superimposed mass of figures I had ever seen, covering the ten-metre-long back wall; a shallow sloping ledge below the paintings bore the silica-polished engravings of early man. People had apparently sat on the ledge and leaned back against the lower painted wall and their oily skins and hair had removed every trace of paint of all lower figures. The process had probably been going on for thousands of years and the sandstone was so impregnated with body oils that any new paints could not permeate into it and were soon rubbed off. The remaining figures and parts of figures were nearly all bright and clear.

It was a secular living place with scores of the usual animal motifs with lots of garfish, eels, catfish and kangaroos. Most of the human figures were of a sorcery or a love-magic nature. There were at least six of the blue figures of men and women in the different layers, and they were all for sorcery, some horizontal and some inverted. The blue paint was actually a pale blue-grey clay, probably stained by a mineral like copper. It had been used to create only sorcery figures and must have had special significance, and came from a special place, like the flood-making clay from Mundoowa.

There was a low recess under the back wall at the east end and in it were some tattered cotton clothing, a piled up fish net made from bush string, and a small hand mirror. The mirror was heavy and in a rusted, handmade tin frame, apparently salvaged from a broken larger mirror. I wondered what dark visage had last gazed from it.

About two hundred metres further east we climbed up among large slabs to the top of the scarp where there was a narrow deep rift, with good shelters under each side of it, and some contained a few bright paintings of crocodiles, and men and women, the latter associated with sorcery. One cleverly arranged portrayal of a woman illustrated that she was not sitting correctly, with heel tucked into crotch, and was thus exposing her vagina. In the shelter opposite there was a similar painting but with the heel more modestly positioned. They were clearly didactic figures.

There was only slight evidence of camping in the shelters and we thought the narrow ravine was a 'safe refuge' place in the days of the black troopers. The main Blue Figures shelter would have been exposed to surprise raids by mounted troopers, while the ravine was hidden and had an escape route out either end. One of the Venturers climbed above the ravine and found part of an old shovel blade, most of which had been cut up for spear tips. Marks on the remnant suggested the steel had been heated until soft, then had a tomahawk placed on it and struck with a heavy implement to cut off a slice nine centimetres long and two wide. The last slice was only half done.

On the way back to camp we walked among big blocks of sandstone on a lower terrace and found a small site sheltered only by a leaning slab. There were four small red and white figures, a woman, a tortoise, a sleepy cod and a barramundi. It seemed to be a women's site associated with fishing.

A fairly common motif in the art of the lower Deighton was a little man, usually in linear dark red, carrying one or more goannas by the tail. On the east side of White Lady Creek we found one of these little men carrying seven goannas. It was in a string of associated small galleries in which all the paintings were micro-figures of people, catfish, eels, echidnas, a kangaroo with a joey in the pouch, three owls, and fruiting vines. In the southernmost small shelter there were five white stencils of tiny men, apparently modelled from wax, and stencils of tiny human feet, and stone axes about four centimetres long. There were five stencils of children's hands, so it may have been a children's play site, or the complex of sites may have been a place where children were taught the techniques of drawing, painting and stencilling.

One of the most exciting discoveries was made by two Venturers, Amanda and Andy. I had sent them to explore the western scarps opposite Blue Figures Gallery, and that evening the two approached me with the query, 'Were there horses or pigs in this country a long time ago?' When told there were no such animals in Australia before 1788, Amanda said, 'Well the painting is much older than that—it is a very old figure,' and produced a small pencil sketch of it. Andy said the drawing was a very good representation of the large animal, painted in faded, solid dark red and near two metres long. I suspected the painting depicted one of the long extinct marsupial megafauna, probably one of the species of diprotodonts. Unfortunately, early next day I had to go to Cairns for a week.

In Cairns I told my rock art colleagues about the new discovery, and Mary decided it was not a chance to miss and returned to the Raleigh camp with me. Early next morning we went up river to inspect the site.

The long cavern, under a dark grey cliff face, was almost two hundred metres above the river, and we hastened toward it. It soon became apparent that a direct approach was not the easiest, and we finally arrived by climbing and scrambling up an almost sheer rock face. We found later that the natural access was down from the top.

The gloomy shelter was about seventy-five metres long, and four metres high in front, but rock ledges filled much of the back of it, and the only clear living place was at the northern end. I saw a large faded red animal on the ceiling and was disappointed to see it had a head like a horse, and turned away to look at other figures further along. Mary said later that she had walked in and looked at the tail of the animal, thought it was a pig, and also walked away in disappointment.

There were decaying sheets of paperbark in the camping area, and a rolled parcel of bark jammed between two small slabs of rock. It contained the bones of a small wallaby. A few paintings on the ceiling above included a sea turtle. Further along a small stick had been lodged in a hole high on the wall to provide a hanging place to keep dillybags of food away from dogs and small children.

We returned to the big red painting and sat down to examine it thoroughly. There was no other painting near it and it was in silhouette dark red with traces of white outline, on a dark grey ceiling. Despite some exfoliation, all contours of the animal were clearly delineated, especially head, feet and tail. It was 1.6 metres long by 1.2 metres high. The thick body was 0.7 metres deep, and the head long and heavy, with face profile curved gently down to a slightly pronounced muzzle. Apart from the marsupial ears the head was horse-like. The legs were short in proportion to the heavy body, and each of the four feet were similar with four toes depicted. Spalling had removed part of the rear toes but enough remained to indicate they were similar to the front feet, which were intact and clear. The two front toes were long and splayed, pointing forward, the two rear toes were shorter and pointed outwards, opposed to each other. The shoulders and back were high, and curved down to a short, pig-like tail, 0.25 metres long, with eight neatly drawn bristles near the end. Genitalia and ears were marsupial in appearance.

Two dark red lines, about a centimetre wide, emanated from the nape of the neck; one line crossed the withers then emerged to curve over the back then down to cross over the body about 0.3 metres above the tail. The upper line emerged from the nape and roughly paralleled the back line about 0.25 metres above it and disappeared just above the tail. The lines appeared to represent ropes, rather than spears sometimes seen protruding from other animals.

The dark red animal above us did not look like any of the thousands of paintings of other animals so far discovered in the Quinkin art body. Despite its horse-like head and pig-like tail, it was clearly neither of those animals, which were also portrayed elsewhere in the art body, and all of them fresh and bright, being less than two hundred years old. The painting of the diprotodon would have been executed long before pigs and horses were domesticated anywhere in the world. The red body colour could be seen on the exfoliated areas which were pale grey in colour; whether it was from repainting or permeation from the original paint, could not be determined.

The front feet of the animal had only four toes portrayed and marsupials have five on their front feet, but a few metres away on the ceiling was a metre-high painting of a woman, in faded dark red with white outline, and looking to be contemporary with the diprotodon; she had only three toes on each foot, so apparently the artists of remote times had also stylised body traits.

It was a very formal figure, carefully and neatly executed for some ceremonial or ritual purpose. Like many ceremonial figures it may have been repainted carefully on more than one occasion especially the white outline, which adhered closely to the body colour all around the figure except under the belly line, where it dipped down to perhaps emphasise what was meant to be the pouch opening of a female animal.

Later on we had discussions with palaeontologists and some thought it could be the species named *zygomaturus trilobus*, a bullock-sized animal, rather than the rhinocerous-sized *diprotodon optatum*. Some anthropologists and archaeologists ignored the obvious antiquity of the painting and decided it was a horse or a pig.

We decided to call it 'Kadimakara', an ancient Aboriginal name for diprotodons.

There were no paintings or stencils in the shelter that had any appearance of being recent, and the paperbark suggested the place may have been used briefly as a safe refuge from the Black Police. A screen of trees and shrubs grew in front of it, but allowed observation of any activities along the river below. It was certainly safe against frontal assault.

We wondered how long ago the kadimakara had been painted and why. The ropes emanating from its neck hinted at animal husbandry. Many of the marsupials were easily tamed, especially wombats, and a kadimakara was very similar to a large wombat. Those gentle giants of the Dreamtime must surely have been one of the world's greatest and most easily harvested meat supplies.

The great droughts of more than 18 000 years ago, apparently turned the lush, green paradise of Australia into arid and semi-arid deserts, with only small pockets of moister country to provide habitats for severely diminished flora and fauna populations, and for man.

The drying out probably commenced gradually and was spread over several thousand years, with the human generations becoming increasingly alarmed over their diminishing food supplies, especially when the very large animals suffered terrible catastrophes like thousands of them dying in the bogs of Lake Callabonna. Those events certainly gave rise to the world's first conservation movement. People began to adapt their religious beliefs and began to conceive that their ancestors had transformed themselves into all the flora and fauna species on earth. Thus each clan would then see to the proper harvesting and conservation of the species of flora and fauna which they regarded as their own ancestors, and were their clan Dreamings.

Willy had told us of how the young men undergoing the man-making ceremonies were warned that if they didn't carry out the ceremony for each Dreaming animal in exactly the same way each year, then that animal would disappear from the face of the earth —and so would the people who depended on it for food. The great droughts had been so horrendous that the fear of their recurrence was burned deep into race memory.

As drought tightened its grip on the entire continent people would have done whatever was possible to enhance the survival of breeding populations of species, just as is done by farmers and graziers of today, by lopping kurrajong, bauhinia and other edible foliage, and driving them to another waterhole when the one they were on was drying up. The ropes portrayed around the neck of the kadimakara may well have been to help move an unwilling animal.

The shelter we were in overlooked a section of the Deighton Valley known to cattlemen as 'the secret pocket', a large area of open forest grazing land virtually walled in by sandstone scarps and rough steep hills, a natural paddock, an asset not likely to be overlooked by the highly intelligent people who had created the well-proportioned, symmetrical figures on the ceiling above.

Ice Age Australia had certainly not been *terra nullius*.

One firm believer in the concept of *terra nullius* had been Dr Robert Logan Jack, government geologist, who in 1895 read a paper on Aboriginal Cave Drawings on the Palmer Goldfield, before the Royal Society of Queensland:

> The figures about to be described are not produced to your notice on account of their artistic merits, which would hardly procure for them a place in the National Gallery. They are, in fact, not much above the level of the dawn of art displayed on school slates. As examples of the art of a race in a stage of intellectual infancy, and which race will certainly die before attaining manhood, they possess, however, a certain interest for ethnologists.

Dr Jack had made drawings of the paintings of animals and people he had seen in sandstone shelters on Chinky and Mun Gin creeks on the Palmer River goldfields, and suggested 'there is internal evidence that they are probably not more than twenty-five years old, and will not outlast a single generation'.

> No. 8 is a group or procession of animals, occurring on a vertical surface beneath a ledge. The peculiarity of the position is, that unless the artist stood ten feet high he must have clung with one hand to a ledge two feet below his 'canvas', while painting with the other, or stood on a platform, or been supported by his assistants. The first animal (in white) may be a pig. The second, third and fifth are unquestionably marsupials. The third has

long hind and short forelegs. The fourth seems to me not a marsupial at all—witness the bison-like head and the hoofed feet. The projections from the head of this animal I take to be horns, while those of the others are probably ears. My friend Peter (Black Trooper), I may mention, calls the whole group 'possum', but I cannot agree with him. The enigmatical fourth animal, if it is to be classed among cattle, is certainly not one of the Palmer breed. It is just possible that the artist may have seen and painted from memory one of the 'buffaloes' descended from the herd imported to Melville Island, by Captain Gordon Bremer.

Dr Jack reasoned that by their state of preservation and the techniques employed, the paintings were all about the same age and possibly the work of a single artist, and went on to say:

When first I lighted on the animal paintings, I thought for a time that I might be privileged to discover paintings of some of the extinct marsupials by contemporary artists, and so provide evidence not only of the co-existence of man and the extinct fauna, but also the forms of the latter. Some of the subjects, although decidedly marsupial, were so grotesquely unlike the present fauna that the hope seemed reasonable, but I was compelled to fall back on the comparatively prosaic explanation of imperfect drawing. The hope was finally dashed to the ground by the discovery of the Palmer cow, and still more by that of the man in the hat, which proved that the drawings did not date further back than the settlement of the district by white man, viz: 1873. It is to be remarked that the hat is the only instance in which the artist has taken any notice of clothing, even on subjects presumably European or Chinese.

Dr Jack's view of the Aborigines as a race in a stage of intellectual infancy was commonly held by most whites of those times, and was perhaps essential to support their own self-respect and creationist religious beliefs. The view that the Aborigines were subhuman was essential to give licence to the indiscriminate killing and dispossession of their land. It was thus logical for Dr Jack to assume that such a race would not be capable of creating any significant art form without exterior influence, and would, out of sheer ignorance, employ such impoverished techniques that 'the pictures can hardly be expected to outlive a single generation'.

Back in 1968, Dick, Caesar and myself had spent three days scouring the rugged Mun Gin Creek gorges for Dr Jack's recorded sites. We found three painted galleries but none of these resembled Dr Jack's description. The largest had about forty-five figures, including large white crocodiles and eight white paintings of a cheeky-looking bird, which Caesar promptly identified as Nungadin, the butcherbird.

After finding the painting of the diprotodon on the Deighton we wondered whether Dr Jack's 'Palmer cow' could be another of them, and decided to search Mun Gin Creek once again.

Seven of us spent two days carefully combing all the rock faces of Mun Gin Creek and found the same three galleries, but no others and arrived back in camp on the second day disappointed and baffled—all except Mary, who was reported to have been sighted edging along the escarpments toward Cradle Creek. She turned up just before dark and from a hundred metres away could be seen to be wearing a grin like she had a coat-hanger stuck across her mouth. The Dr Jack sites were on a branch of Cradle Creek.

Next morning we went across to inspect them and it was immediately obvious that the paintings described by Dr Jack in 1895 had changed very little—if at all, and that he had been selective in choosing the ones he drew, as there were scores of other paintings in four sites along the adjacent cliff face, and at least four more sites further round to the east.

The 'Palmer cow' was located in an excellent, much-used living site, no doubt located by Trooper Peter tracking people into it. Peter had identified the 'cow' panel as all possums, which they certainly were. The high withers on the one which suggested water-buffalo to Jack was actually caused by an exfoliation silhouetting a piece of unpainted sandstone above the shoulders, the actual painted backline of the animal was as straight as the other three. The two front feet of the 'cow' clearly had four toes each, not hoofs as Jack described them. The rear feet were more faded and could have been mistaken for hooves. Jack's group 6, 'a man and a woman carrying a log', was a red and white bichrome snake superimposed on older human figures. Other figures were Imjim-type Quinkins.

It could be assumed that Dr Jack wrote his paper years after having visited the site, relying heavily on imperfect memory and his few sketched figures. His eyesight must also have been less than perfect because signs of a great durability and antiquity were all about him. Only a couple of metres left of the 'Palmer cow', were two distinct rows of regularly spaced, deep, engraved egg pits, most of them having a smooth, thick silica skin, surely a curiosity to any geologist. About twenty metres to the west of the shelter there were large, faded red paintings of men, including an almost life-size guardian figure, painted on the side of a large slab of sandstone and exposed to every shower of rain. They were almost certainly the same when Dr Jack saw them a hundred years before. It is a curious fact that most people see only what they expect to see, and seldom more.

'We found three painted galleries . . . the largest had about 45 figures, including large white crocodiles . . .'

'The late afternoon sun was just at the right angle to sidelight a larger
than life engraved dingo . . .'

17

A ceremonial amphitheatre

Our next big discovery sprang from Noelene Cole's decision to do a thesis for a degree in archaeology, on the art sites of Shepherd and Brady creeks, for comparison with Jo Flood's report on the Koolburra plateau rock art. We made it a family affair during the Easter school holidays to show Noelene the sites on Jowalbinna she had not yet seen.

One of the tributaries of Shepherd Creek had been named Dingo Creek, not only because it was dominated by the towering Dingo Rocks, but because it was where old Dingo had taken her last bush-walk with me and Dick. On the western scarps of its headwaters we had found several small sites containing a few paintings, and one large ceremonial site containing scores of mainly faded, small, red hand stencils, which we had taken to be a 'boy seclusion' place.

Two of the sites were on either side of a shallow gorge in the top of the plateau, and we sat about among huge sandstone slabs while Noelene made drawings of the few figures. Her son Jeremy suddenly leapt to his feet and said, 'Look at the big dingo!' We all expected to see a big orange dingo slipping away among the rocks, but Jeremy said, 'There—on the rock wall.' The late afternoon sun was just at the right angle to sidelight a larger-than-life engraved dingo, making it stand out in sharp relief. It was fully abraded out, like a cameo in reverse.

It immediately dawned on me there would be more engravings and I began to search the floor of the gorge between the two painted sites, and saw that I was standing on large engraved figures of men and women nearly two metres tall. They had been fully pecked out and abraded smooth, and had patinated back to the same colour as the surrounding surface, and like it, were largely covered with lichen. Further in the gorge, Beverley and Mary were calling excitedly, and over near the dingo, our grandson, Matthew and the Cole family were obviously making exciting finds. I realised that I had walked over the large human figures several times in the past. They were difficult to see, and I, like Dr Jack, saw only what I expected to see—lichen-covered sandstone.

It was a stunning and totally unexpected discovery, nothing quite like it had been found anywhere in Australia. The fully pecked and abraded, larger-than-life figures of people, emus and dingo, were unique, and added an exciting new facet to the massive assemblage of the Quinkin art body. Being our bicentennial year, 1988, it was an apt discovery, coming almost exactly two hundred years after our ancestors had declared the continent to be *terra nullius*.

The first International Rock Art Congress was scheduled for Darwin the following August, where Noelene and I were to read papers, so we decided to compile a joint paper on the new find for the Congress. We decided to return to the site in the June school holidays to do an intensive recording of all the figures.

We had to camp in the site to record the engravings at night, using low side lighting to obtain sharp relief. There was no water on the plateau so Mary and I decided to backpack a total of 50 litres into the site the afternoon before we all carried camping and recording gear up there.

After storing the water in one of the rock shelters we noted that the upper end of the shallow gorge was choked with an impenetrable mass of spinifex, dead wood and shrubs, apparently isolated from bushfires by broad slabs of rock. Before we left we set it alight so we could examine the rest of the gorge next day.

We returned to an astonishing sight. The spinifex had burned fiercely and swept the gorge clear of shrubs and dead wood, to reveal a great natural amphitheatre. It was oval in shape, about eighty metres long and up to thirty-five metres wide. A passage into the north-western side led to a natural wing for the entry of staged ceremonial performances. The walls of the amphitheatre were from four to six metres high, and in the western end there was a shallow cave with a small tunnel in the back. A broad sandstone ramp on the east side gave access to it, and on the southern or left side, a shallow cave about forty metres long provided an excellent camping place. A few paintings of people and snakes were scattered about the back wall and ceiling. There was another small shelter on the right side, with a red Imjim Quinkin among other figures.

Deposits of sandy loam up to half a metre deep covered much of the inner amphitheatre, and there was a large nesting mound made by scrub turkeys in the centre of it. We swept a lot of burnt grass and litter away and found more engraved figures under it, and it appeared that the entire floor may contain engravings.

The human figures disappearing under the loam deposits were much smoother and appeared worn, more so than the engravings nearer the broad entrance slab, where there were two incomplete emus. Their outlines had been pecked and abraded out, but only their legs were fully abraded, and for some reason the work had been abandoned before completion.

There were many large emu and kangaroo tracks, apparently engraved at random. A panel of large human figures appeared to be an associated composition, with three figures side by side and another engraved horizontally across them, perhaps representing the ceremonial human table with initiate person lying across them. A smaller figure among them may represent a child.

One engraved footprint was about the size of a human hand with short fingers. We had previously identified such engraved figures as human hand and foot prints, and some may be just that, but it was likely that most of them represented front and rear tracks of the extinct megafauna of marsupials, giant wombats, diprotodons etc. A large engraved site at Wall Creek, recorded by G. Walsh had similar, but smaller, figures to the amphitheatre ones, and he also recorded 'human tracks'.

The large engraved dingo was an outstanding figure. It was over a metre long, with tail curled over its back. It was deeply engraved and sanded to a very smooth finish, perhaps in some annual ritual. It also appeared to be part of a large composition, with its nose almost in the armpit of an inverted man about 1.5 metres tall. About two metres behind the dingo was a large figure of a robust man over two metres tall, with what appeared to be a spear parallel to his right side. Perhaps it was a portrayal of the giant devil dingo legend. From the top of the amphitheatre the Dingo Rocks could be seen glowing rose in the setting sun, a short kilometre away.

The potential of the natural amphitheatre as a ceremonial site had not been lost on the ancient Australians. About two hundred metres north of it was the large shelter in the Dingo Creek escarpment, containing hundreds of small red hand stencils, most of them rather faded. They were on all available surfaces but most were placed in several deep, womb-like niches. There were stencils of boomerangs and dillybags, and two extremely faded red dingoes. It appeared to be another place where initiates were shown how they would be born again into life after death.

Although the painted shelters in the amphitheatre appeared to have been used as occasional living sites during fairly recent times it seemed that it had been abandoned as a ceremonial site a very long time ago. In the present climatic conditions ceremonies could only have been carried out during the wet season when water was readily available, and the size of the amphitheatre suggested that it would have needed at least a couple of hundred people to make a satisfactory human impact for ceremonial ritual and spectacle.

We may never be able to estimate the human population of Australia at the onset of the humid phase 60 000 years ago, but after another 20 000 years of optimum living conditions among the vast food supply of the marsupial megafauna, there would have been a great number of people, certainly enough in Quinkin country to fill every available shelter. How many of them survived the droughts to 15 000 years ago, can also only be guessed, but it was probably only a few thousand across the entire continent, eking out an existence on the few permanent waters remaining.

Where the amphitheatre fitted into the ebb and flow of people populations was another difficult guess. At present there appears to be no means to date its engravings, as, like those in Early Man site, they lack silica skins. Many students of Australian rock art would place them in the minor humid phase beginning about 8000 years ago, but the probable diprotodon track engraved in the amphitheatre, and the sophisticated painting of the diprotodon on the Deighton, infer that the first figures were engraved in the amphitheatre in much more remote times.

Shortly after we found the amphitheatre, Dr Mike Morwood, an archaeologist from the University of New England, arrived on an inspection tour of potential dig sites for the following year, when they would commence a three-year project to carry out a multidisciplined investigation of the prehistory of the Laura-Cooktown Basin. He was very impressed with the amphitheatre but equally at a loss as to how its art could be dated.

Mike Morwood and his team chose Yam Camp on Jowalbinna for their first excavation, and established a base camp below it on Shepherd Creek. The deeply patinated, pecked engravings on the back wall indicated great antiquity, while the charcoal floor, layers of superimposed paintings, and remains of a bone burial in a sandstone tunnel indicated it had been in constant use as a wet season living site.

Other members of the expedition were to make detailed assessments of local resource structures and ethnographic information to investigate how systems of Aboriginal resource use had developed over time. Another team was investigating evidence for palaeo-climatic change by the study of pollen sequences from the excavations and local swamps.

Another team from Canberra, led by Dr Alan Watchman, a geologist from ANU, was to investigate silica skins, their age, and the conditions of their formation over paintings and engravings. It had been discovered that oxalates, or micro-organisms, had been deposited in some silica skins as they were forming, and could be dated.

I greeted Alan Watchman with great enthusiasm, telling him I had been waiting for him for over twenty years, anxious to test my theories on the antiquity of the oldest paintings and engravings. He said the first step was to ascertain whether the oxalates were embedded in the local silica skins, and if they were he would be back the following year to collect a series of samples for dating.

We had a list of the best sites for silica sampling and Sandy Creek was at the top because its enigmatic, silica-coated geometric engravings had haunted us for over twenty years. Mike Morwood expressed interest in seeing the site and came along.

The only change at Rainbow Serpent Rock was where one of the old lady-apple trees had died and crashed down. While Alan was checking the engravings I showed Mike the limits of our excavation of the 1960s, and described how we had found the cemented rubble about two metres down, penetrated it for nearly a metre to bedrock, and found an edge-ground stone axe, grooved for hafting, under it.

Mike's jaw dropped and he became animated: 'Three metres! That would have to be the world's oldest hafted axe!' We had guessed that it was, but could not prove it as we did not find charcoal. Mike was already selecting a site to excavate alongside our dig, obviously hoping he would get lucky with charcoal.

We had treasured the pink quartzite axe and it had occupied pride of place on a book case for at least a decade, when I noticed it was missing. Beverley thought that Patty had taken it to school to 'show and tell' and it had gone astray. Fortunately Eddy had taken good photographs of it sitting on my hand and we were able to measure it.

We had found an extremely rich collection of stone artifacts in the excavation and Mike was keen to see these and have his students study and classify them. They were all tagged and bagged to identify the layer and spot each item had occupied, and were stored at Jowalbinna. But a thorough search failed to find the boxes of artifacts, which had been moved about several times during building works. Stephen finally suggested they may have got mixed up with the gravel during concrete pouring. Mike's jaw dropped again when I told him the artifacts were probably in the concrete slab he was standing on.

The oldest date for human occupation of Cape York peninsula was still Andrée Rosenfeld's 13 200 B.P. at Early Man, but we hoped for an earlier date at Yam Camp because of the silica-skinned engravings. Later on Mike was very pleased to announce the bottom charcoal yielded a date of about 17 000 years B.P., with lower artifacts down to bedrock at 130 cm and suggesting about 25 000 B.P. for the initial Aboriginal use of the site.

The archaeologists excavated two more sites after Yam Camp, at Red Bluff and Magnificent galleries. Red Bluff yielded a date of about 7500 B.P., but Mike thought it probably dated a rock-fall which formed a comfortable windbreak, rather than the initial use of the shelter. An unusual find in the uppermost layer was the trimmed end of a small hollow log, which someone identified as a by-product of didjeridoo making. When it was shown to me I recalled that Dick had been with Frank Woolston and myself when we recorded the site about twenty-five years ago. Industrious Dick was never without his tomahawk, so he could make something useful while he sat about. Mike announced a basal date of about 13 000 B.P. for Magnificent with a fluctuating intensity of occupation reflecting major weather changes occurring over those millennia.

The last excavation for the year was at Sandy Creek in the Rainbow Serpent shelter, and my visit there coincided with an exciting discovery. They had almost reached the base of the cemented rubble layer and found utilised quartz crystals among charcoal. After more than twenty years the stone axe could be dated, and so too could the lost Dreamtime of the old people, on the far side of the droughts.

Quartz crystals were often associated with rain-making magic and the discovery of them near bedrock was consistent with our identification of the large 'pitchfork' design on the buried boulder as representing rain-making magic.

Mike obtained a series of carbon dates from various levels. The oldest, from just above bedrock at about 240 cm, was 31 900 ± 700 B.P. The next date was from the top of the rubble layer and was about 12 500 years ago, and there was minimal evidence for the use of the site between those two dates.

My interpretation of the evidence offering was that the 20 000-year-long hiatus between the two human populations was consistent with Dr J. Bowler's chronological sequence of weather patterns for more southern parts of the continent, and that it indicated the chronology also applied to Cape York peninsula.

The chronological sequence of human activity in Rainbow Serpent site appeared as follows:

1   Early man chose the shelter in the massive snake-like rock for a ceremonial site and engraved his mysterious symbols on a boulder among a rock-fall. The time was probably before 40 000 years ago, either prior to, or during Bowler's 60 000 to 40 000 years ago humid phase, during which time the silica skin formed over the engravings. This engraving would have been motivated by religion, and possibly symbolised the travels of ancestors, the ancestral beings, or was associated with the Rainbow Serpent.

The first engravers were probably living in shelters among big slabs of sandstone a little further out on the outwash sand plain, where they would have sandy floors more suited to camping. Excavation of them may yield appropriate dates.

2   The next engraving artists arrived during an increasingly arid period, probably about 35 000 years ago. The shelter was still rock-floored, and they engraved their rain-making symbols of thunderstorms on boulders in the shelter. Conditions were never again humid enough to provide them with silica skins.

3   About 32 000 years ago the site was abandoned to drought for the next 20,000 years.

4   Around 12 500 years ago climatic conditions had recovered sufficiently to permit hunter–gatherers to return. They found the floor to be composed of sandy rubble and adapted it as a camping site. The first paintings may have been added to the site at that time. The boulder bearing the large Gothic-shaped engraving protruded from the floor and was apparently used as a seat and working platform, which damaged and eroded parts of the engraving.

5   The second excavation uncovered the same sequence of stone artifact technology as our first one, with large cores and flakes of quartzite and silcrete in the lower levels over the hiatus rubble, with utilised pieces of haematite for painting, then finer tools of chert, ribbon-stone and agate in the upper levels. The stratified layers held evidence of the ebb and flow of human populations, consistent with weather fluctuations of the Holocene epoch.

6   The last engraving to be added to the site was a pair of kangaroo rear foot-tracks, probably added during the last few thousand years. The last Aboriginal people to occupy the site, probably about the 1940s, left behind artifacts made of steel, quart pots and an iron yam-digging stick, thus ending the long human saga at Sandy Creek.

'The strange design was covered with a thick layer of smooth dark brown silica, a state which indicated considerable antiquity . . .'

18

Dream roads and rock art

After three decades of following my own Dream road, criss-crossing many of the ancient ones, and stumbling upon the temples of Dreamtime, it had slowly dawned in my mind that the declaration of a *terra nullius* Australia, had, perhaps unknowingly, been one of the world's greatest injustices, when inflicted on the first Australians.

They were a people who had not been nomadic for many millennia; their land tenure was an interlocked system of clan holdings covering the entire continent, and dividing it up in much the same way as it is now divided into shire and council lands. The clans managed their clan estates with the greatest care, having a deep knowledge of every animal and plant resource in their care, and governed by strict laws. 'Your clan land is all that you, your children, and your children's children, will ever have. Look after your land and your land will look after you. Take what you need from your land. Need what you take.'

All life was governed by the seasons, and the clans followed naturally, moving about the clan country harvesting the resources in such a manner as to keep them ever renewable, and sharing large resources with neighbouring clans while they enriched their spiritual and social lives by performing rituals associated with their religion, land, and animals.

Many of the Dream roads are clearly associated with animal husbandry, where an animal such as the antilopine kangaroo was jointly managed by many clans over its entire habitat, and harvested as a wet season food according to ritual laid down in 'swearing the kangaroo foot'. There were sanctuaries for each species which gave shelter during times of stress, like Spring Creek on Ngalculli's Dream road, where the kangaroo could not be hunted and so was safe during droughts.

Animal husbandry would have its roots in the 20 000 years of severe aridity during the late Pleistocene, when the Dream roads slowly evolved, and the clans also realised that they had to control their own population in accordance with what their clan land could support, no matter how seemingly cruel the methods. They became the first, perhaps the only, people in the world that controlled all populations for the good of all species.

The Aboriginal concept of Genesis (that in the beginning every living thing was human) portrays their belief that they were related to every species of flora and fauna on Earth, and being the progenitors of all life they were responsible for the wellbeing of all species.

The engraved and painted rock faces of Australia, especially northern Australia, are a spectacular graphic recording of history, not only of recent times but extending back to remote ages to record events in times we term prehistoric. The engraved and painted symbols serve as the memory banks which contain the associated mythology. Together they form the literature created by ancient peoples and they can serve equally well, and sometimes better than written records, to inform us of the events and concerns of their times.

The true meaning of the symbols of early man cannot be fully understood or interpreted until they are accurately dated and arranged in a chronological order, which can then be matched with a chronological sequence of weather patterns covering the same time spans. Weather was ever the dominant concern in the daily life of a hunter–gatherer.

One of the most lucid messages from remote times is surely borne by the faded bichrome painting of the diprotodon on the ceiling of the Deighton River cave. It is a beautifully drawn, very formal figure which clearly expresses ceremonial concern about those animals, which we now know gradually became extinct during severe aridity and droughts extending over more than 20 000 years and ending about 15 000 years ago. Far away in southern Australia, at Alabena on Cooper Creek, there is a spectacular stone arrangement which was the ancient sacred bora ground of the kadimakara, a species of the extinct diprotodons. The stone omphaloi of the bora ground mark a story place on the kadimakara Dream road, but now there is no key to unlock the vast store of knowledge contained within them. They are mute forever.

The chronological sequence of art styles appears to commence with the engraved meandering lines and geometric shapes of early man. The style must have continued over many millennia and changes in weather patterns. Engravings covered by silica skins appear to be older than similar ones which do not have skins. It is probable that those with silica skins were executed some time before or during the very humid phase from 60 000 to 40 000 years ago, and those without silica skins were created after the end of the humid phase.

At one engraved site on the upper reaches of the Kennedy River we recorded a large panel of rows of engraved round pits. Both ends of the panel bore a thick brown silica skin, but the mid-section had been battered out again and the silica completely removed. This reworking of an ancient panel illustrates that the designs retained their significance over many millennia, and seemingly younger engravings may merely have had their ancient skins removed. So let the student beware.

The motivations for the creation of the first art form can only be speculated upon. Those in the Deighton Lady shelter, Yam Camp, Lakes Creek, Sandy Creek etc, are composed of meandering lines and geometric shapes, with no identifiable figurative shapes. They may be symbolised maps representing the putative travels of the ancestral beings as they moved across the country in creation times.

I have a bark painting of the travels of Thuwathu the Rainbow Serpent, painted by Burrud of the Lardil clan on Mornington Island. The main design is a symbolic map of the local Dugong River and its tributaries, with large round dots representing important story places along the way. The tributaries were made as Thuwathu encountered difficulties like hills or hard ground, forcing him to return and try another direction. As an engraving the map would lie comfortably with the ancient meandering engravings.

Some of the meandering line and geometric engravings have emu and scrub turkey tracks incorporated in the design, along with round shallow pits, notably in Early Man, Yam Camp, Emu Dreaming, Death Adder and others. Although round pits can symbolise many things, when in conjunction with bird tracks they may represent eggs in a maintenance ritual concerning those birds, which are easily domesticated.

Most of the extensively engraved ancient sites have had one pair of kangaroo rear footprints engraved on or near the main design in much more recent times, as all the kangaroo tracks are unpatinated. It seemed that the later artists understood the nature and purpose of the old engravings and added the new symbol to include kangaroos.

Sites containing engraved figures which do not have silica skins cannot be dated other than where excavations have revealed them in association with charcoal. That was achieved by Rosenfeld at Early Man and yielded a minimum date of 13 000 years BP for those engravings.

Kershaw et al. postulate a minor humid phase from about 8000 to 5000 years ago, which allowed the return of rainforest to the Atherton Tablelands and for people to resettle country long abandoned to drought, but it was obviously not wet enough to produce silica skins on sandstone. These climatic patterns may bracket the unskinned approximately to more than 13 000 years, but less than 40 000 years, with the proviso that some of the ancient engravings may have been reworked in more recent times.

Two sites, Hann River and Death Adder on Jowalbinna, have engravings which have been outlined or infilled with red ochre paint, probably to update them. This is convincing evidence that the engravings are still meaningful.

The engraved two-metre-tall human figures, and other animal figures and tracks in the amphitheatre present an enigma. Apart from a much smaller site recorded by Walsh at Wall Creek there is no other comparable site yet found in Australia; if the fully abraded out figures were infilled with red ochre they would match perfectly with the tall painted figures in the locality. The large engraved dingo appears to be worn smooth with time and exposure, as are a few human figures near it and others which disappear under an earth deposit in the western floor of the amphitheatre, but the rest convey no feeling of any great antiquity, not even a large four-toed engraving of a footprint, probably of one of the extinct megafauna.

There are no silica skins on any of the figures and many are covered by lichen. The amphitheatre is so large that it would require the impact of many people to create a ceremonial atmosphere. It is possible that it was first in use during the latter part of the great humid phase, then eventually abandoned to drought and not used again until some time in the lesser humid phase between 8000 and 5000 years ago when most of the engravings were added. One of the large emus is only partly abraded out, and the amphitheatre may have been again abandoned about 5000 years ago.

Dating of some engravings covered with desert varnish or under silica skins has been attempted. Using a catiron ratio technique Dorn and Nobbs sampled desert varnish over engravings in the Olary region in South Australia, resulting at first in dates of up to 31 000 years, but they later postulated dates of up to 45 000 years B.P.

Alan Watchman's examination of silica skins has yielded some scientifically obtained dates. He removed a minute sample of unpainted crust from the rear wall of a Sandy Creek site, and under high power magnification of the flake cross-section he identified several layers of paint separated by mineral deposits. This evidence showed that this section of the rockshelter wall had been repainted at least three times.

Using a technique which can date minute quantities of organic matter present in the mineral coatings on the wall, Watchman obtained a series of radiocarbon dates which show that the wall was painted by Aboriginal artists on at least three occasions—6500 years ago, 16 000 years ago and 24 600 years ago. This is the oldest dated evidence for rock painting in Australia and it may be the oldest direct radiocarbon date for rock painting anywhere in the world.

The dating techniques for desert varnish and silica skins are still in the early stages and will eventually yield much older dates. This is indicated by archaeologist Rhys Jones, who used the technique of thermoluminescence (TL), to date a layer in an excavation in Arnhem Land. TL is the release in the form of light of stored energy from a substance when it is heated.

The layer in the excavation contained pieces of utilised ochre material, and it was dated at 56 000 years B.P., but there was no indication of how the paint material was being used.

The most significant date for human occupation of Australia came from a 1991–92 scientific expedition to investigate the age and origin of the Great Barrier Reef off the coast of Cairns. It was led by Professor Peter Davies. On Euston Reef they used high-tech equipment to drill core samples from deep coralite rock. The work involved biological calcium carbonate testing of core samples. This chemical acts as a time capsule recording the environmental conditions existing at a particular time in history. Peter Kershaw recovered fossil pollen and charcoal samples taken from cores of dated rock and marine sediment, and he has concluded that between 150 000 and 100 000 years ago conifer-dominated rainforests in the area were frequently burned following more than one million years of relative stability. He cites this as evidence that humans were deliberately setting fire to the rainforest, and his findings support those of Gurdip Singh who argued that deliberate burning of forests took place at least 120 000 years ago around the shores of Lake George near Canberra (Interview, *Cairns Post*, 29 April 1992).

When in 1960 we set out to seek and investigate the lost world of the Quinkin art body, the consensus of academic opinion was that the Aborigines had been in Australia less than 10 000 years, had not been contemporaries of the extinct megafauna, and their art forms were bracketed within the last 3000 years. The first Australians were still thought to be the world's most backward race, and there was much sage discussion on whether or not they were capable of abstract thought. For too long they had been isolated from the mainstreams of mankind, unchanging savages in an unchanging land.

Blinded by ignorance and Eurocentric arrogance, our logic and thinking shackled by our own modern religions, some 200 years after the monstrous declaration of *terra nullius*, we still are having trouble focusing on the picture.

The message that the thick-boned, almost opalised skull of Willandra Lakes hominid No. 50 is trying to convey to us, is that his ancestors came riding on the magic carpet of the Leeuwin Current hundreds of thousands of years ago, to be followed over the millennia by numerous bands of adventurous sailors seeking a new land.

After decades of studying and musing over the painted sandstone faces of Quinkin country it became obvious that the oldest engravings and paintings were very old indeed—geomorphological evidence insists upon it. Weathering in many places has left engravings and faded paintings high out of reach, and it is clear that the erosion occurred a long time ago, probably during the great humid phase of the last Ice Age, 40 000 to 60 000 years ago. The layer of sandstone composing the floor of some shelters was apparently more friable and porous than other layers and carried seepage water which froze in the colder winters and shattered the sandstone. Geologist Bob Henderson closely examined the painted surfaces in the early 1970s and concluded that some exfoliation had occurred in the long past but very little was happening now.

Ferruginous concretions containing the multicoloured ochre pigments outcrop everywhere from the Jurassic Age conglomerate sandstones which underlie the Cretaceous sandstone notable for its smooth-walled shelters. With paints and canvas side by side, and fire-shattered nodules of the concretions revealing their pretty colours, it is logical to assume that the use of them began very early in Quinkin country. If Robust early man, engrossed with his engravings, took no notice of them, the advent of the Mungo-type Graciles would have soon seen them in use.

Red ochre, or haematite, occurs in many shades, from light bright red to dark purple-red, and the oldest figures are always haematite, which is so fine-grained that given the right conditions it will penetrate and stain sandstone millimetres deep. In open sites some red figures are exposed to rain, sun and wind, and some go under floodwater every year but still persist without apparent damage. Protected in shelters and sometimes with a hard silica skin, many of them will survive as long as the rocks stand—the oldest works of man visible on Earth.

The first use of the ochres was probably as a dry pigment used to do simple linear figures, and its use as such continued to recent times. The use of mixed paint may have stemmed from stencilling, where a piece of ochre was chewed to mix with saliva and then mouth-sprayed to create a hand stencil.

Paint was prepared by filling a shallow stone pit with water then abrading a selected piece of ochre in it until the required thickness of paint was achieved.

The first paintings appear to be linear style figures, sometimes applied by finger-painting; good examples of the style can be seen in the light red, first portrayal of ancestral beings, predecessors to the later, much larger, portrayal of them in the Split Rock ceremonial site. Another good example is the linear horizontal woman under the tall, dark red Timara figures in the Quinkin Cave.

At Sandy Creek there is a panel of paintings which is not heavily superimposed and several figures in the old linear style can be clearly

198

seen; they include a dingo apparently pursuing a kangaroo, and an echidna.

The painting styles progressed predictably through monochrome silhouettes, then to bichrome silhouettes by adding outlines and decorations of a different colour. The latter style truly blossomed during the minor humid phase, probably about 5000 years ago when the stone tool industry also underwent changes, and the introduction of the microlithic industry which employed pretty material like agate and ribbonstone occurred.

Most of the large white figures were intricately decorated with fine red outlines, interior bars and dots, portraying people, kangaroos, emus, crocodiles, saw-sharks, beehives etc. The white body colour seems to have been mainly barite, which adhered better and was much less fugitive than white clay, and occurs as thin seams in the Jurassic sandstone. The large well-executed figures reflect an affluent people with time for philosophy and religion.

One of the most striking changes to occur in the art body was the switch from red hand stencils to white. All red hand stencils appear to be old and we have not seen any that appear to be recent; it seems that sometime in the past a tabu was placed on red hand stencils. It was probably at the beginning of the minor humid phase when people were able to return to country abandoned to searing drought for many millennia. The astonishment at the discovery of the ancient galleries, and the awe concerning the mysterious people who had created them, is reflected in mythology all over the continent. It was generally concluded that the ancestral spirits had created them by placing themselves within the rock walls. Since then, out of respect for the ancient ones, only white hand stencils have been employed.

The paintings on top of the big white figures are usually in red and generally not as well drawn or decorated. A significant increase in the number of sorcery figures reflects the harder times following the lush humid era.

The final, dramatic upsurge of artistic activity in Quinkin country was to record the fatal impact of the European invasion. The enormity of the trauma is evidenced by the giant yellow and white horse, almost six metres long and three metres tall.

The artists recorded the arrival of pigs released at Cooktown by Cook, and the giant horse probably records the passage of the ill-fated Edmund Kennedy expedition. In coastal sites, especially the islands in Princess Charlotte Bay, they recorded sailing ships which passed by, a beche-de-mer lugger near Cooktown, and on Clack and Stanley islands several ships that look like Chinese junks.

The ferocity of the quarter-century-long guerilla warfare that raged through the hills of Quinkin country was powerfully recorded by paintings of the hated Black Police. Some are two and three metres tall, armed, booted, massive and threatening—the most compelling sorcery figures in the entire art body.

Atrocities perpetrated by the mounted native police eventually came to public notice and the outcry compelled their disarming and restriction to tracking duties only.

The decimated tribes had been driven into the rough inaccessible parts of their clan land, their numbers dwindling under the impact of influenza and other introduced diseases. The last additions to the Quinkin art during that time were rather impoverished figures in clay slurry, usually motivated by sorcery or love-magic. In the 1920s the remaining few tribes were rounded up and settled at mission stations located around the coastline. The painted ancestral beings gazed out over a silent land.

In 1992, about 115 years after the bloody scenes at Battle Camp, the Queensland Government ceremoniously handed over the title deeds of the Quinkin Reserves to the descendants of the former owners. The 1000 square kilometres contain the major body of the Quinkin art treasures. The deeds were received by the Chairman of the Ang Gnarra Aboriginal Corporation, on behalf of the Aboriginal people. The temples of Dreamtime are again with their traditional owners.

Bibliography

Ardrey, R. 1976, *The Hunting Hypothesis*, Collins.

Berndt, R.M. and C.H. 1964, *The World of the First Australians*, Ure Smith, Australia.

Berndt, R.M. and C.H. 1989, *The Speaking Land*, Penguin.

Bowler, J.M. 1987, 'Water and Sand: climate in ancient Australia', in J.D. Mulvaney and J.P. White (eds), *Australians to 1788*, pp. 25–45, Fairfax, Syme and Weldon Associates, Broadway, NSW.

Bowler J.M. and Thorne, A.G. 1976, 'Human remains from Lake Mungo: discovery of Lake Mungo III', in R.L Kirk and A.G. Thorne (eds) *The Origin of the Australians*, pp. 55–77.

Brunnschweiler, R.D. 1984, *Ancient Australia*, Angus and Robertson, Sydney.

Cresswell, G.R. and Golding, T.J. 1980, 'Observations of a south-flowing current in the southeastern Indian Ocean', *Deep Sea Research*, vol. 27A, Pergamon Press.

Flood, J.M. and Horsfall, N. 1986, 'Excavation of Green Ant and Echidna Shelters, Cape York Peninsula', *Queensland Archaeological Research*, 3: pp. 4–64.

Holthouse, H. 1967, *River of Gold*, Angus and Robertson.

Jack, R.L. 1895, 'On Aboriginal cave-drawings on the Palmer Goldfield', *Proceedings of the Royal Society of Queensland* II (Part 2).

Jones, Rhyss, 'A date for utilised ochre material in an archaeological excavation in Arnhem Land', Personal Comm.

Langloh Parker, K. 1953, *Australian Legendary Tales*, Angus and Robertson, Sydney.

McCarthy, F. 1979, *Australian Rock Art*, Australian Museum, Sydney.

McConnel, U. 1957, *Myths of the Munkan*, Melbourne University Press.

MacKenzie, G. 1981, *Aurukun Diary*, The Aldersgate Press, Melbourne.

Morwood, M.J. and Trezise, P.J. 1989, 'Edge-ground axes in Pleistocene Australia: new evidence from S.E. Cape York Peninsula', *Queensland Archaeological Research* 6: 77–90.

Mountford, C.P. 1965, 'The Pungalungas', in *Australian Dreaming* J. Isaacs (ed.) Landsdowne Press, 1980, Australia.

Murray, P. and Chaloupka, G. 1984, 'The Dreamtime Animals: extinct megafauna in Arnhem land rock art', *Archaeology in Oceania* 19, pp. 105–16.

Nobbs, M.F. and Dorn, R.I. 1988, 'Age determination from rock varnish formation within petroglyphs: cation-ratio dating of 24 motifs from the Olary Region, South Australia', *Rock Art Research* 5, pp. 108–24.

Reed, A.E. 1965, *Myths and Legends of Australia*, A.H. & A.W. Reed.

Reynolds, H. 1982, *The Other Side of the Frontier: Aboriginal Resistance to the European Invasion of Australia*, Penguin, Victoria.

Rich, P.V. and van Tets, G.V. (eds) 1985, *Kadimakara*, Pioneer Design Press.

Rosenfeld, A.D., Horton, D. and Winter, J. 1981, *Early Man in North Queensland*, Department of Prehistory, Research School of Pacific Studies, The Australian National University, Canberra.

Singh, G., Kershaw, A.P. and Clark, R. 1981, 'Quaternary vegetation and fire in Australia', in A.M. Gill, R.H. Groves and I.R. Noble (eds) *Fire and the Australian biota*, pp. 23–54, The Australian National University, Canberra.

Tindale, N.T. 1974, *Aboriginal Tribes of Australia; their terrain environmental controls, distribution, limits, and proper names*, Australian National University Press, Canberra.

Trezise, P.J. 1969, *Quinkan Country*, Reed, Sydney.

—— 1971, *Rock Art of South-east Cape York Peninsula*, Australian Institute of Aboriginal Studies, Canberra.

—— 1987a, 'Paintings of extinct animals in Quinkan rock art', paper presented to 57th ANZAAS Conference, August 1987 Townsville.

—— 1987b, 'Comment on J. Flood, 'Rock Art of the Koolburra Plateau, north Queensland', *Rock Art Research* 4, p. 124.

Watchman, A., Sirois, J. and Cole, N.A. (in press) 'Mineralogical examinations of rock painting pigments near Laura, north Queensland', proceedings of Archaeometry Conference, Canberra, January 1991.

Woolston, F.P. and Trezise, P.J. 1969, 'Petroglyphs of Cape York Peninsula', *Mankind* 7, p. 120–7.

Index